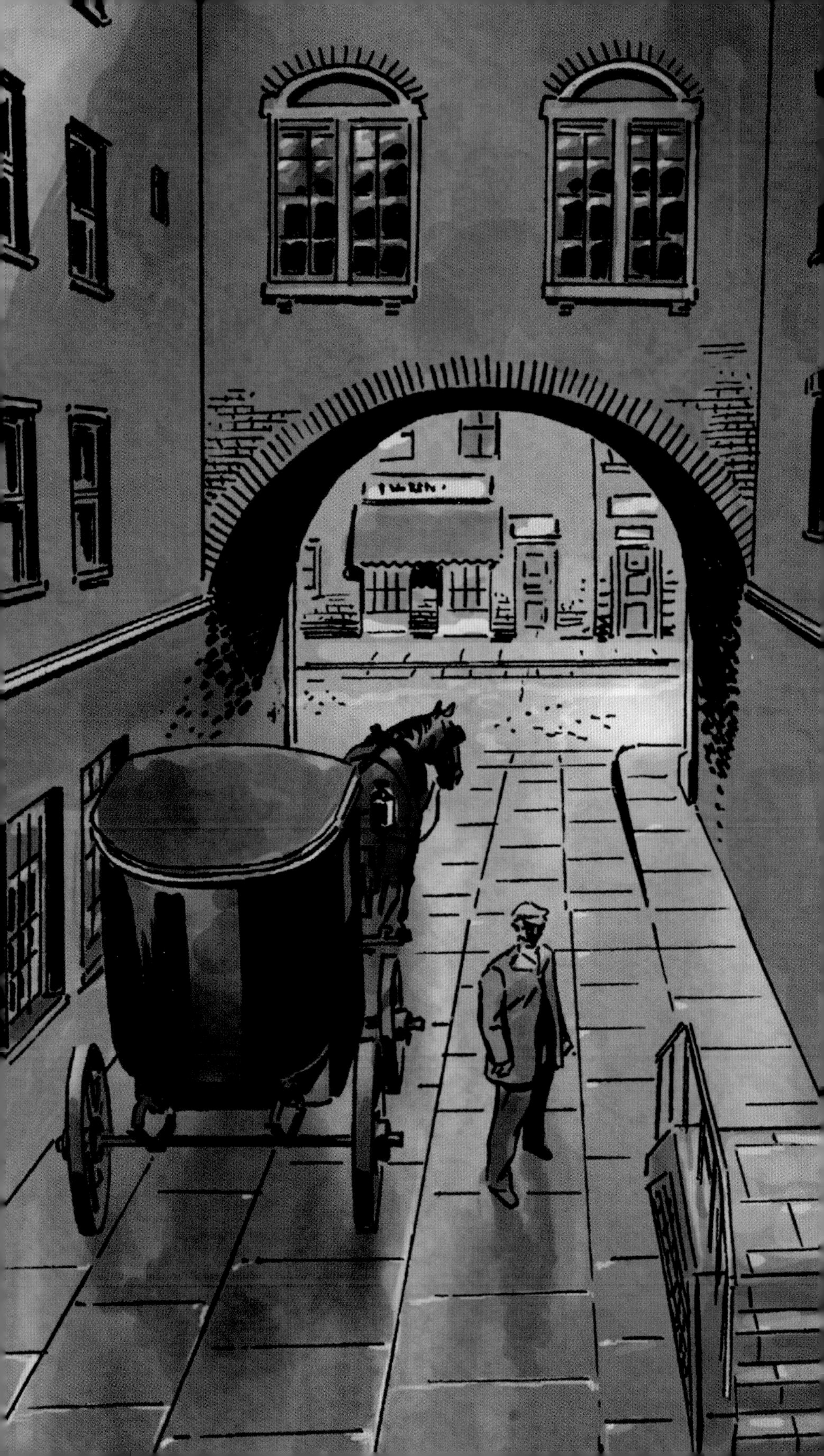

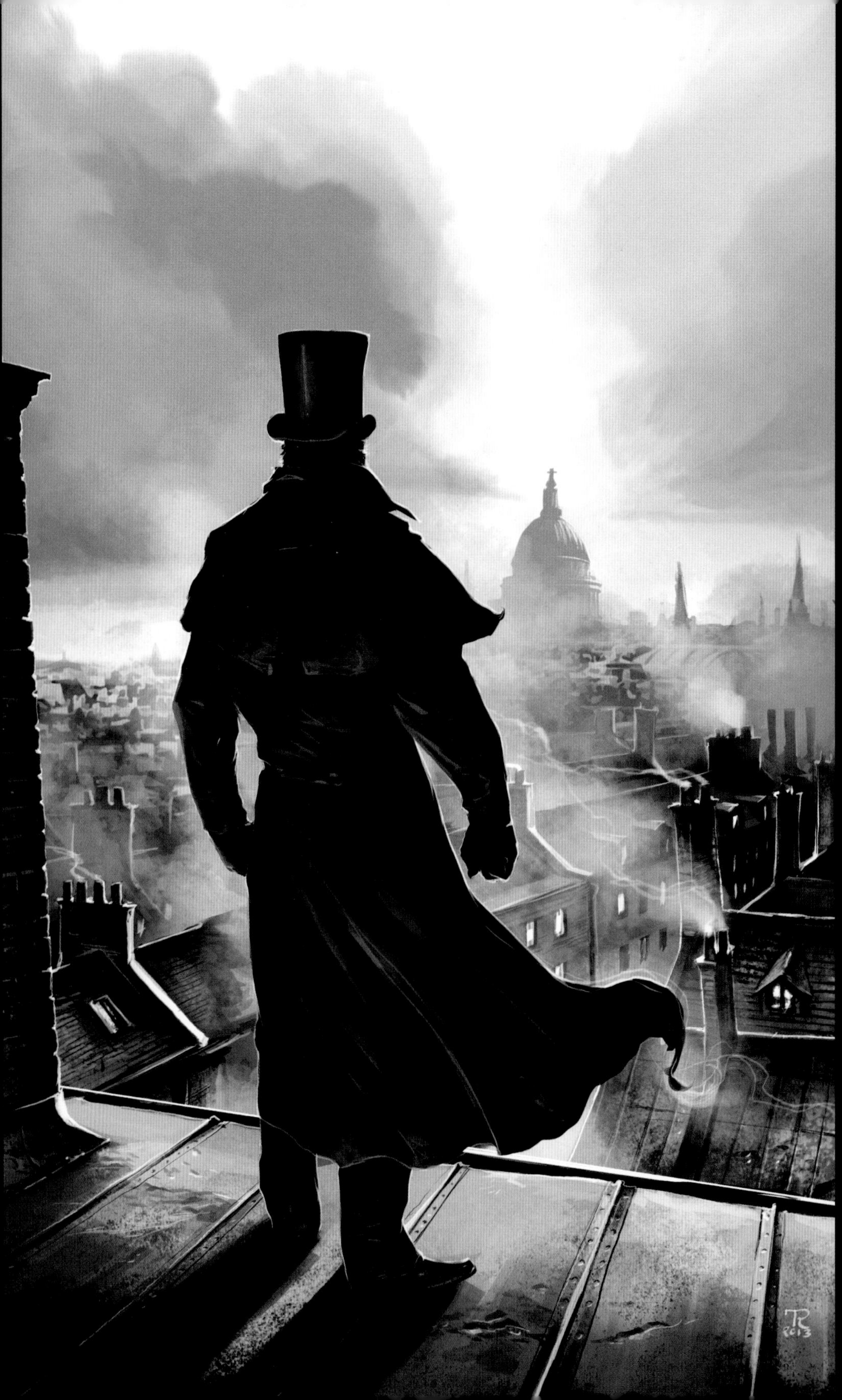

SHERLOCK HOLMES
CRIME ALLEYS

President and Publisher MIKE RICHARDSON

Editor DANIEL CHABON

Assistant Editor IAN TUCKER

Designer RICK DeLUCCO

Digital Art Technician CHRISTINA McKENZIE

Translation by LAURE DUPONT
Localization by ANDY GROSSBERG
Lettering & Retouch by SUSIE LEE

Neil Hankerson executive vice president • Tom Weddle chief financial officer • Randy Stradley vice president of publishing • Michael Martens vice president of book trade sales • Scott Allie editor in chief • Matt Parkinson vice president of marketing • David Scroggy vice president of product development • Dale LaFountain vice president of information technology • Ken Lizzi general counsel • Davey Estrada editorial director • Chris Warner senior books editor • Cary Grazzini director of print and development • Lia Ribacchi art director • Cara Niece director of scheduling • Mark Bernardi director of digital publishing

Published by Dark Horse Books
A division of Dark Horse Comics, Inc.
10956 SE Main Street
Milwaukie, OR 97222

First edition: February 2016
ISBN 978-1-61655-826-0

10 9 8 7 6 5 4 3 2 1
Printed in China

International Licensing: (503) 905-2377
Comic Shop Locator Service: (888) 266-4226

This volume collects *Sherlock Holmes: Crime Alleys* Books 1 and 2, originally published by Éditions Soleil.

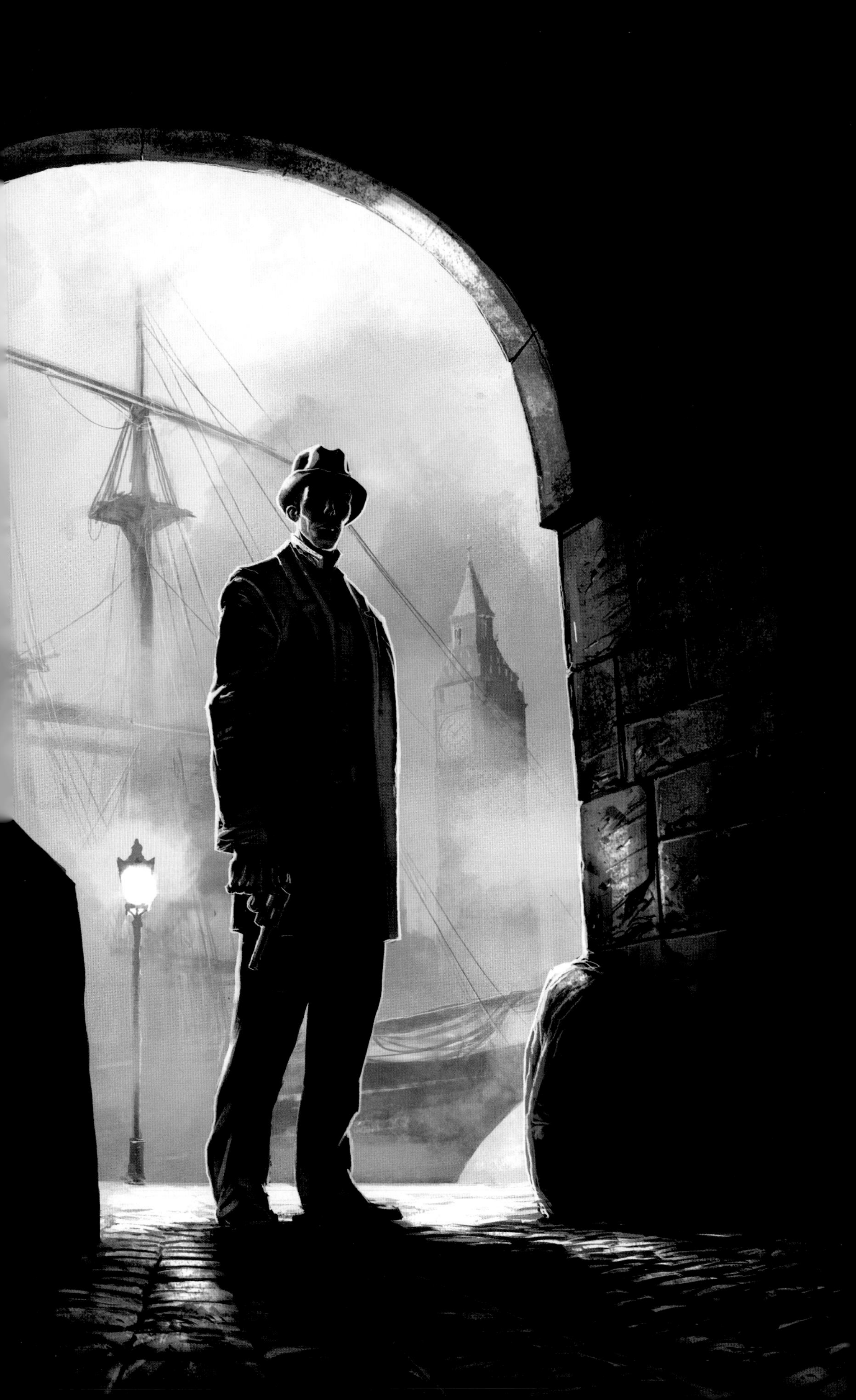

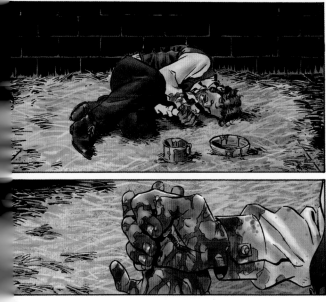

NAPTIME IS OVER.
IT'S YOUR TURN,
GENIUS!

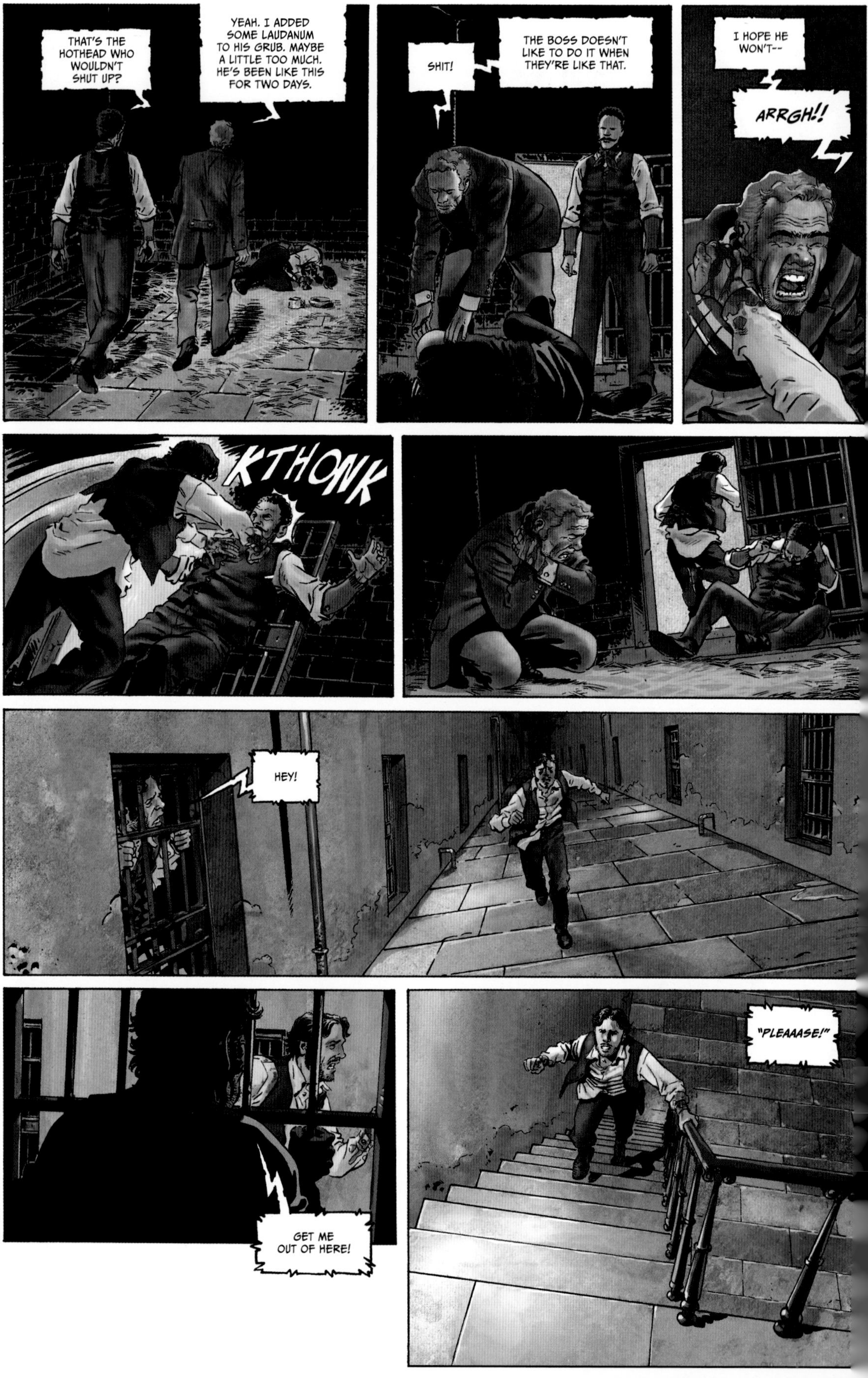
THAT'S THE HOTHEAD WHO WOULDN'T SHUT UP?
YEAH. I ADDED SOME LAUDANUM TO HIS GRUB. MAYBE A LITTLE TOO MUCH. HE'S BEEN LIKE THIS FOR TWO DAYS.
SHIT!
THE BOSS DOESN'T LIKE TO DO IT WHEN THEY'RE LIKE THAT.
I HOPE HE WON'T--
ARRGH!!
KTHONK
HEY!
GET ME OUT OF HERE!
"PLEAAASE!"

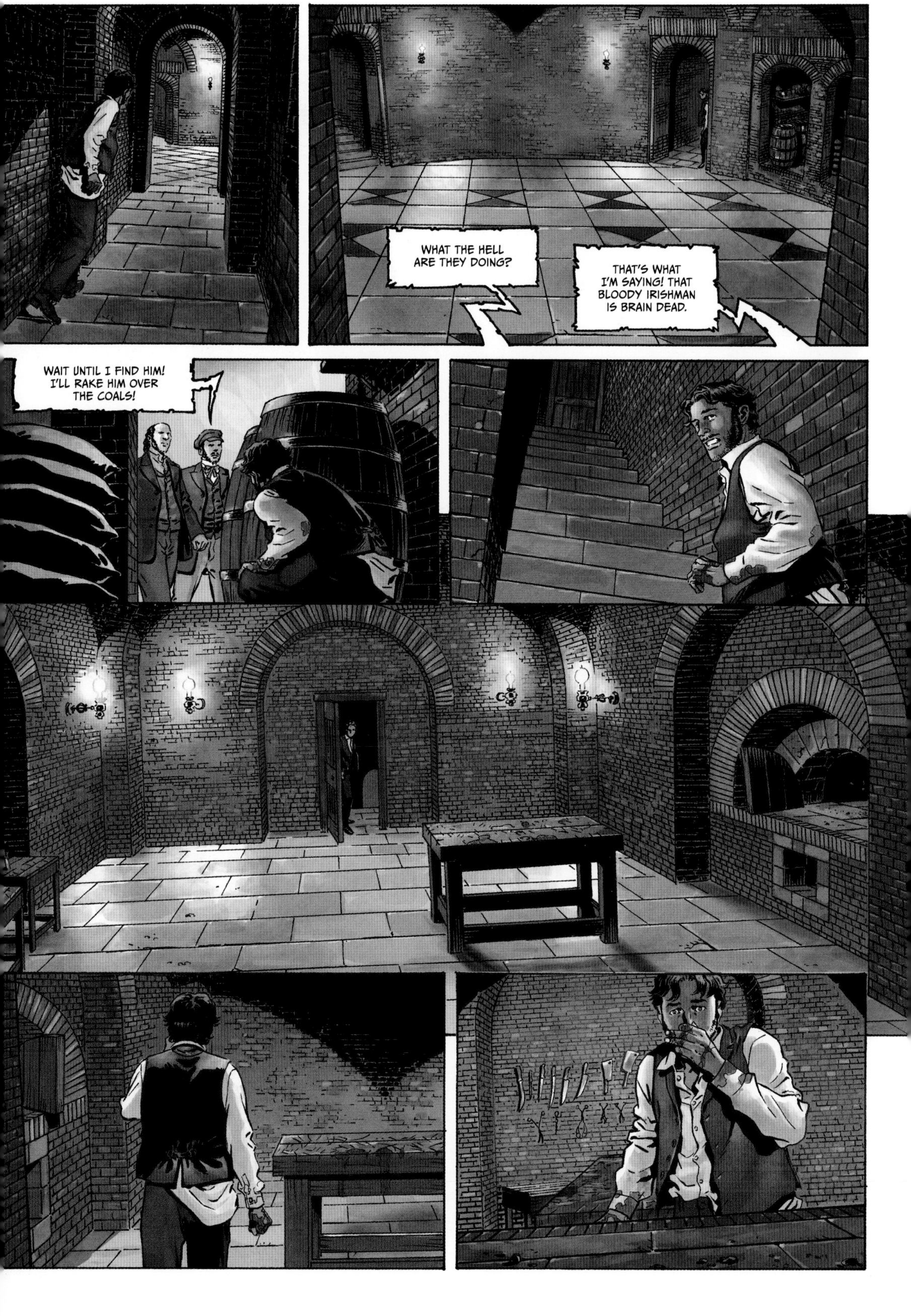
WHAT THE HELL ARE THEY DOING?
THAT'S WHAT I'M SAYING! THAT BLOODY IRISHMAN IS BRAIN DEAD.
WAIT UNTIL I FIND HIM! I'LL RAKE HIM OVER THE COALS!

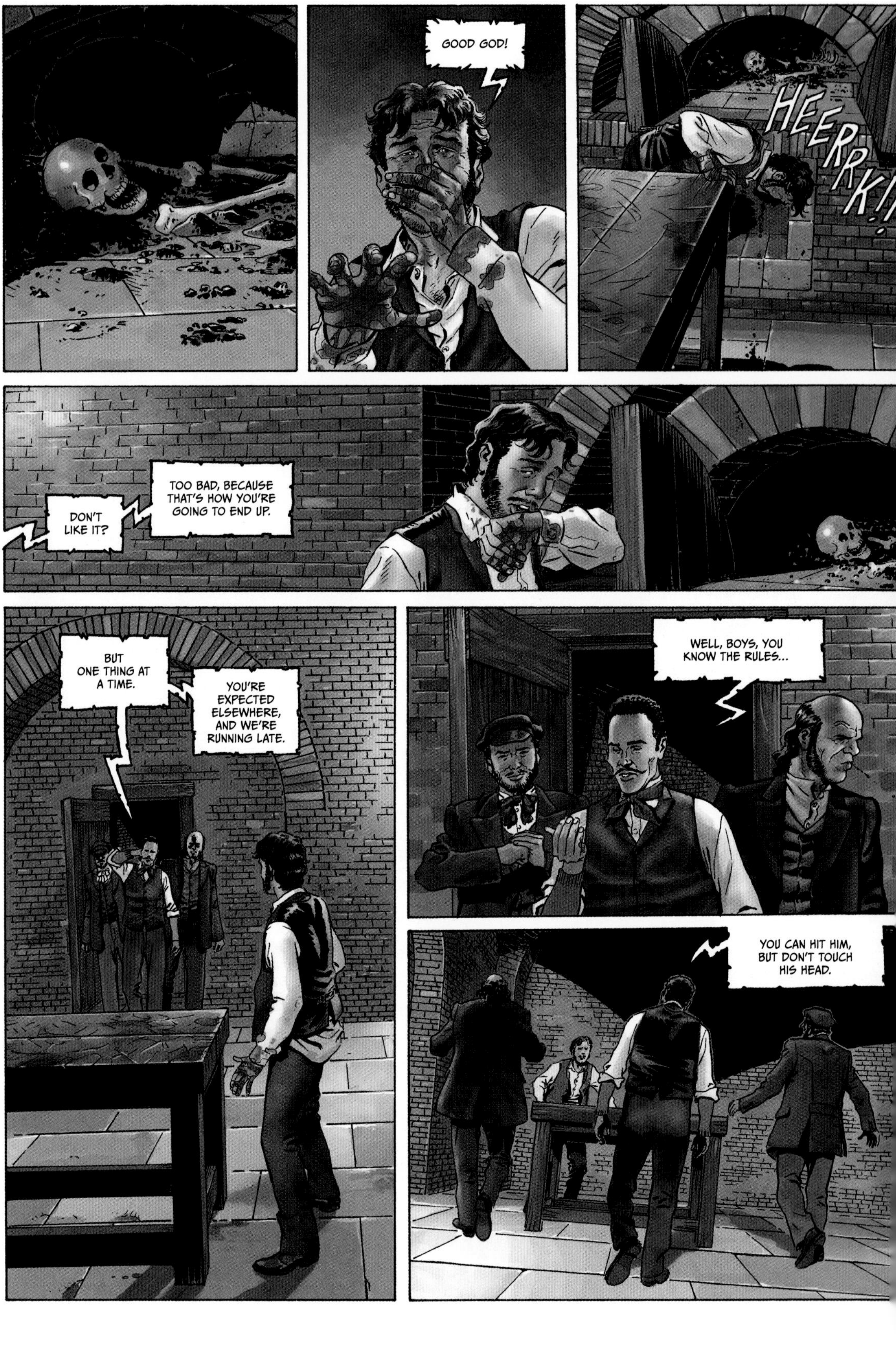
GOOD GOD!
HEERRK!!
DON'T LIKE IT?
TOO BAD, BECAUSE THAT'S HOW YOU'RE GOING TO END UP.
BUT ONE THING AT A TIME.
YOU'RE EXPECTED ELSEWHERE, AND WE'RE RUNNING LATE.
WELL, BOYS, YOU KNOW THE RULES...
YOU CAN HIT HIM, BUT DON'T TOUCH HIS HEAD.

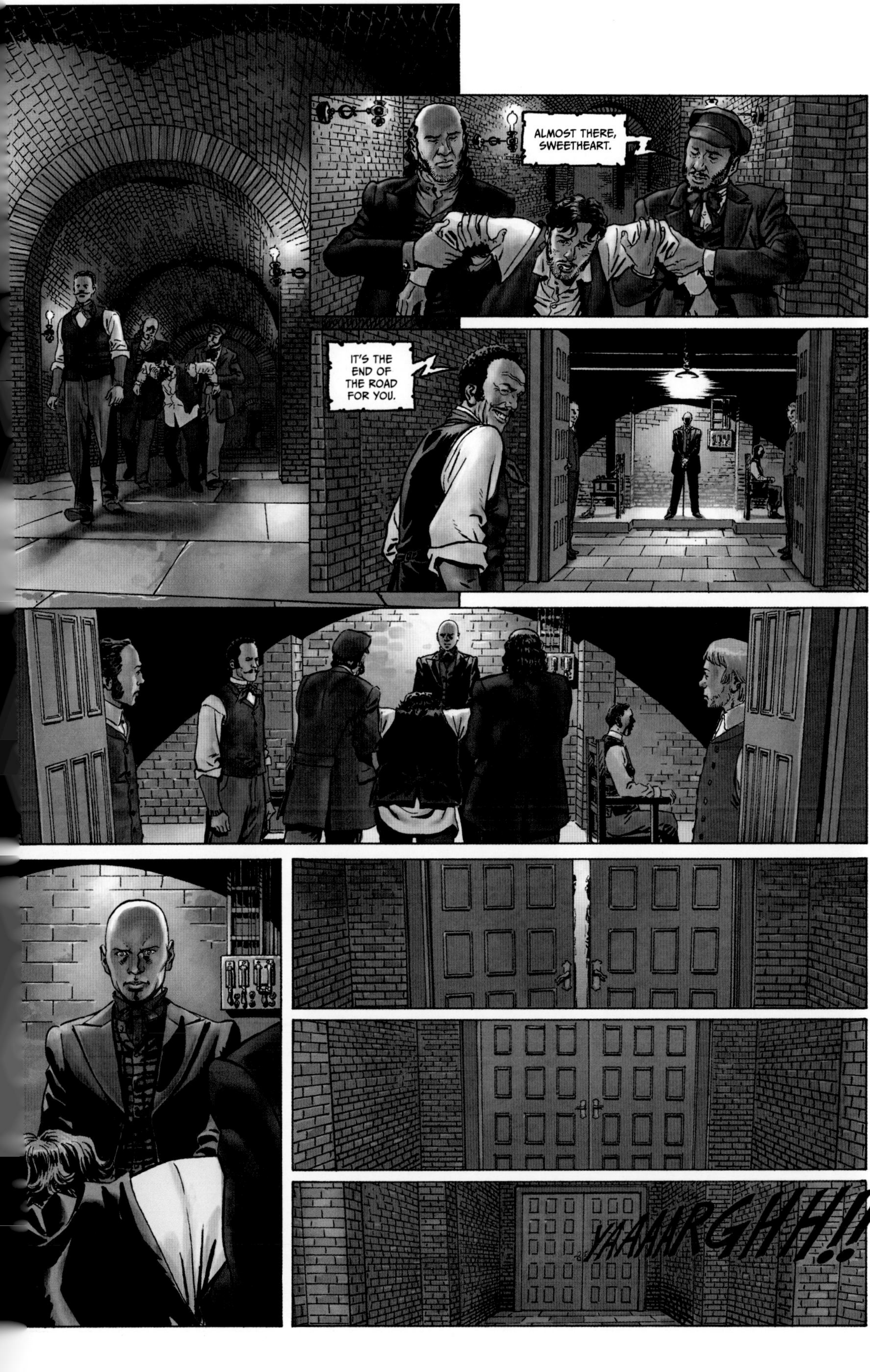
ALMOST THERE, SWEETHEART.
IT'S THE END OF THE ROAD FOR YOU.
YAAAARGHH!!

MAY 1876. LONDON.

MY FRIENDS SAY I AM A MISANTHROPE. THEY ARE WRONG. IT IS SIMPLY THAT FOR SOMEONE TO CATCH MY ATTENTION, HE MUST HAVE QUALITIES BEYOND THE ORDINARY.

HE MUST HAVE SOME LITTLE THING THAT MAKES HIM SPECIAL, IF NOT EXCEPTIONAL.

RON JANTSCHER IS ONE OF THEM. HE'S NOT ONLY A CHARMING BOY, BUT ALSO A VIRTUOSO.

HE IS SO POISED, HE MAKES PLAYING THE VIOLIN SEEM EASY. I AM IN A POSITION TO SAY IT IS NOT.

I COULD PRACTICE FOR TEN YEARS, BUT I WOULD NEVER ACHIEVE THIS PERFECTION.

I DON'T ENVY HIM. ON THE CONTRARY, I AM A GOOD AUDIENCE. IT IS BETTER TO ENJOY THE TALENT OF OTHERS THAN TO BE JEALOUS OF IT.

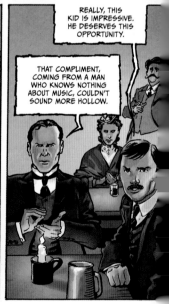

REALLY, THIS KID IS IMPRESSIVE. HE DESERVES THIS OPPORTUNITY.

THAT COMPLIMENT, COMING FROM A MAN WHO KNOWS NOTHING ABOUT MUSIC, COULDN'T SOUND MORE HOLLOW.

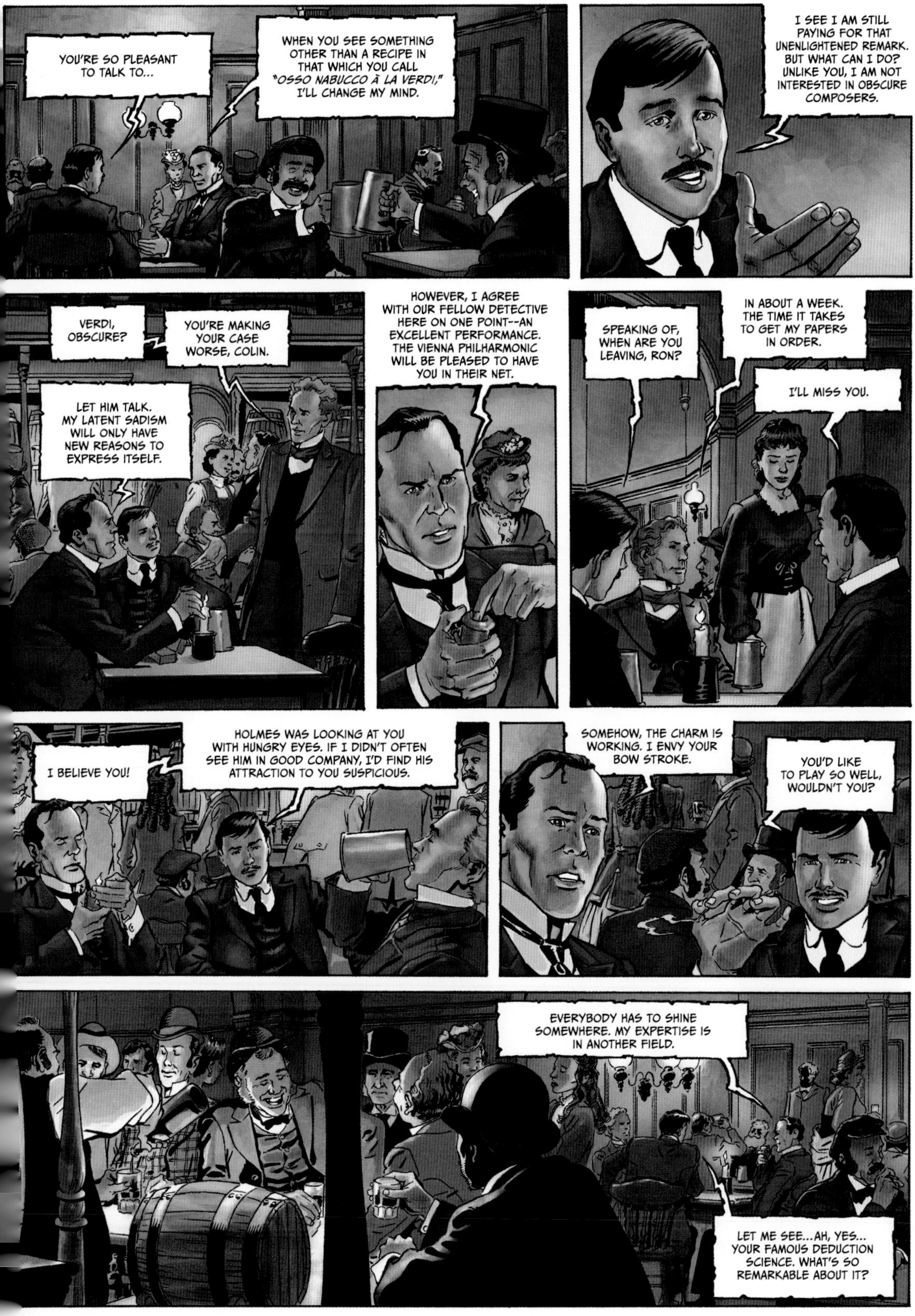
YOU'RE SO PLEASANT TO TALK TO...
WHEN YOU SEE SOMETHING OTHER THAN A RECIPE IN THAT WHICH YOU CALL "OSSO NABUCCO À LA VERDI," I'LL CHANGE MY MIND.
I SEE I AM STILL PAYING FOR THAT UNENLIGHTENED REMARK. BUT WHAT CAN I DO? UNLIKE YOU, I AM NOT INTERESTED IN OBSCURE COMPOSERS.
VERDI, OBSCURE?
YOU'RE MAKING YOUR CASE WORSE, COLIN.
LET HIM TALK. MY LATENT SADISM WILL ONLY HAVE NEW REASONS TO EXPRESS ITSELF.
HOWEVER, I AGREE WITH OUR FELLOW DETECTIVE HERE ON ONE POINT--AN EXCELLENT PERFORMANCE. THE VIENNA PHILHARMONIC WILL BE PLEASED TO HAVE YOU IN THEIR NET.
SPEAKING OF, WHEN ARE YOU LEAVING, RON?
IN ABOUT A WEEK. THE TIME IT TAKES TO GET MY PAPERS IN ORDER.
I'LL MISS YOU.
I BELIEVE YOU!
HOLMES WAS LOOKING AT YOU WITH HUNGRY EYES. IF I DIDN'T OFTEN SEE HIM IN GOOD COMPANY, I'D FIND HIS ATTRACTION TO YOU SUSPICIOUS.
SOMEHOW, THE CHARM IS WORKING. I ENVY YOUR BOW STROKE.
YOU'D LIKE TO PLAY SO WELL, WOULDN'T YOU?
EVERYBODY HAS TO SHINE SOMEWHERE. MY EXPERTISE IS IN ANOTHER FIELD.
LET ME SEE...AH, YES... YOUR FAMOUS DEDUCTION SCIENCE. WHAT'S SO REMARKABLE ABOUT IT?

NOT MERELY DEDUCTION. FIRST, I OBSERVE...

"THE DRUNKARD AT THE BAR IS WITHOUT A DOUBT A TERRIBLE HUSBAND, PERHAPS A BAD FATHER AS WELL. FROM HIS APPEARANCE, WE MIGHT SEE ONLY THE FIGHTER IN HIM. BUT THE BLOOD ON HIS BELT SUGGESTS HE BEATS UP THOSE WEAKER THAN HIM.

"THAT WOMAN COMES HERE BECAUSE SHE KNOWS RICH YOUNG MEN FREQUENT THIS PLACE. SHE'S DOING HER BEST TO SEDUCE THIS COXCOMB. SUBTLY, BUT NOT ENOUGH TO ESCAPE MY NOTICE, SHE'S EVALUATING THE NUMBER AND THE VALUE OF HIS POSSESSIONS. I WOULDN'T BE SURPRISED IF THE POOR GUY WAKES UP ALONE AND WITH LIGHTER POCKETS."

"THE MAN NEXT TO THE DOOR WON'T TAKE HIS EYES OFF RON. SHORTLY AFTER HE ARRIVED AT THE TAVERN, HE BEGAN TAKING NOTES. HOWEVER, HE DOESN'T HAVE THAT LIGHT IN HIS EYES ONE SEES IN THOSE WHO HUNT FOR SOLOISTS. HE INTRIGUES ME..."

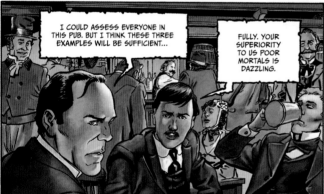

I COULD ASSESS EVERYONE IN THIS PUB. BUT I THINK THESE THREE EXAMPLES WILL BE SUFFICIENT...

FULLY. YOUR SUPERIORITY TO US POOR MORTALS IS DAZZLING.

OBSERVATION AND DEDUCTION, COLIN. SKILLS YOU AT SCOTLAND YARD ARE PAINFULLY LACKING.

PLEASE, NOT TONIGHT!

WE ARE HERE TO ENJOY RON'S FINAL RECITAL...

...WHO IS NOW RETURNING TO THE STAGE AND LEAVING YOU TO YOUR BATTLE OF THE EXPERTS.

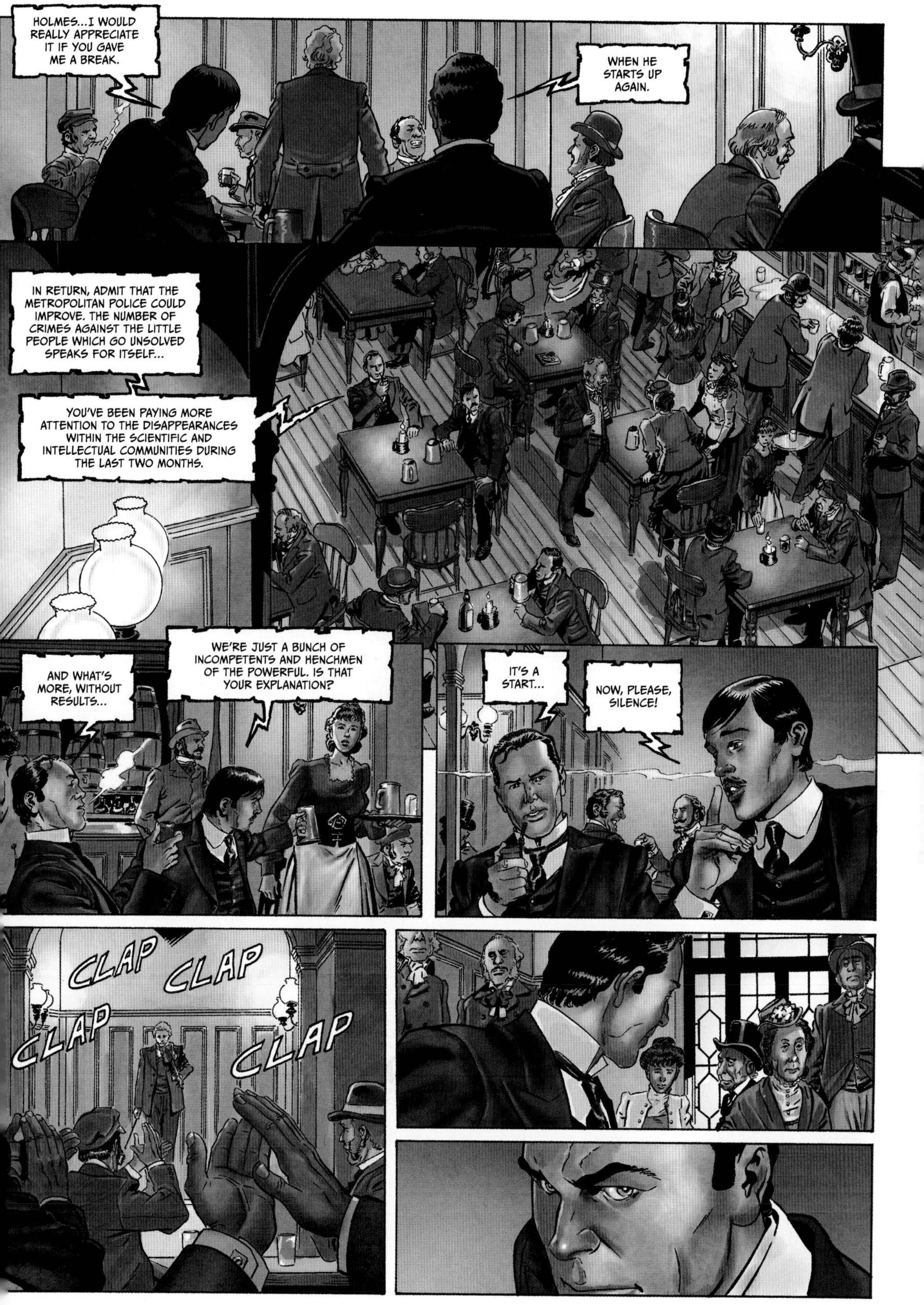
HOLMES...I WOULD REALLY APPRECIATE IT IF YOU GAVE ME A BREAK.
WHEN HE STARTS UP AGAIN.
IN RETURN, ADMIT THAT THE METROPOLITAN POLICE COULD IMPROVE. THE NUMBER OF CRIMES AGAINST THE LITTLE PEOPLE WHICH GO UNSOLVED SPEAKS FOR ITSELF...
YOU'VE BEEN PAYING MORE ATTENTION TO THE DISAPPEARANCES WITHIN THE SCIENTIFIC AND INTELLECTUAL COMMUNITIES DURING THE LAST TWO MONTHS.
AND WHAT'S MORE, WITHOUT RESULTS...
WE'RE JUST A BUNCH OF INCOMPETENTS AND HENCHMEN OF THE POWERFUL. IS THAT YOUR EXPLANATION?
IT'S A START...
NOW, PLEASE, SILENCE!
CLAP
CLAP
CLAP
CLAP

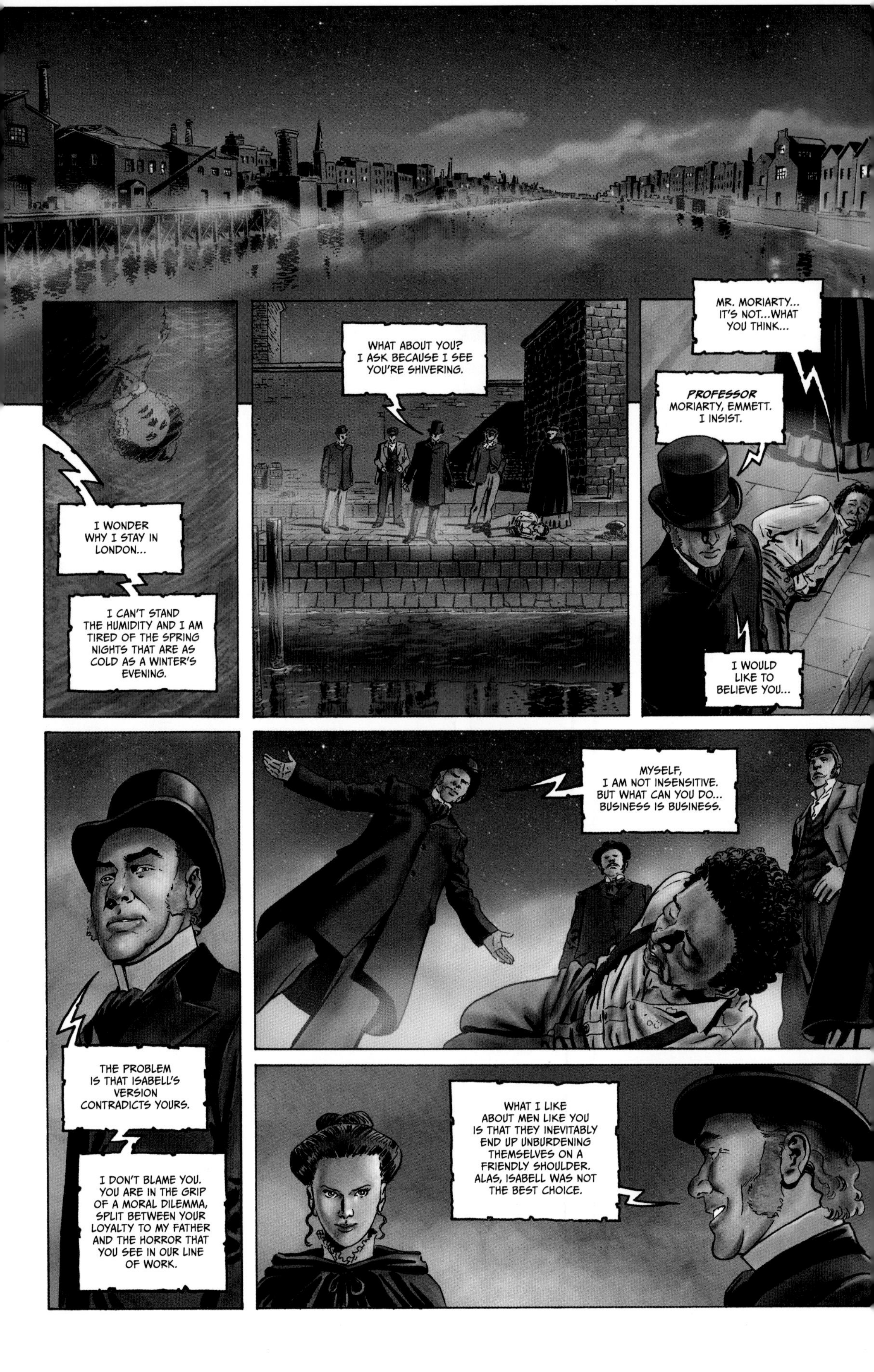
I WONDER WHY I STAY IN LONDON...
I CAN'T STAND THE HUMIDITY AND I AM TIRED OF THE SPRING NIGHTS THAT ARE AS COLD AS A WINTER'S EVENING.
WHAT ABOUT YOU? I ASK BECAUSE I SEE YOU'RE SHIVERING.
MR. MORIARTY... IT'S NOT...WHAT YOU THINK...
PROFESSOR MORIARTY, EMMETT. I INSIST.
I WOULD LIKE TO BELIEVE YOU...
THE PROBLEM IS THAT ISABELL'S VERSION CONTRADICTS YOURS.
I DON'T BLAME YOU. YOU ARE IN THE GRIP OF A MORAL DILEMMA, SPLIT BETWEEN YOUR LOYALTY TO MY FATHER AND THE HORROR THAT YOU SEE IN OUR LINE OF WORK.
MYSELF, I AM NOT INSENSITIVE. BUT WHAT CAN YOU DO... BUSINESS IS BUSINESS.
WHAT I LIKE ABOUT MEN LIKE YOU IS THAT THEY INEVITABLY END UP UNBURDENING THEMSELVES ON A FRIENDLY SHOULDER. ALAS, ISABELL WAS NOT THE BEST CHOICE.

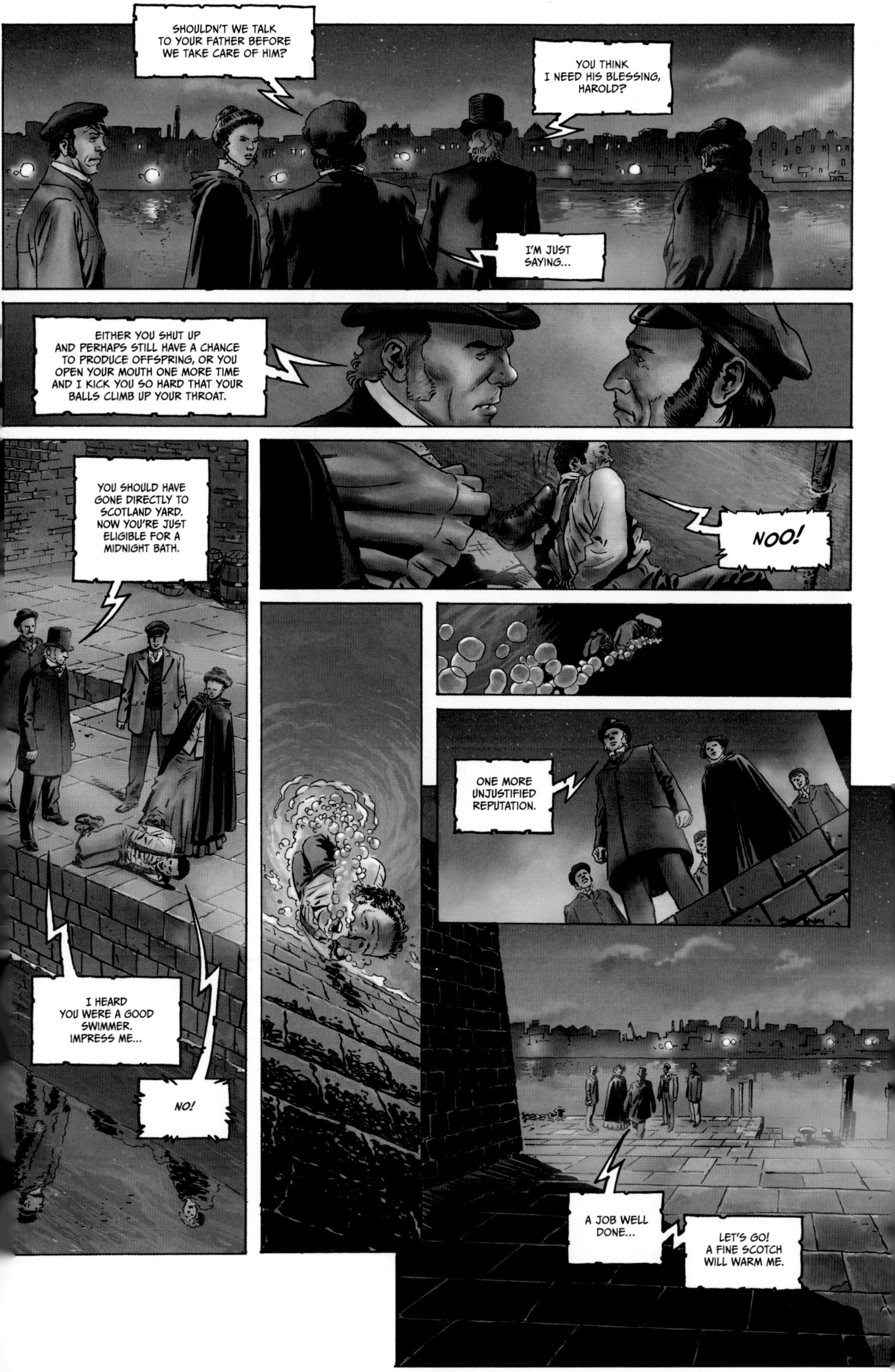
SHOULDN'T WE TALK TO YOUR FATHER BEFORE WE TAKE CARE OF HIM?
YOU THINK I NEED HIS BLESSING, HAROLD?
I'M JUST SAYING...
EITHER YOU SHUT UP AND PERHAPS STILL HAVE A CHANCE TO PRODUCE OFFSPRING, OR YOU OPEN YOUR MOUTH ONE MORE TIME AND I KICK YOU SO HARD THAT YOUR BALLS CLIMB UP YOUR THROAT.
YOU SHOULD HAVE GONE DIRECTLY TO SCOTLAND YARD. NOW YOU'RE JUST ELIGIBLE FOR A MIDNIGHT BATH.
I HEARD YOU WERE A GOOD SWIMMER. IMPRESS ME...
NO!
NOO!
ONE MORE UNJUSTIFIED REPUTATION.
A JOB WELL DONE...
LET'S GO! A FINE SCOTCH WILL WARM ME.

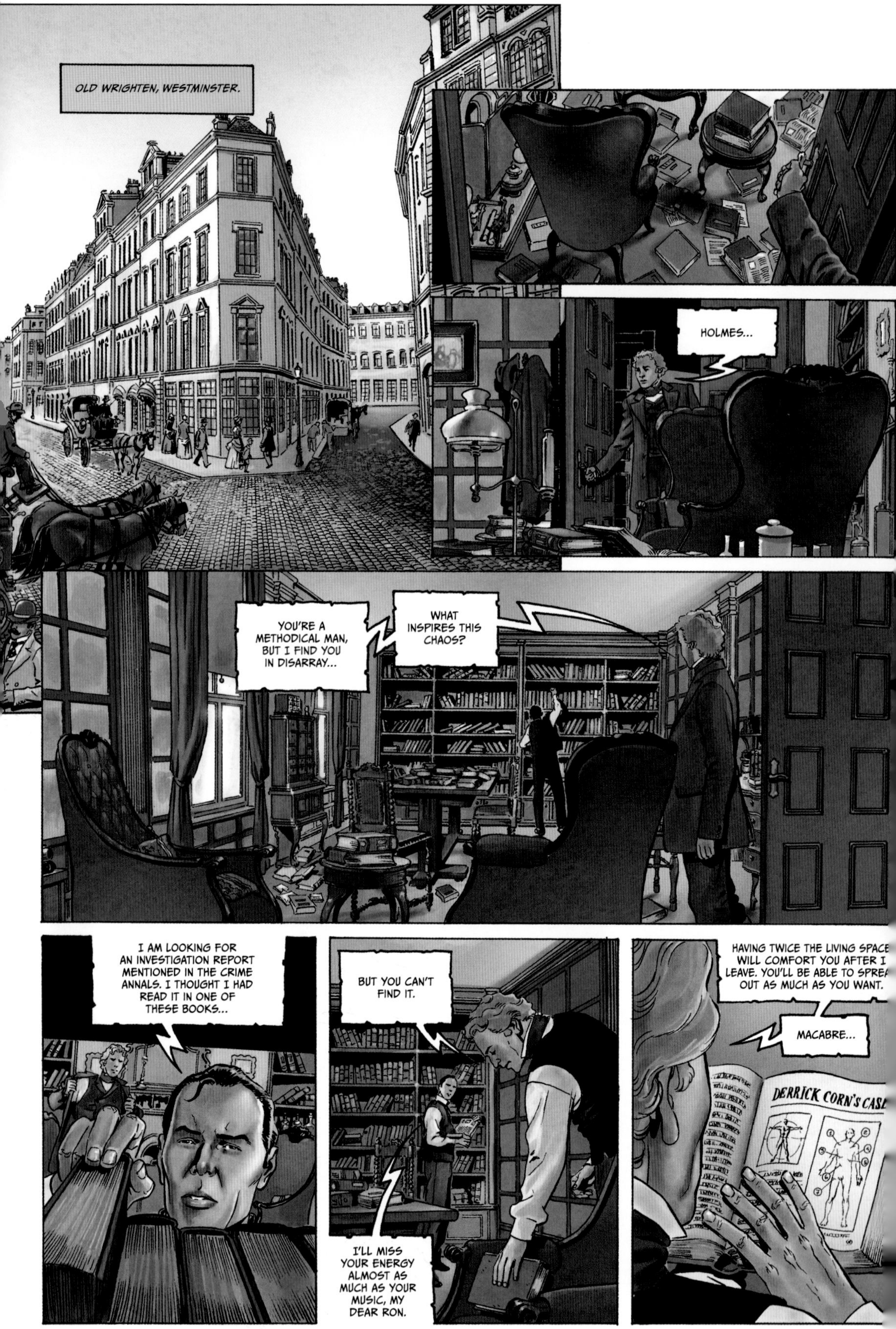

OLD WRIGHTEN, WESTMINSTER.
HOLMES...
YOU'RE A METHODICAL MAN, BUT I FIND YOU IN DISARRAY...
WHAT INSPIRES THIS CHAOS?
I AM LOOKING FOR AN INVESTIGATION REPORT MENTIONED IN THE CRIME ANNALS. I THOUGHT I HAD READ IT IN ONE OF THESE BOOKS...
BUT YOU CAN'T FIND IT.
I'LL MISS YOUR ENERGY ALMOST AS MUCH AS YOUR MUSIC, MY DEAR RON.
HAVING TWICE THE LIVING SPACE WILL COMFORT YOU AFTER I LEAVE. YOU'LL BE ABLE TO SPREA OUT AS MUCH AS YOU WANT.
MACABRE...
DERRICK CORN'S CASE

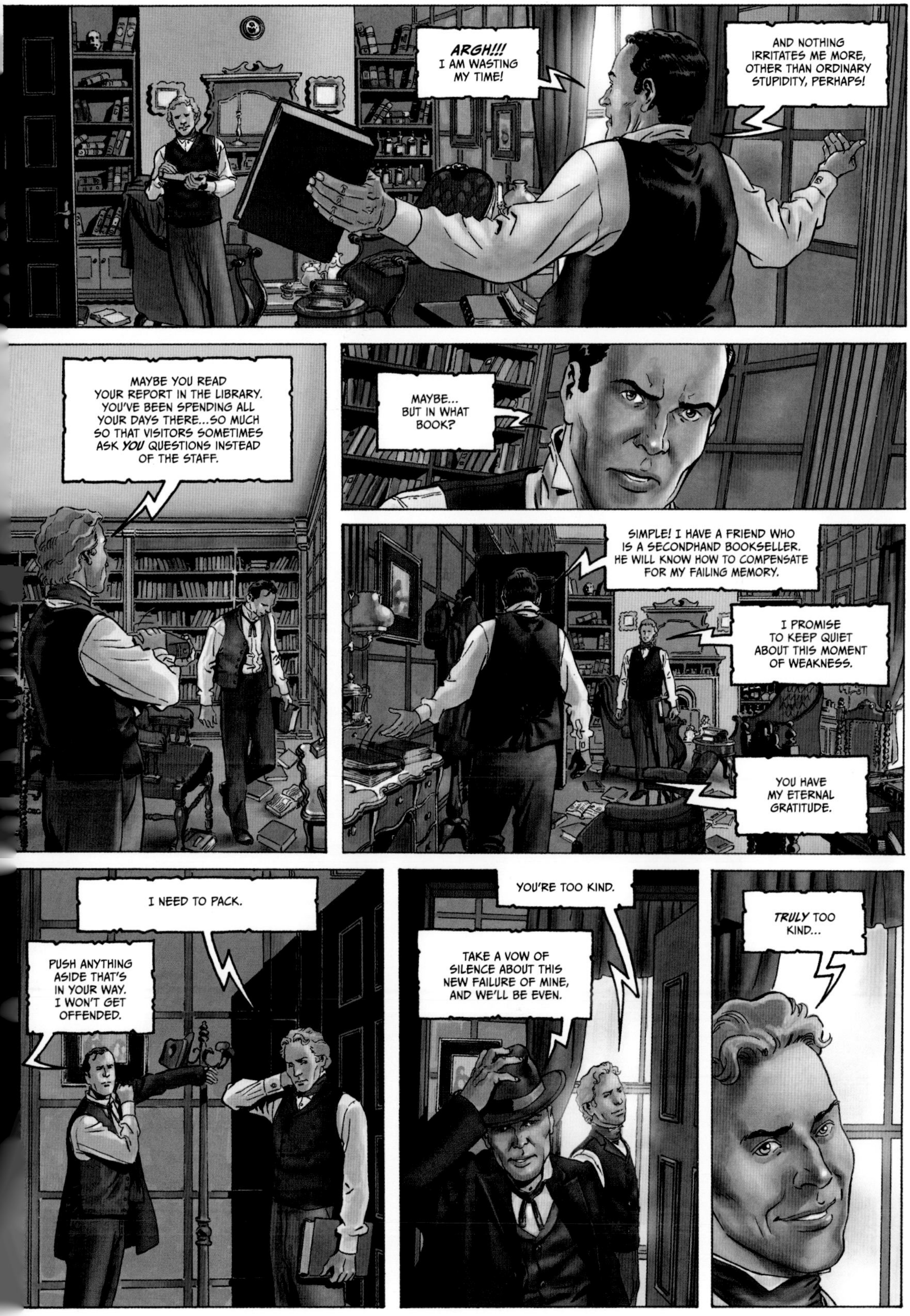
ARGH!!! I AM WASTING MY TIME!
AND NOTHING IRRITATES ME MORE, OTHER THAN ORDINARY STUPIDITY, PERHAPS!
MAYBE YOU READ YOUR REPORT IN THE LIBRARY. YOU'VE BEEN SPENDING ALL YOUR DAYS THERE...SO MUCH SO THAT VISITORS SOMETIMES ASK YOU QUESTIONS INSTEAD OF THE STAFF.
MAYBE... BUT IN WHAT BOOK?
SIMPLE! I HAVE A FRIEND WHO IS A SECONDHAND BOOKSELLER. HE WILL KNOW HOW TO COMPENSATE FOR MY FAILING MEMORY.
I PROMISE TO KEEP QUIET ABOUT THIS MOMENT OF WEAKNESS.
YOU HAVE MY ETERNAL GRATITUDE.
I NEED TO PACK.
PUSH ANYTHING ASIDE THAT'S IN YOUR WAY. I WON'T GET OFFENDED.
YOU'RE TOO KIND.
TAKE A VOW OF SILENCE ABOUT THIS NEW FAILURE OF MINE, AND WE'LL BE EVEN.
TRULY TOO KIND...

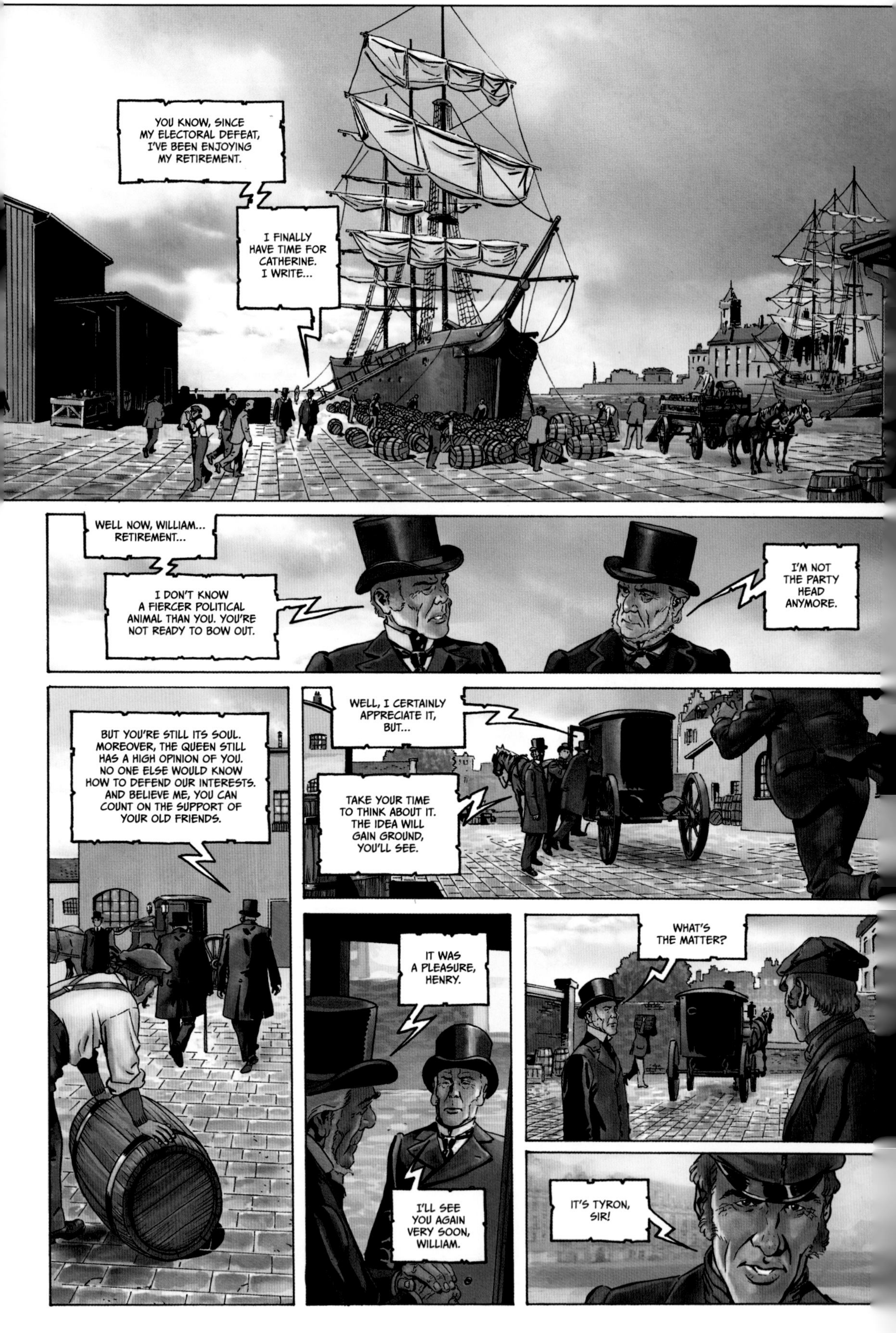

YOU KNOW, SINCE MY ELECTORAL DEFEAT, I'VE BEEN ENJOYING MY RETIREMENT.
I FINALLY HAVE TIME FOR CATHERINE. I WRITE...
WELL NOW, WILLIAM... RETIREMENT...
I DON'T KNOW A FIERCER POLITICAL ANIMAL THAN YOU. YOU'RE NOT READY TO BOW OUT.
I'M NOT THE PARTY HEAD ANYMORE.
BUT YOU'RE STILL ITS SOUL. MOREOVER, THE QUEEN STILL HAS A HIGH OPINION OF YOU. NO ONE ELSE WOULD KNOW HOW TO DEFEND OUR INTERESTS. AND BELIEVE ME, YOU CAN COUNT ON THE SUPPORT OF YOUR OLD FRIENDS.
WELL, I CERTAINLY APPRECIATE IT, BUT...
TAKE YOUR TIME TO THINK ABOUT IT. THE IDEA WILL GAIN GROUND, YOU'LL SEE.
IT WAS A PLEASURE, HENRY.
I'LL SEE YOU AGAIN VERY SOON, WILLIAM.
WHAT'S THE MATTER?
IT'S TYRON, SIR!

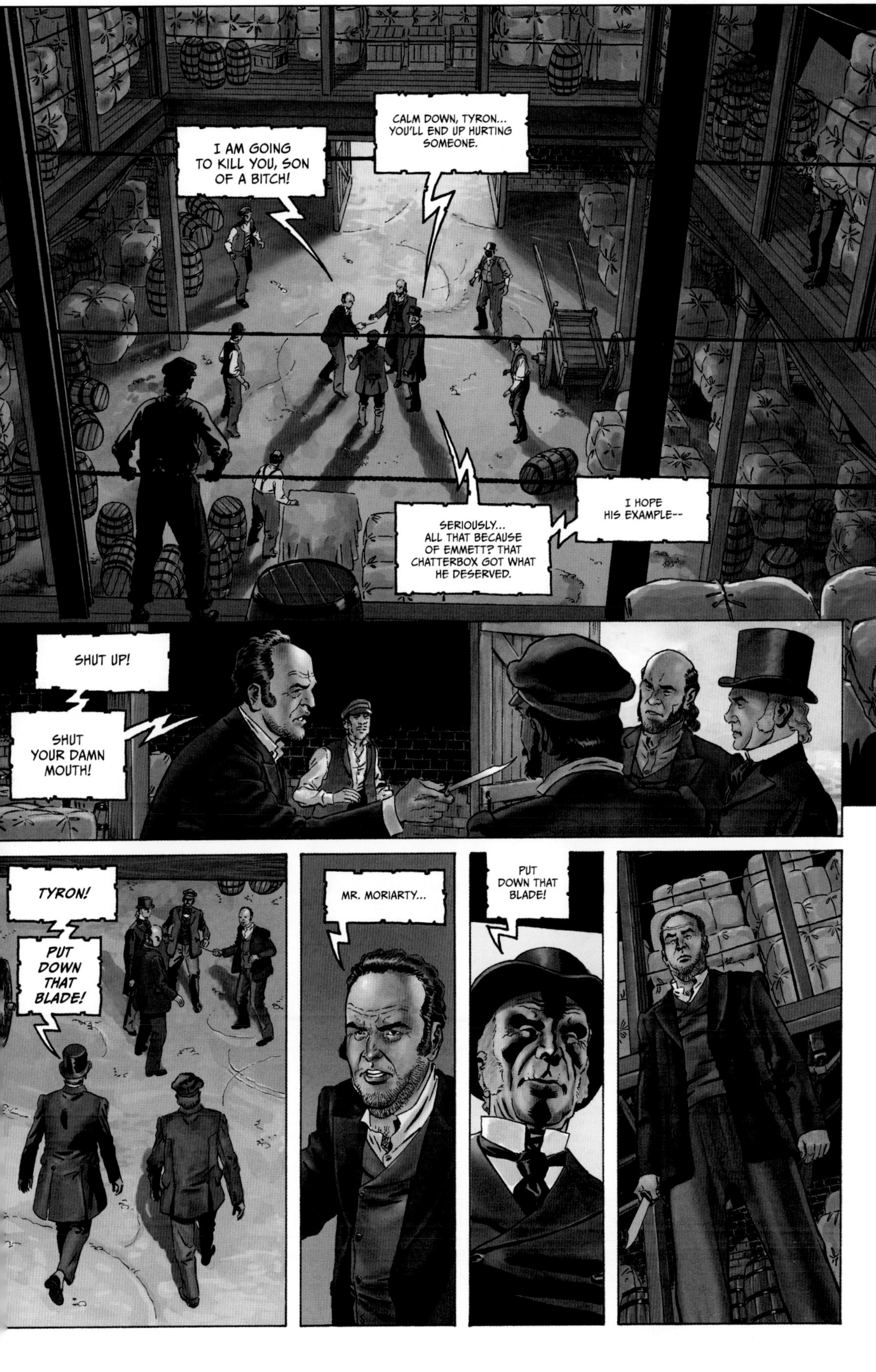

I AM GOING TO KILL YOU, SON OF A BITCH!
CALM DOWN, TYRON... YOU'LL END UP HURTING SOMEONE.
SERIOUSLY... ALL THAT BECAUSE OF EMMETT? THAT CHATTERBOX GOT WHAT HE DESERVED.
I HOPE HIS EXAMPLE--
SHUT UP!
SHUT YOUR DAMN MOUTH!
TYRON!
PUT DOWN THAT BLADE!
MR. MORIARTY...
PUT DOWN THAT BLADE!

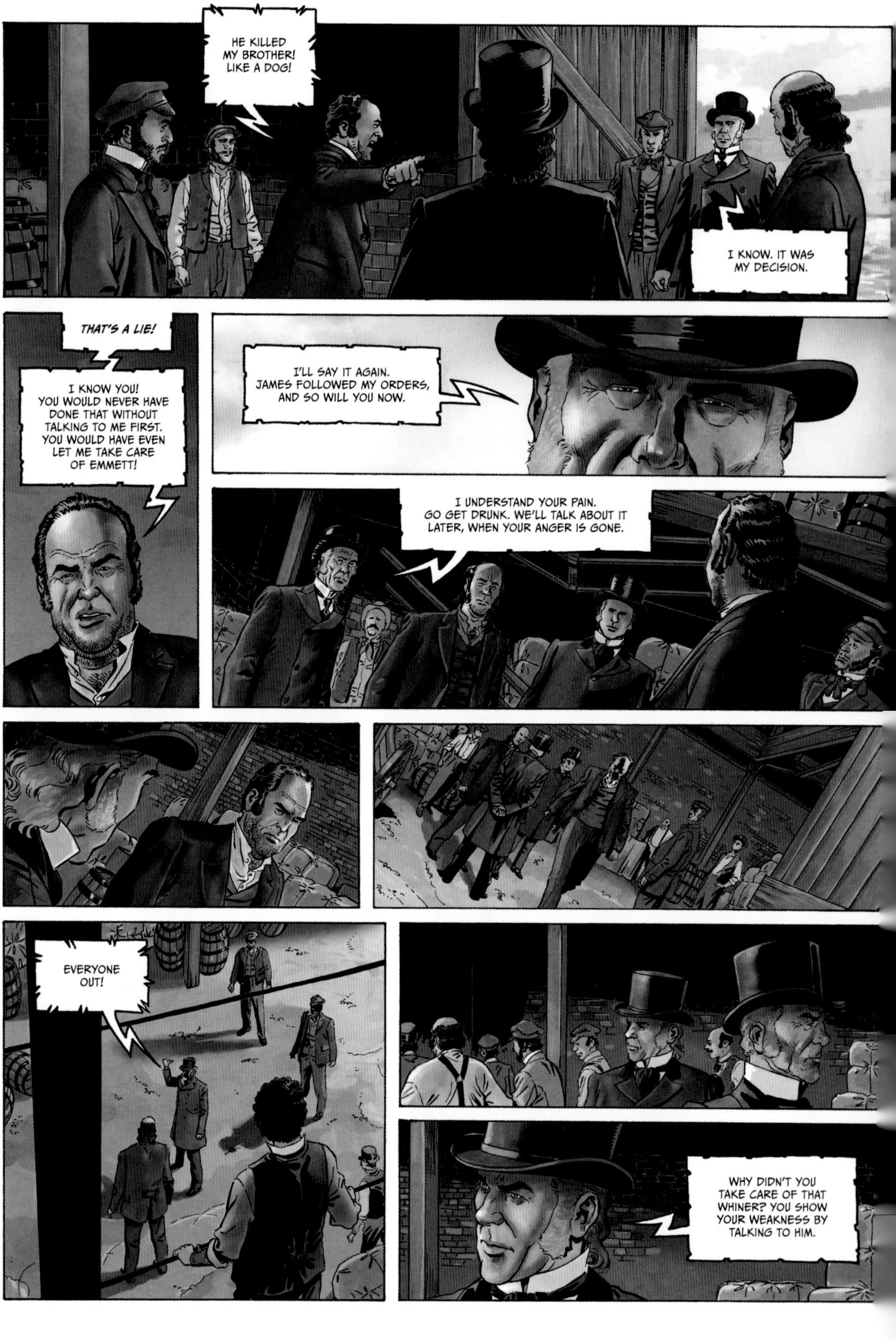
HE KILLED MY BROTHER! LIKE A DOG!
I KNOW. IT WAS MY DECISION.
THAT'S A LIE!
I KNOW YOU! YOU WOULD NEVER HAVE DONE THAT WITHOUT TALKING TO ME FIRST. YOU WOULD HAVE EVEN LET ME TAKE CARE OF EMMETT!
I'LL SAY IT AGAIN. JAMES FOLLOWED MY ORDERS, AND SO WILL YOU NOW.
I UNDERSTAND YOUR PAIN. GO GET DRUNK. WE'LL TALK ABOUT IT LATER, WHEN YOUR ANGER IS GONE.
EVERYONE OUT!
WHY DIDN'T YOU TAKE CARE OF THAT WHINER? YOU SHOW YOUR WEAKNESS BY TALKING TO HIM.

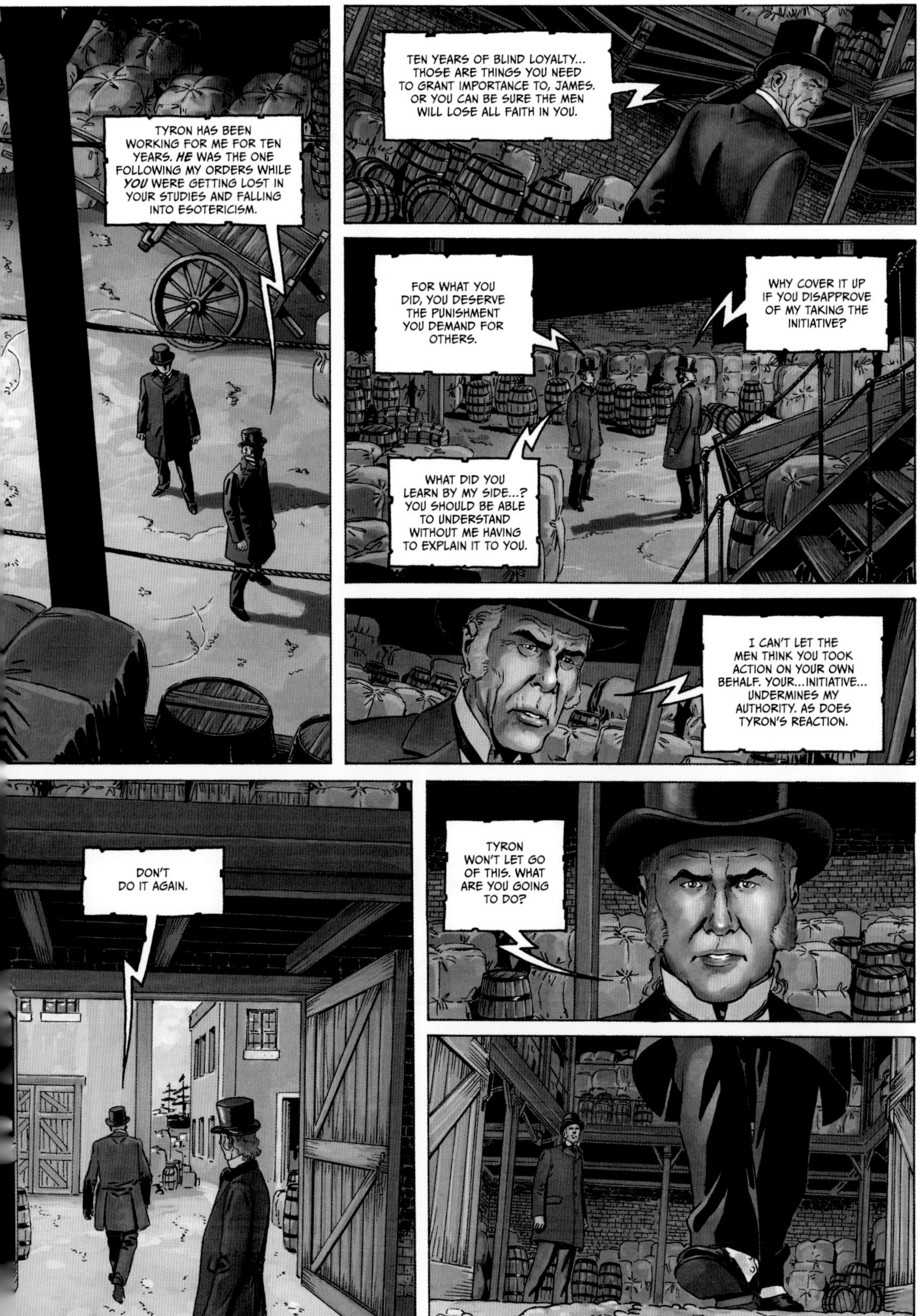
TYRON HAS BEEN WORKING FOR ME FOR TEN YEARS. HE WAS THE ONE FOLLOWING MY ORDERS WHILE YOU WERE GETTING LOST IN YOUR STUDIES AND FALLING INTO ESOTERICISM.
TEN YEARS OF BLIND LOYALTY... THOSE ARE THINGS YOU NEED TO GRANT IMPORTANCE TO, JAMES. OR YOU CAN BE SURE THE MEN WILL LOSE ALL FAITH IN YOU.
FOR WHAT YOU DID, YOU DESERVE THE PUNISHMENT YOU DEMAND FOR OTHERS.
WHY COVER IT UP IF YOU DISAPPROVE OF MY TAKING THE INITIATIVE?
WHAT DID YOU LEARN BY MY SIDE...? YOU SHOULD BE ABLE TO UNDERSTAND WITHOUT ME HAVING TO EXPLAIN IT TO YOU.
I CAN'T LET THE MEN THINK YOU TOOK ACTION ON YOUR OWN BEHALF. YOUR...INITIATIVE... UNDERMINES MY AUTHORITY. AS DOES TYRON'S REACTION.
DON'T DO IT AGAIN.
TYRON WON'T LET GO OF THIS. WHAT ARE YOU GOING TO DO?

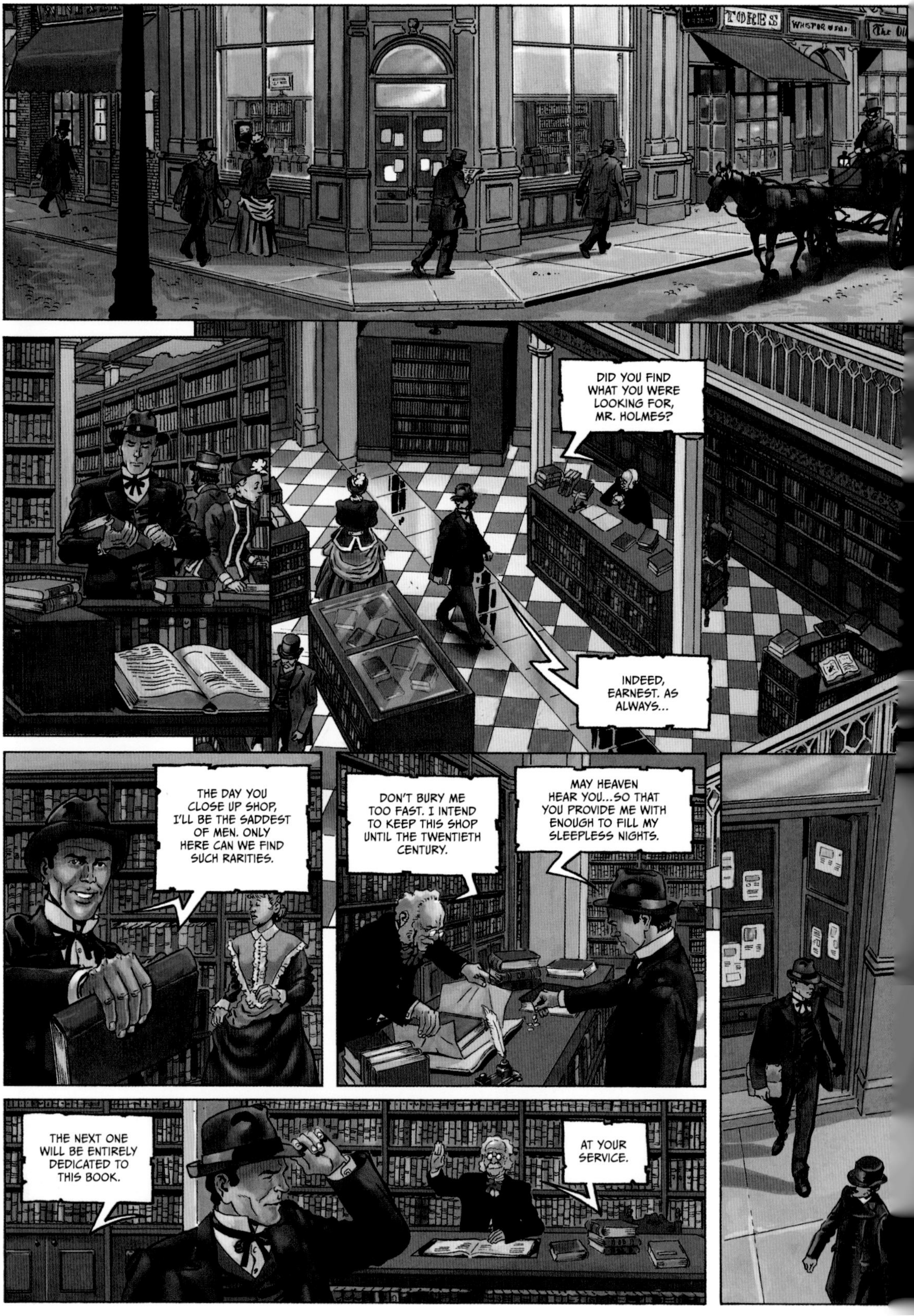

DID YOU FIND WHAT YOU WERE LOOKING FOR, MR. HOLMES?
INDEED, EARNEST. AS ALWAYS...
THE DAY YOU CLOSE UP SHOP, I'LL BE THE SADDEST OF MEN. ONLY HERE CAN WE FIND SUCH RARITIES.
DON'T BURY ME TOO FAST. I INTEND TO KEEP THIS SHOP UNTIL THE TWENTIETH CENTURY.
MAY HEAVEN HEAR YOU...SO THAT YOU PROVIDE ME WITH ENOUGH TO FILL MY SLEEPLESS NIGHTS.
THE NEXT ONE WILL BE ENTIRELY DEDICATED TO THIS BOOK.
AT YOUR SERVICE.

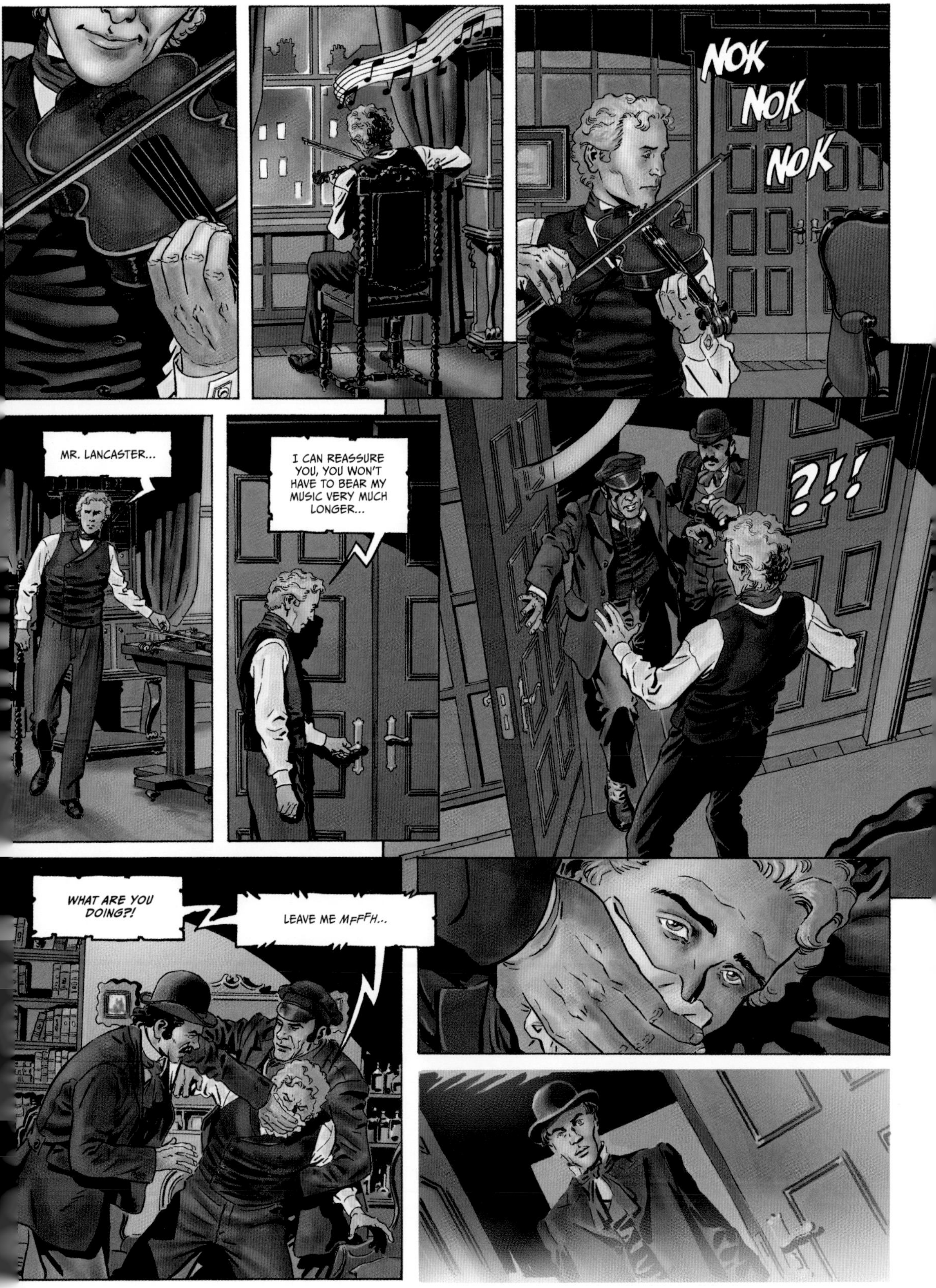
NOK
NOK
NOK
MR. LANCASTER...
I CAN REASSURE YOU, YOU WON'T HAVE TO BEAR MY MUSIC VERY MUCH LONGER...
?!!
WHAT ARE YOU DOING?!
LEAVE ME MFFFH...

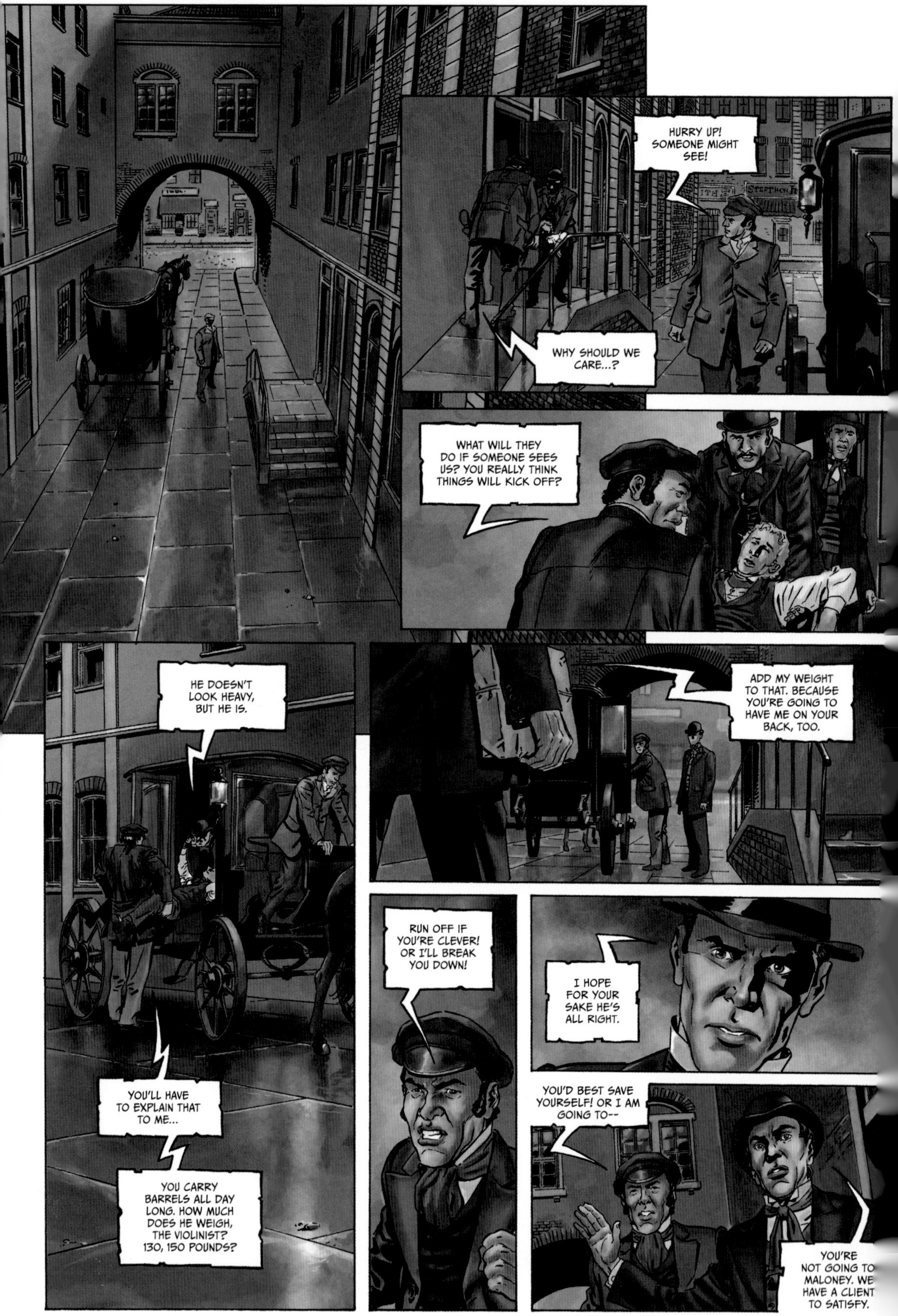
HURRY UP! SOMEONE MIGHT SEE!
WHY SHOULD WE CARE...?
WHAT WILL THEY DO IF SOMEONE SEES US? YOU REALLY THINK THINGS WILL KICK OFF?
HE DOESN'T LOOK HEAVY, BUT HE IS.
YOU'LL HAVE TO EXPLAIN THAT TO ME...
YOU CARRY BARRELS ALL DAY LONG. HOW MUCH DOES HE WEIGH, THE VIOLINIST? 130, 150 POUNDS?
ADD MY WEIGHT TO THAT. BECAUSE YOU'RE GOING TO HAVE ME ON YOUR BACK, TOO.
RUN OFF IF YOU'RE CLEVER! OR I'LL BREAK YOU DOWN!
I HOPE FOR YOUR SAKE HE'S ALL RIGHT.
YOU'D BEST SAVE YOURSELF! OR I AM GOING TO--
YOU'RE NOT GOING TO MALONEY. WE HAVE A CLIENT TO SATISFY.

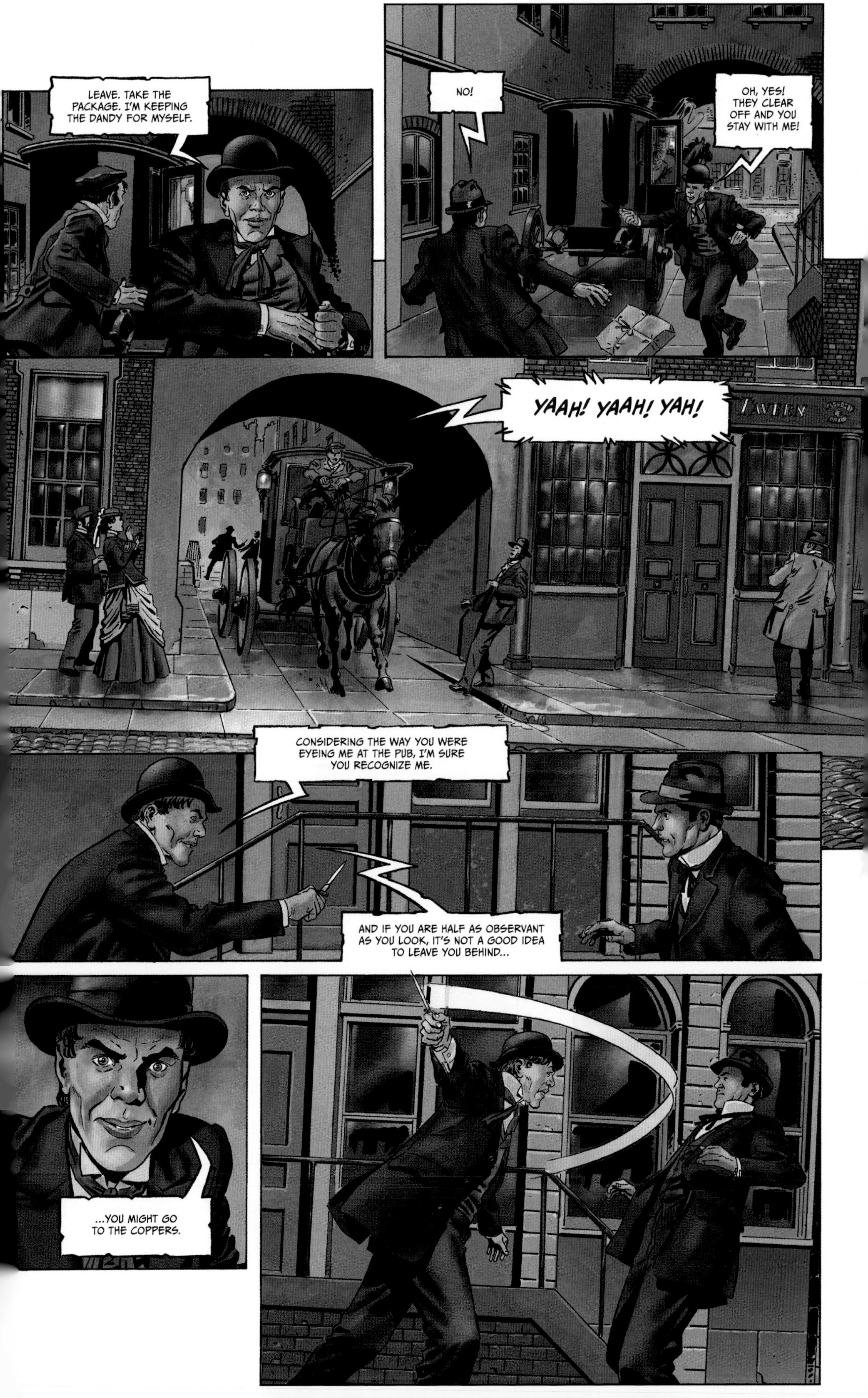
LEAVE. TAKE THE PACKAGE. I'M KEEPING THE DANDY FOR MYSELF.
NO!
OH, YES! THEY CLEAR OFF AND YOU STAY WITH ME!
YAAH! YAAH! YAH!
TAVERN
CONSIDERING THE WAY YOU WERE EYEING ME AT THE PUB, I'M SURE YOU RECOGNIZE ME.
AND IF YOU ARE HALF AS OBSERVANT AS YOU LOOK, IT'S NOT A GOOD IDEA TO LEAVE YOU BEHIND...
...YOU MIGHT GO TO THE COPPERS.

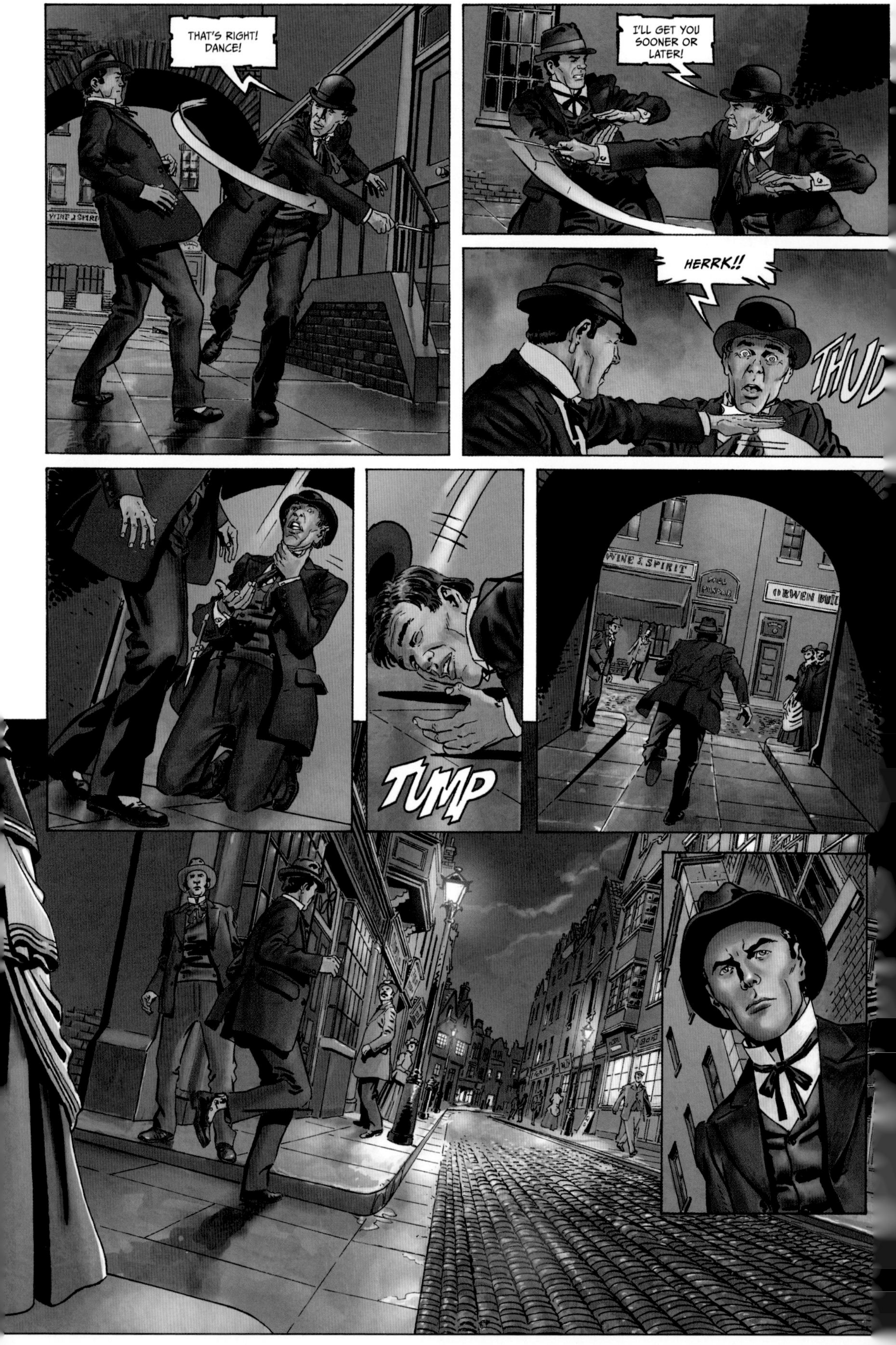
THAT'S RIGHT! DANCE!
I'LL GET YOU SOONER OR LATER!
HERRK!!
THUD
TUMP
WINE & SPIRIT
ORWEN BUIL

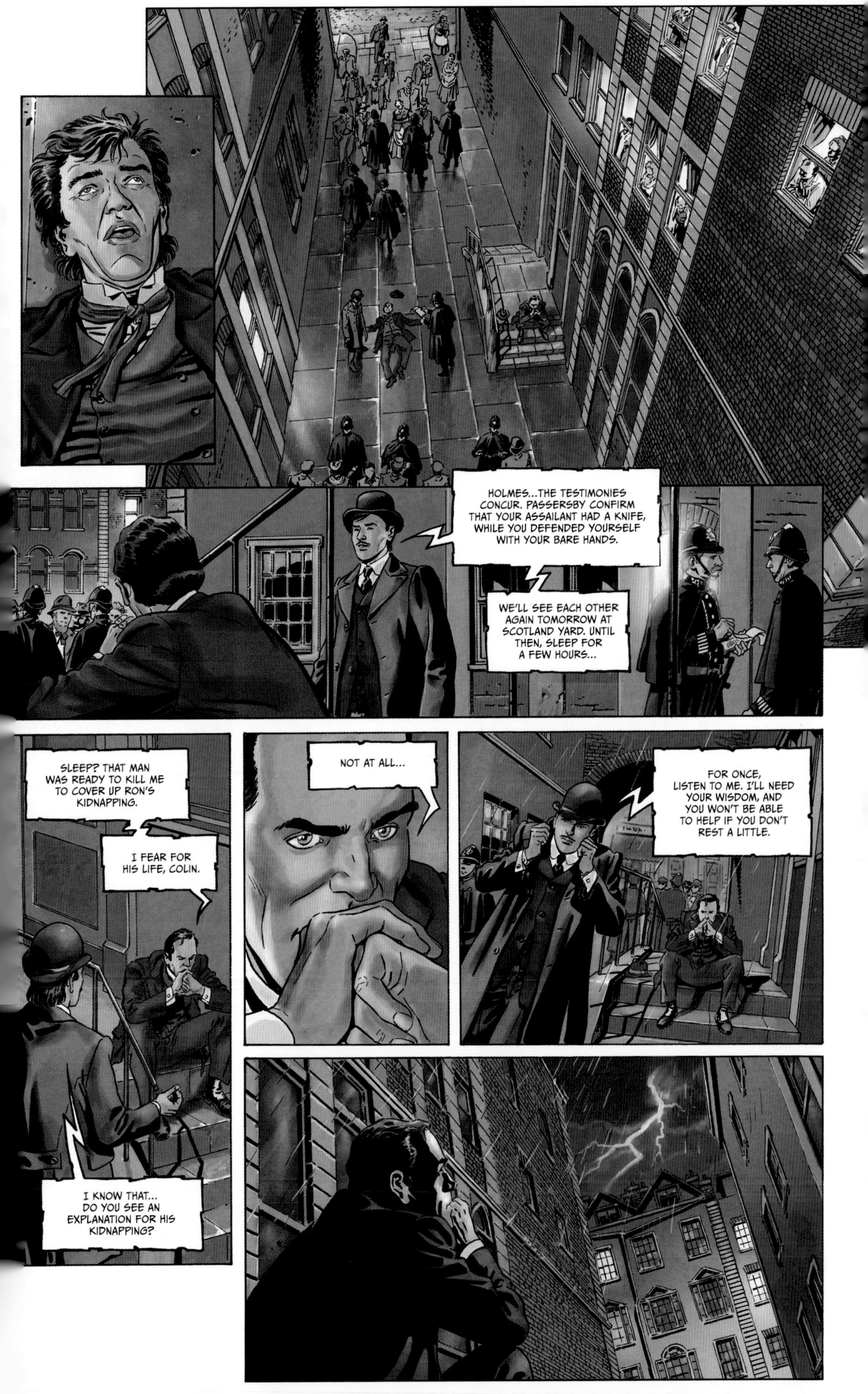

HOLMES...THE TESTIMONIES CONCUR. PASSERSBY CONFIRM THAT YOUR ASSAILANT HAD A KNIFE, WHILE YOU DEFENDED YOURSELF WITH YOUR BARE HANDS.
WE'LL SEE EACH OTHER AGAIN TOMORROW AT SCOTLAND YARD. UNTIL THEN, SLEEP FOR A FEW HOURS...
SLEEP? THAT MAN WAS READY TO KILL ME TO COVER UP RON'S KIDNAPPING.
I FEAR FOR HIS LIFE, COLIN.
I KNOW THAT... DO YOU SEE AN EXPLANATION FOR HIS KIDNAPPING?
NOT AT ALL...
FOR ONCE, LISTEN TO ME. I'LL NEED YOUR WISDOM, AND YOU WON'T BE ABLE TO HELP IF YOU DON'T REST A LITTLE.

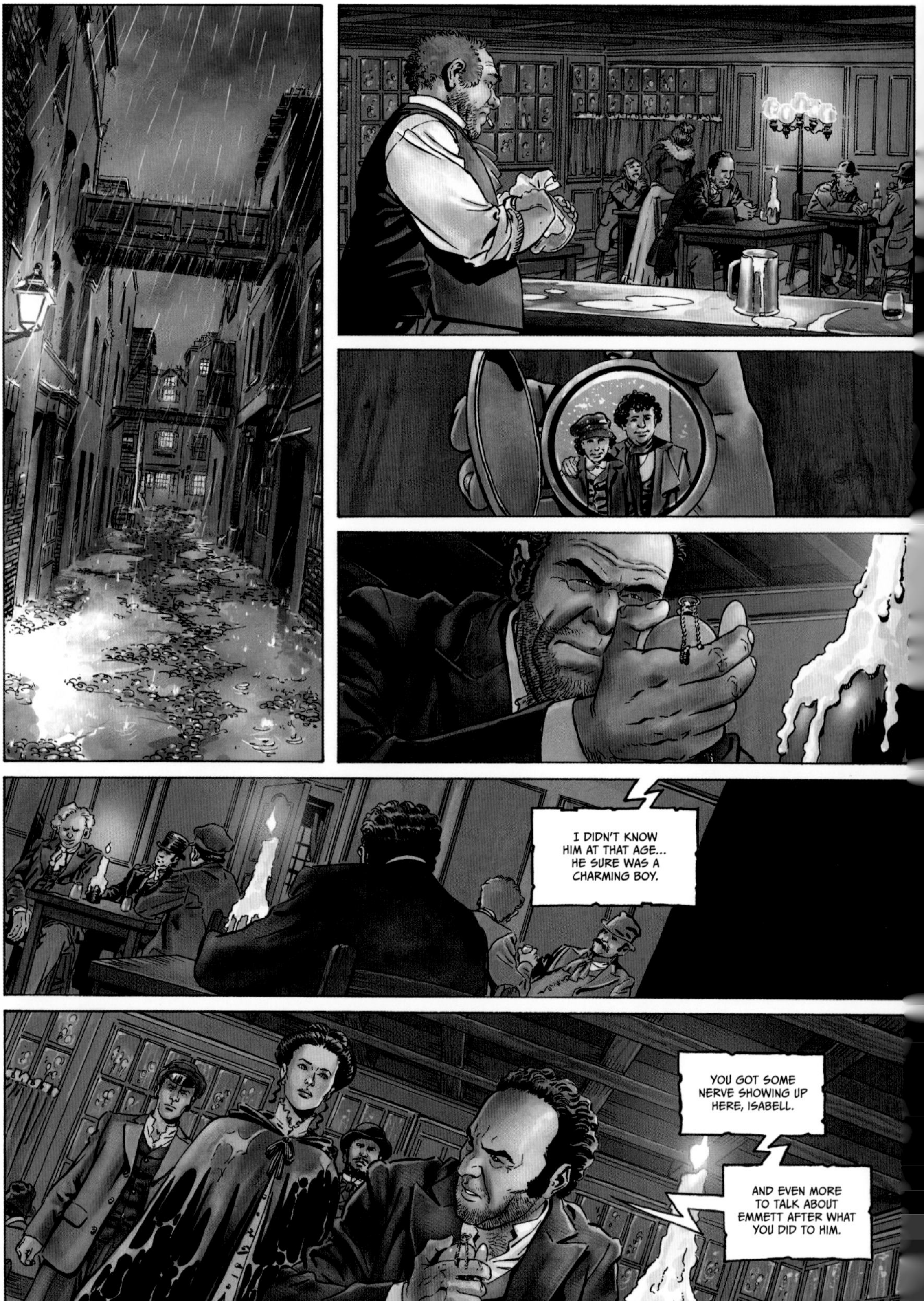
I DIDN'T KNOW HIM AT THAT AGE... HE SURE WAS A CHARMING BOY.
YOU GOT SOME NERVE SHOWING UP HERE, ISABELL.
AND EVEN MORE TO TALK ABOUT EMMETT AFTER WHAT YOU DID TO HIM.

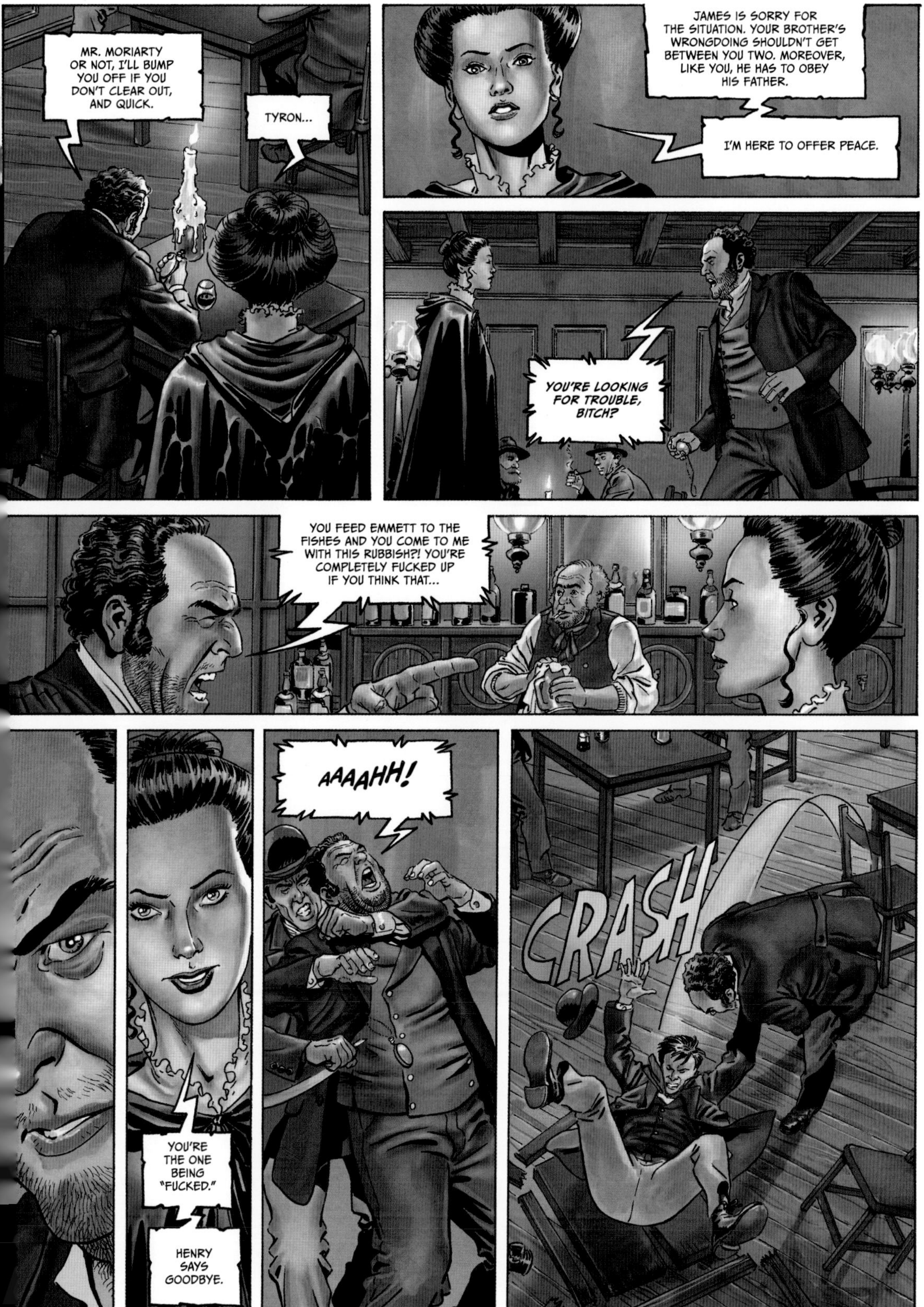
MR. MORIARTY OR NOT, I'LL BUMP YOU OFF IF YOU DON'T CLEAR OUT, AND QUICK.
TYRON...
JAMES IS SORRY FOR THE SITUATION. YOUR BROTHER'S WRONGDOING SHOULDN'T GET BETWEEN YOU TWO. MOREOVER, LIKE YOU, HE HAS TO OBEY HIS FATHER.
I'M HERE TO OFFER PEACE.
YOU'RE LOOKING FOR TROUBLE, BITCH?
YOU FEED EMMETT TO THE FISHES AND YOU COME TO ME WITH THIS RUBBISH?! YOU'RE COMPLETELY FUCKED UP IF YOU THINK THAT...
YOU'RE THE ONE BEING "FUCKED."
HENRY SAYS GOODBYE.
AAAAHH!
CRASH

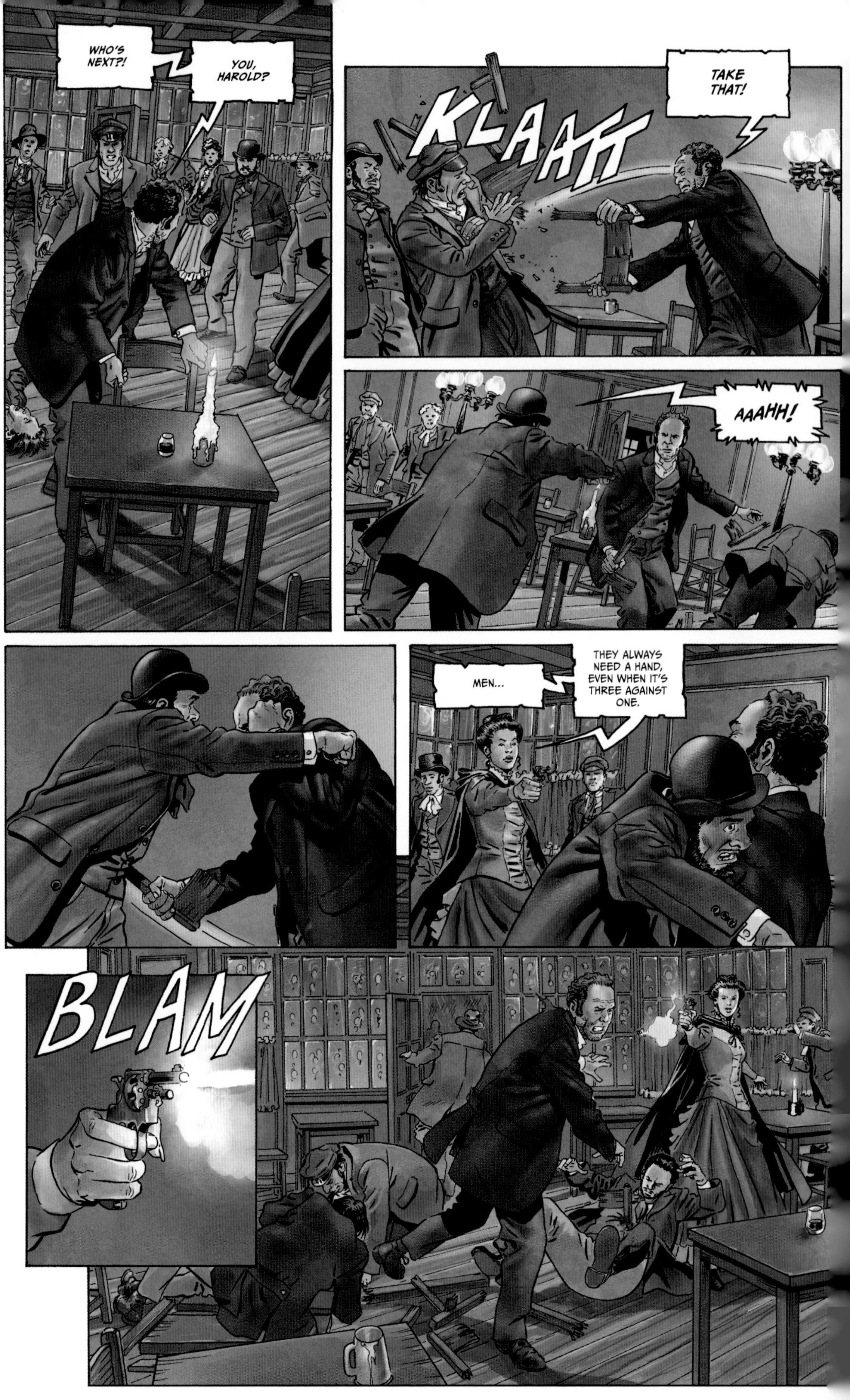
WHO'S NEXT?!
YOU, HAROLD?
KLAATT
TAKE THAT!
AAAHH!
MEN...
THEY ALWAYS NEED A HAND, EVEN WHEN IT'S THREE AGAINST ONE.
BLAM

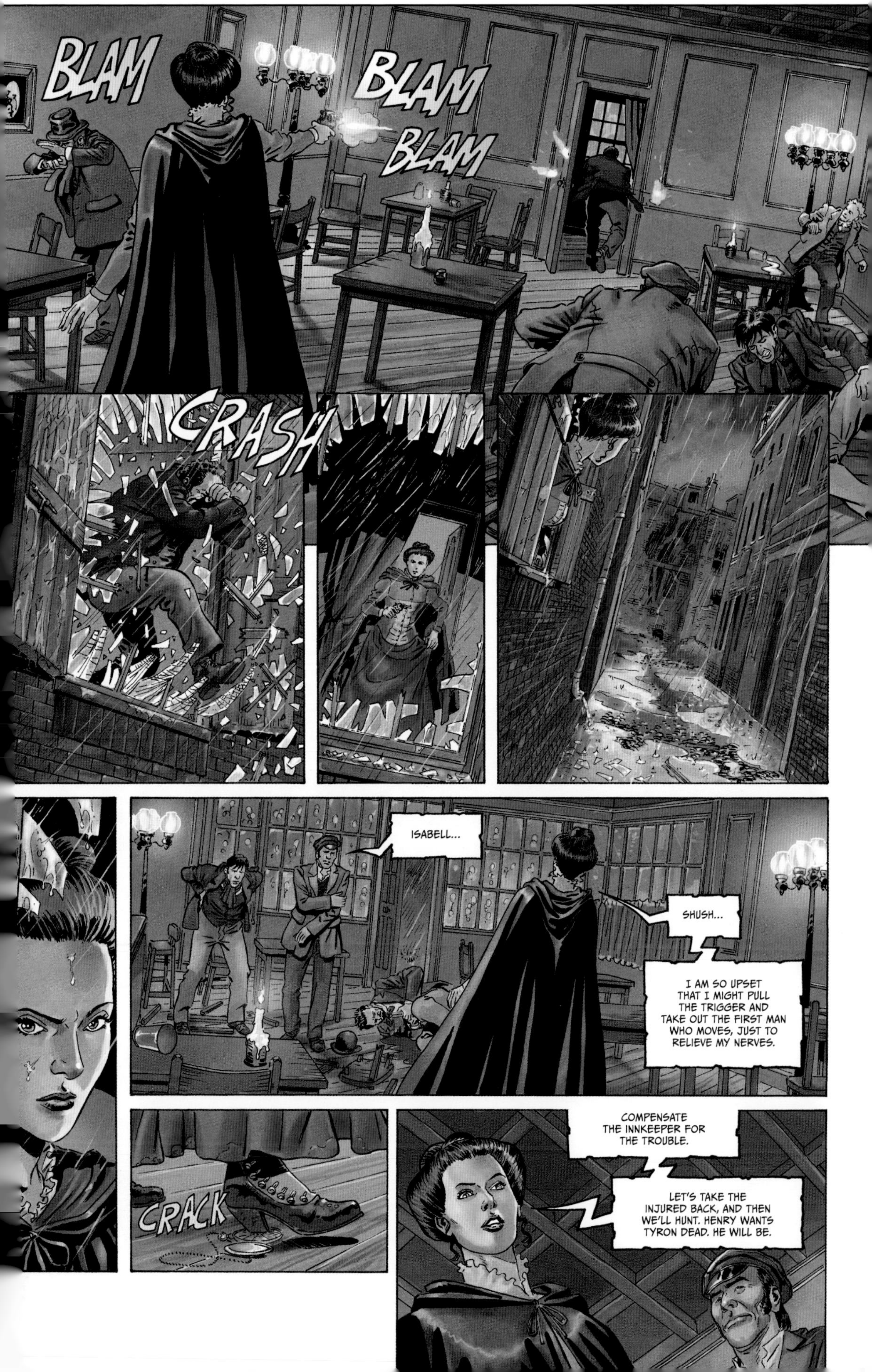
BLAM
BLAM
BLAM
CRASH
ISABELL...
SHUSH...
I AM SO UPSET THAT I MIGHT PULL THE TRIGGER AND TAKE OUT THE FIRST MAN WHO MOVES, JUST TO RELIEVE MY NERVES.
CRACK
COMPENSATE THE INNKEEPER FOR THE TROUBLE.
LET'S TAKE THE INJURED BACK, AND THEN WE'LL HUNT. HENRY WANTS TYRON DEAD. HE WILL BE.

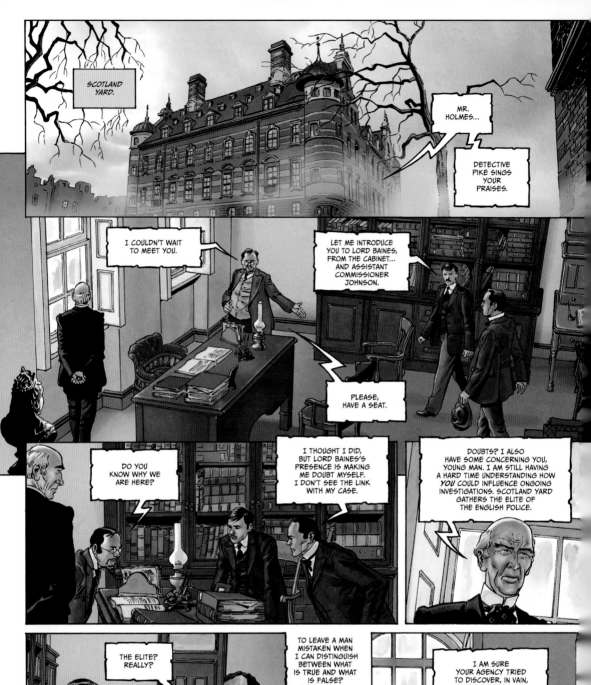

SCOTLAND YARD.

MR. HOLMES...

DETECTIVE PIKE SINGS YOUR PRAISES.

I COULDN'T WAIT TO MEET YOU.

LET ME INTRODUCE YOU TO LORD BAINES, FROM THE CABINET... AND ASSISTANT COMMISSIONER JOHNSON.

PLEASE, HAVE A SEAT.

DO YOU KNOW WHY WE ARE HERE?

I THOUGHT I DID, BUT LORD BAINES'S PRESENCE IS MAKING ME DOUBT MYSELF. I DON'T SEE THE LINK WITH MY CASE.

DOUBTS? I ALSO HAVE SOME CONCERNING YOU, YOUNG MAN. I AM STILL HAVING A HARD TIME UNDERSTANDING HOW *YOU* COULD INFLUENCE ONGOING INVESTIGATIONS. SCOTLAND YARD GATHERS THE ELITE OF THE ENGLISH POLICE.

THE ELITE? REALLY?

TO LEAVE A MAN MISTAKEN WHEN I CAN DISTINGUISH BETWEEN WHAT IS TRUE AND WHAT IS FALSE? WELL, COLIN...

HOLMES. PLEASE...

I AM SURE YOUR AGENCY TRIED TO DISCOVER, IN VAIN, THE IDENTITIES OF THE PROVIDENTIAL PEN FRIENDS WHO SIGNED THESE MISSIVES-- MELCHOR KHOLSES, CHLOE RELKHMOSS, AND SO ON.

LORD BAINES, I IMAGINE MY COOPERATION IS POTENTIALLY AS VALUABLE AS THE SERIES OF LETTERS SCOTLAND YARD HAS RECEIVED OVER THE PAST THREE YEARS-- LETTERS THAT REVEALED PLENTY OF CLUES TO THE SO-CALLED ELITES, WHO WERE STUCK IN THEIR ENDLESS INVESTIGATIONS.

34

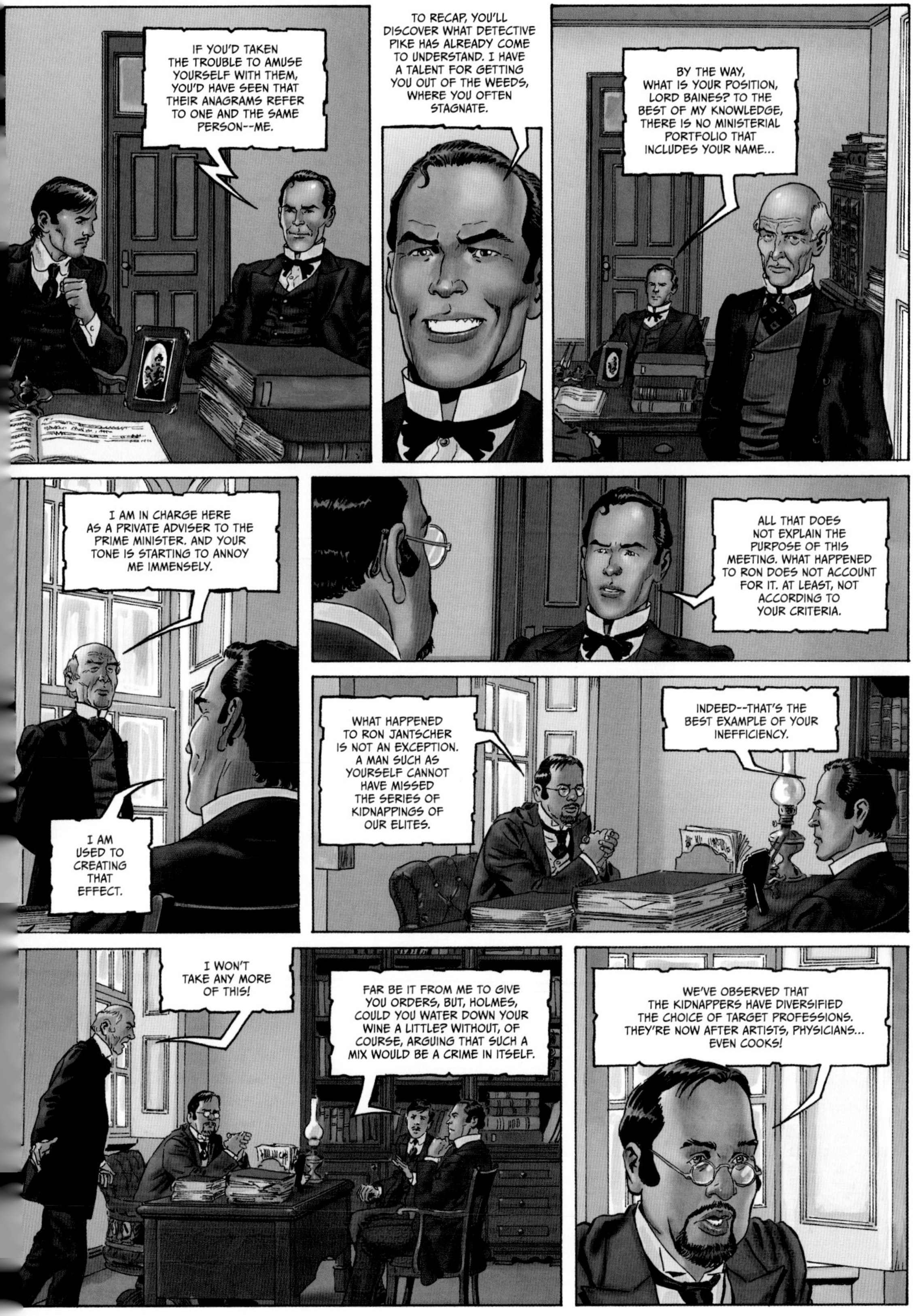
IF YOU'D TAKEN THE TROUBLE TO AMUSE YOURSELF WITH THEM, YOU'D HAVE SEEN THAT THEIR ANAGRAMS REFER TO ONE AND THE SAME PERSON--ME.
TO RECAP, YOU'LL DISCOVER WHAT DETECTIVE PIKE HAS ALREADY COME TO UNDERSTAND. I HAVE A TALENT FOR GETTING YOU OUT OF THE WEEDS, WHERE YOU OFTEN STAGNATE.
BY THE WAY, WHAT IS YOUR POSITION, LORD BAINES? TO THE BEST OF MY KNOWLEDGE, THERE IS NO MINISTERIAL PORTFOLIO THAT INCLUDES YOUR NAME...
I AM IN CHARGE HERE AS A PRIVATE ADVISER TO THE PRIME MINISTER. AND YOUR TONE IS STARTING TO ANNOY ME IMMENSELY.
I AM USED TO CREATING THAT EFFECT.
ALL THAT DOES NOT EXPLAIN THE PURPOSE OF THIS MEETING. WHAT HAPPENED TO RON DOES NOT ACCOUNT FOR IT. AT LEAST, NOT ACCORDING TO YOUR CRITERIA.
WHAT HAPPENED TO RON JANTSCHER IS NOT AN EXCEPTION. A MAN SUCH AS YOURSELF CANNOT HAVE MISSED THE SERIES OF KIDNAPPINGS OF OUR ELITES.
INDEED--THAT'S THE BEST EXAMPLE OF YOUR INEFFICIENCY.
I WON'T TAKE ANY MORE OF THIS!
FAR BE IT FROM ME TO GIVE YOU ORDERS, BUT, HOLMES, COULD YOU WATER DOWN YOUR WINE A LITTLE? WITHOUT, OF COURSE, ARGUING THAT SUCH A MIX WOULD BE A CRIME IN ITSELF.
WE'VE OBSERVED THAT THE KIDNAPPERS HAVE DIVERSIFIED THE CHOICE OF TARGET PROFESSIONS. THEY'RE NOW AFTER ARTISTS, PHYSICIANS... EVEN COOKS!

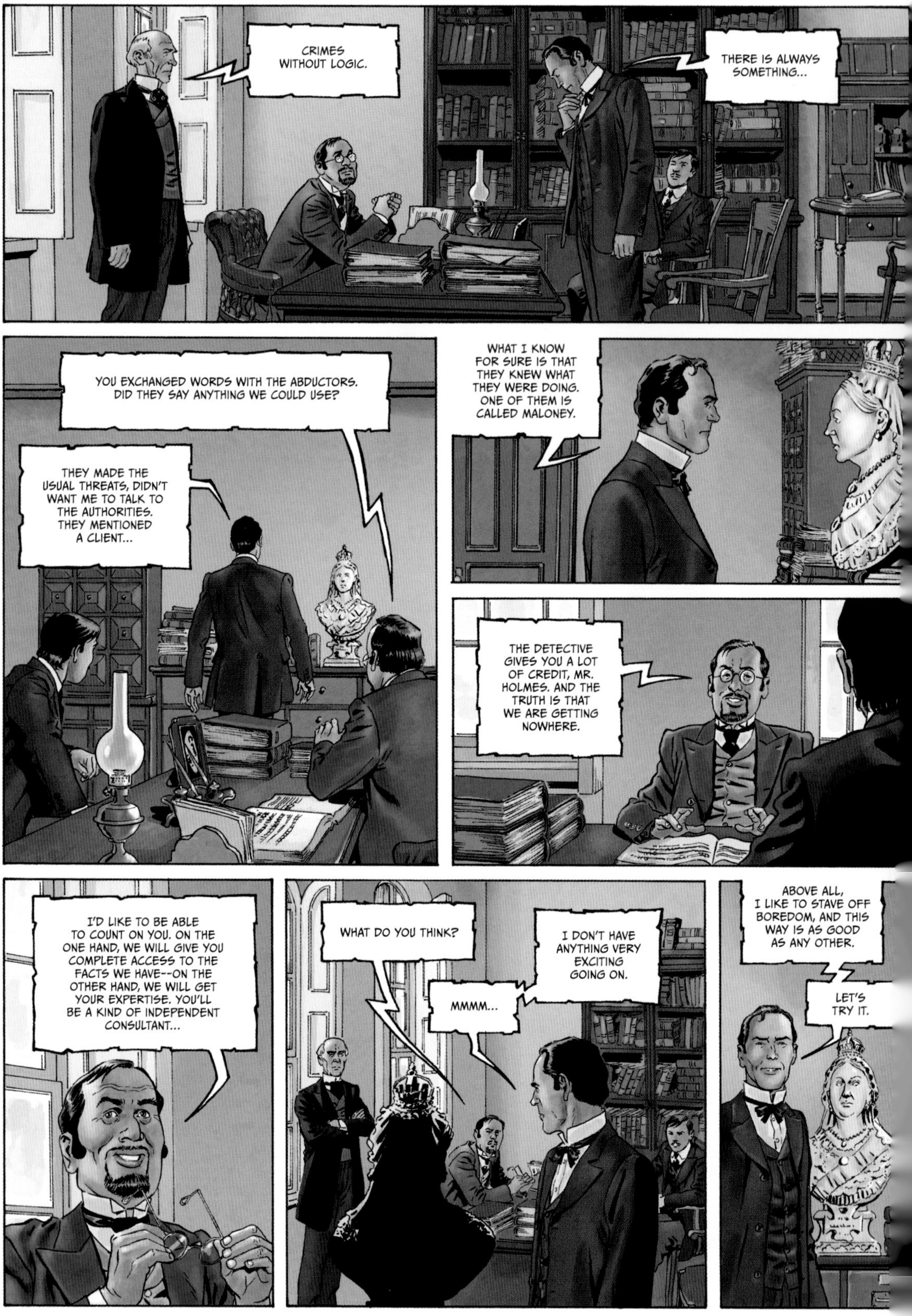
CRIMES WITHOUT LOGIC.
THERE IS ALWAYS SOMETHING...
YOU EXCHANGED WORDS WITH THE ABDUCTORS. DID THEY SAY ANYTHING WE COULD USE?
THEY MADE THE USUAL THREATS, DIDN'T WANT ME TO TALK TO THE AUTHORITIES. THEY MENTIONED A CLIENT...
WHAT I KNOW FOR SURE IS THAT THEY KNEW WHAT THEY WERE DOING. ONE OF THEM IS CALLED MALONEY.
THE DETECTIVE GIVES YOU A LOT OF CREDIT, MR. HOLMES. AND THE TRUTH IS THAT WE ARE GETTING NOWHERE.
I'D LIKE TO BE ABLE TO COUNT ON YOU. ON THE ONE HAND, WE WILL GIVE YOU COMPLETE ACCESS TO THE FACTS WE HAVE--ON THE OTHER HAND, WE WILL GET YOUR EXPERTISE. YOU'LL BE A KIND OF INDEPENDENT CONSULTANT...
WHAT DO YOU THINK?
MMMM...
I DON'T HAVE ANYTHING VERY EXCITING GOING ON.
ABOVE ALL, I LIKE TO STAVE OFF BOREDOM, AND THIS WAY IS AS GOOD AS ANY OTHER.
LET'S TRY IT.

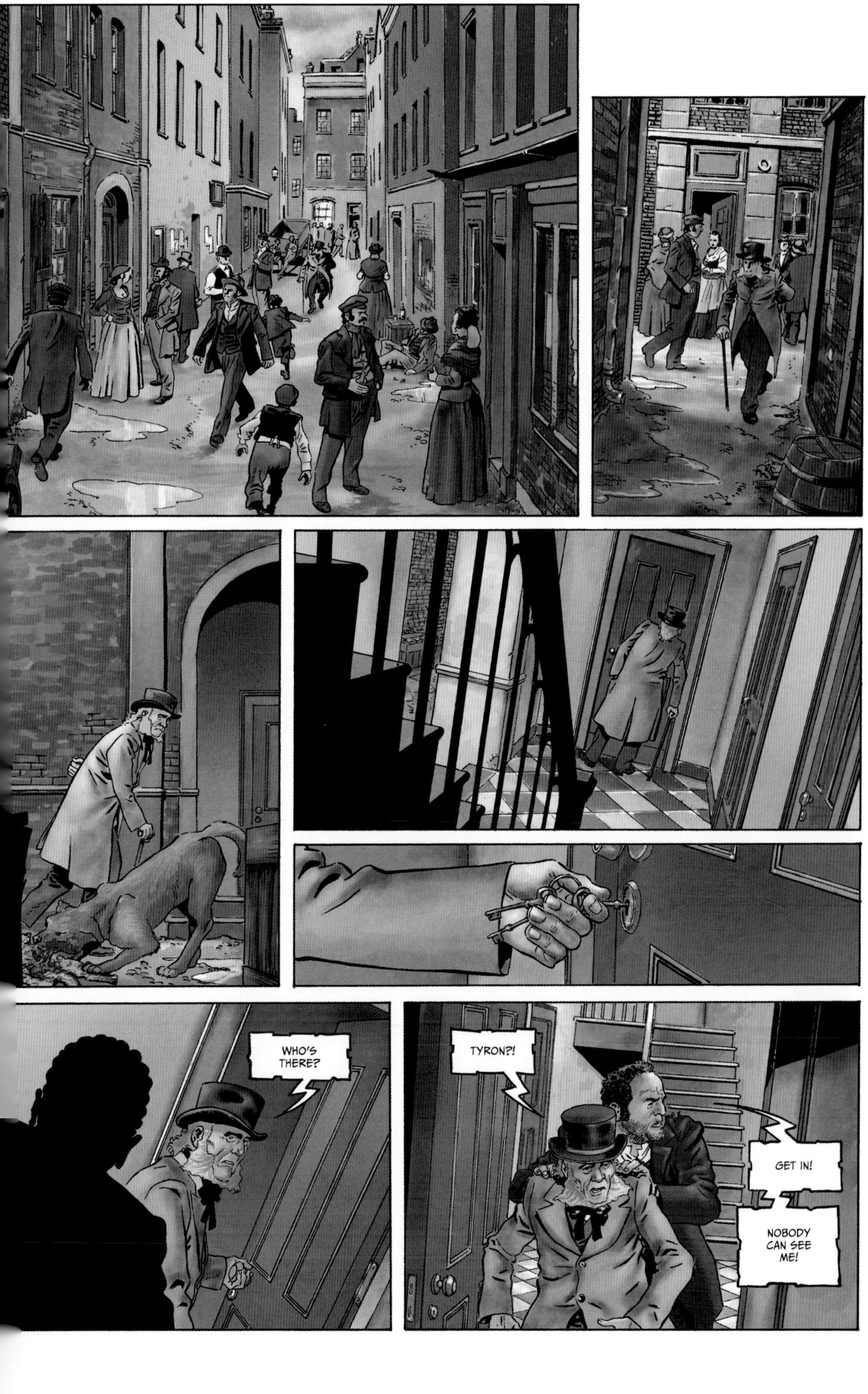
WHO'S THERE?
TYRON?!
GET IN!
NOBODY CAN SEE ME!

YOU GOT LUCKY.

THE BULLET JUST GRAZED YOU. AND THE KNIFE WOUND COULD HAVE DONE SOME SERIOUS DAMAGE...FORTUNATELY, THE INJURY IS SUPERFICIAL.

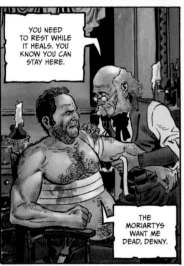

YOU NEED TO REST WHILE IT HEALS. YOU KNOW YOU CAN STAY HERE.

THE MORIARTYS WANT ME DEAD, DENNY.

IF THEY FIND ME HERE, YOU'LL BE IN TROUBLE. JUST FOR HELPING ME.

I CAN'T STAY...

AND WHAT WILL YOU DO INSTEAD? HIDE IN SOME CORNER?

KEEP MOVING.

AND MAKE YOUR CONDITION WORSE AT THE SAME TIME.

DO YOU AT LEAST HAVE A PLAN?

FIRST, I AM GOING TO AVOID BEING A TARGET. THAT'S A GOOD START...

IF THE MORIARTY FAMILY IS AFTER YOU, THE ONLY REASONABLE THING TO DO IS TO LEAVE LONDON.

YOU THINK THAT WILL SAVE ME? IF HENRY AND JAMES WANT ME, THEY'LL HAVE ME.

NO...THE ONLY WAY TO GET OUT OF THIS IS TO STRIKE FIRST.

THOSE WHO TRIED AREN'T HERE ANYMORE TO TALK ABOUT IT. I DON'T SEE WHY YOU'D FARE BETTER.

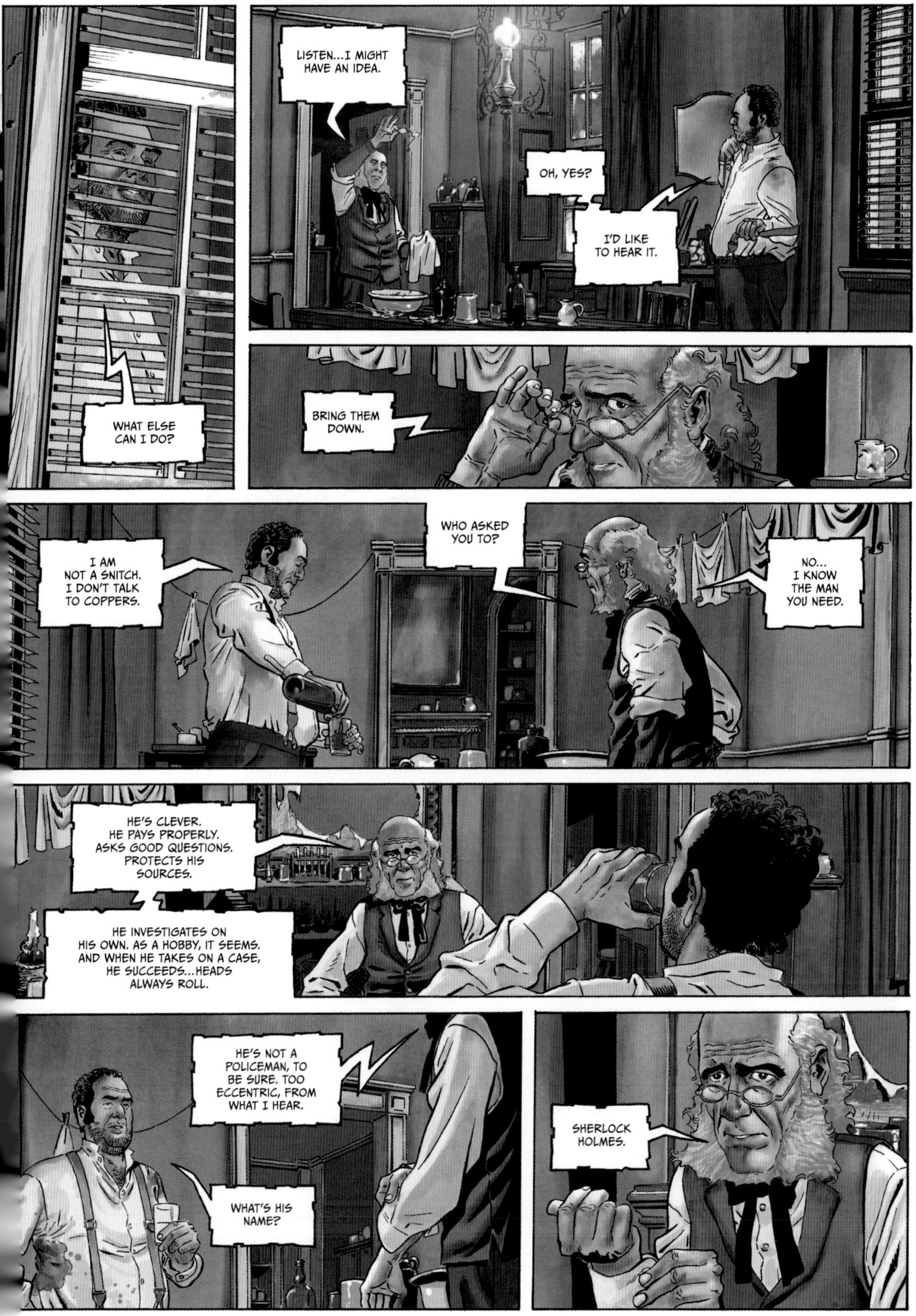
LISTEN...I MIGHT HAVE AN IDEA.
OH, YES?
I'D LIKE TO HEAR IT.
WHAT ELSE CAN I DO?
BRING THEM DOWN.
I AM NOT A SNITCH. I DON'T TALK TO COPPERS.
WHO ASKED YOU TO?
NO... I KNOW THE MAN YOU NEED.
HE'S CLEVER. HE PAYS PROPERLY. ASKS GOOD QUESTIONS. PROTECTS HIS SOURCES.
HE INVESTIGATES ON HIS OWN. AS A HOBBY, IT SEEMS. AND WHEN HE TAKES ON A CASE, HE SUCCEEDS...HEADS ALWAYS ROLL.
HE'S NOT A POLICEMAN, TO BE SURE. TOO ECCENTRIC, FROM WHAT I HEAR.
WHAT'S HIS NAME?
SHERLOCK HOLMES.

COLLABORATING IS ONE THING. SHARING ALL MY INFORMATION WITH SCOTLAND YARD IS ANOTHER.

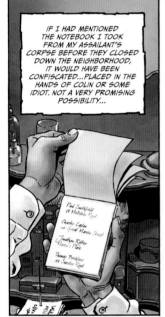

IF I HAD MENTIONED THE NOTEBOOK I TOOK FROM MY ASSAILANT'S CORPSE BEFORE THEY CLOSED DOWN THE NEIGHBORHOOD, IT WOULD HAVE BEEN CONFISCATED...PLACED IN THE HANDS OF COLIN OR SOME IDIOT. NOT A VERY PROMISING POSSIBILITY...

AFTER CHECKING INTO THE MATTER, I'VE DISCOVERED ALL THE PEOPLE NAMED HERE ARE ALREADY MISSING.

TOO BAD...PUTTING A POTENTIAL TARGET UNDER SURVEILLANCE COULD HAVE LED TO CATCHING THE ABDUCTORS IN THE ACT AND TO THEIR SUBSEQUENT ARRESTS.

THE NOTEBOOK CONFIRMS JOHNSON'S WORDS. THE MOST RECENT VICTIMS ARE FROM INCREASINGLY VARIED TRADES. BUT THEY ALL HAVE SOMETHING IN COMMON HE DID NOT EMPHASIZE. THEY'RE THE BEST IN THEIR RESPECTIVE FIELDS.

INTERESTING...

ALSO INTRIGUING... THE KIDNAPPERS' MOTIVES ARE UNKNOWN. THERE HAVE BEEN NO DEMANDS FOR RANSOM SINCE THEY STARTED.

THAT LEADS ME TO A SIMPLE QUESTION... WHY THESE ABDUCTIONS?

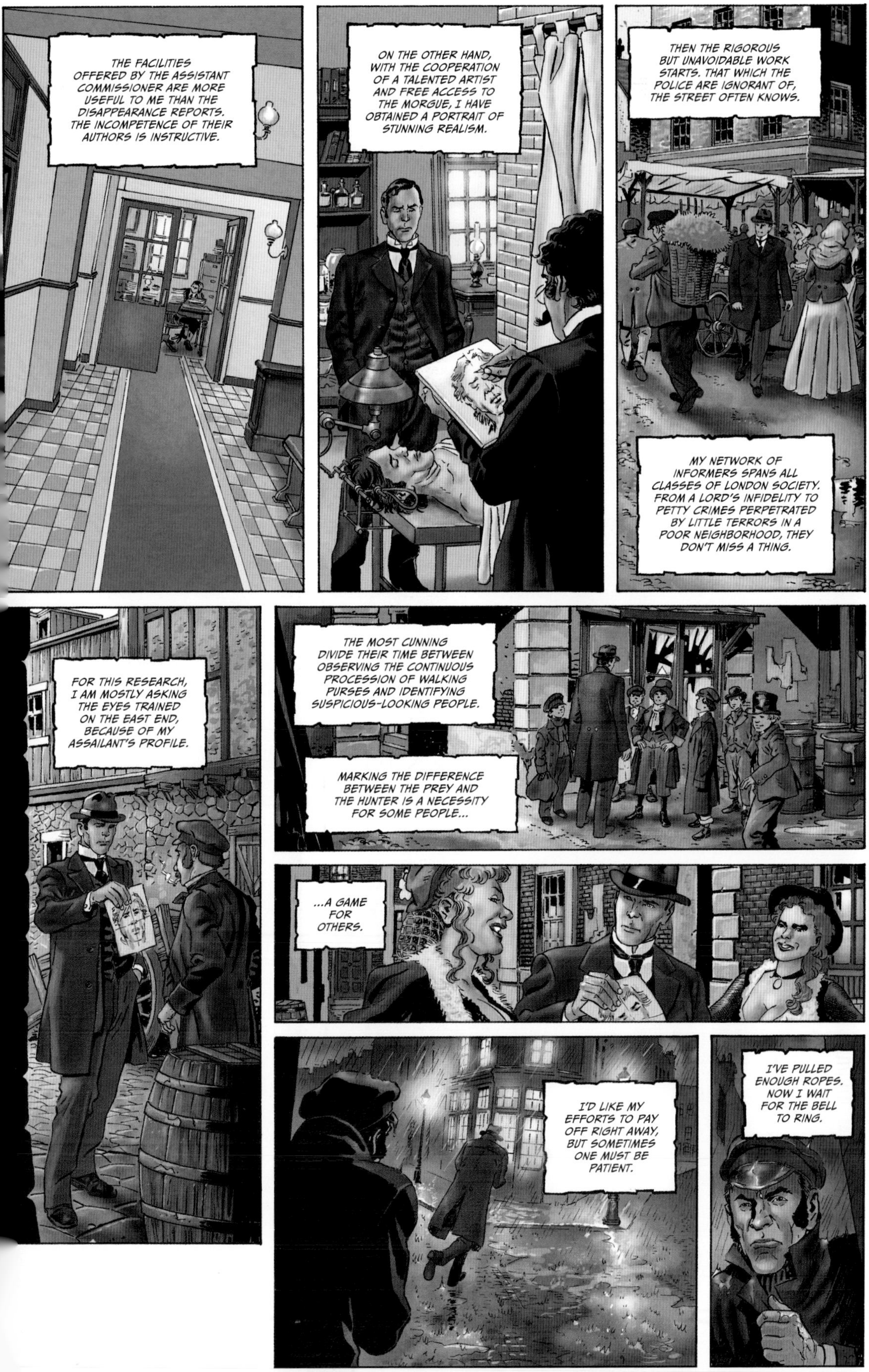
THE FACILITIES OFFERED BY THE ASSISTANT COMMISSIONER ARE MORE USEFUL TO ME THAN THE DISAPPEARANCE REPORTS. THE INCOMPETENCE OF THEIR AUTHORS IS INSTRUCTIVE.
ON THE OTHER HAND, WITH THE COOPERATION OF A TALENTED ARTIST AND FREE ACCESS TO THE MORGUE, I HAVE OBTAINED A PORTRAIT OF STUNNING REALISM.
THEN THE RIGOROUS BUT UNAVOIDABLE WORK STARTS. THAT WHICH THE POLICE ARE IGNORANT OF, THE STREET OFTEN KNOWS.
MY NETWORK OF INFORMERS SPANS ALL CLASSES OF LONDON SOCIETY. FROM A LORD'S INFIDELITY TO PETTY CRIMES PERPETRATED BY LITTLE TERRORS IN A POOR NEIGHBORHOOD, THEY DON'T MISS A THING.
FOR THIS RESEARCH, I AM MOSTLY ASKING THE EYES TRAINED ON THE EAST END, BECAUSE OF MY ASSAILANT'S PROFILE.
THE MOST CUNNING DIVIDE THEIR TIME BETWEEN OBSERVING THE CONTINUOUS PROCESSION OF WALKING PURSES AND IDENTIFYING SUSPICIOUS-LOOKING PEOPLE.
MARKING THE DIFFERENCE BETWEEN THE PREY AND THE HUNTER IS A NECESSITY FOR SOME PEOPLE...
...A GAME FOR OTHERS.
I'D LIKE MY EFFORTS TO PAY OFF RIGHT AWAY, BUT SOMETIMES ONE MUST BE PATIENT.
I'VE PULLED ENOUGH ROPES. NOW I WAIT FOR THE BELL TO RING.

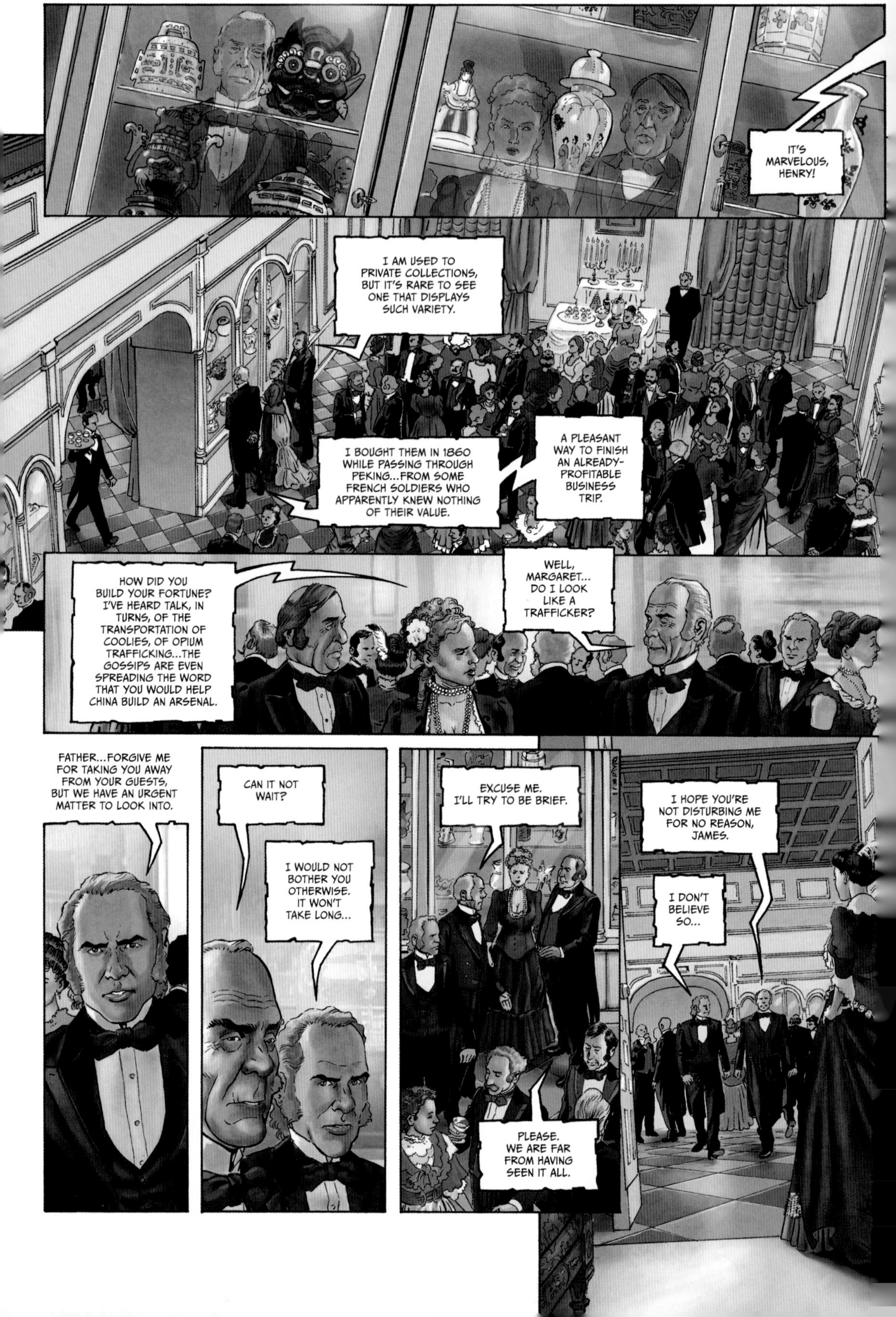
IT'S MARVELOUS, HENRY!
I AM USED TO PRIVATE COLLECTIONS, BUT IT'S RARE TO SEE ONE THAT DISPLAYS SUCH VARIETY.
I BOUGHT THEM IN 1860 WHILE PASSING THROUGH PEKING...FROM SOME FRENCH SOLDIERS WHO APPARENTLY KNEW NOTHING OF THEIR VALUE.
A PLEASANT WAY TO FINISH AN ALREADY-PROFITABLE BUSINESS TRIP.
HOW DID YOU BUILD YOUR FORTUNE? I'VE HEARD TALK, IN TURNS, OF THE TRANSPORTATION OF COOLIES, OF OPIUM TRAFFICKING...THE GOSSIPS ARE EVEN SPREADING THE WORD THAT YOU WOULD HELP CHINA BUILD AN ARSENAL.
WELL, MARGARET... DO I LOOK LIKE A TRAFFICKER?
FATHER...FORGIVE ME FOR TAKING YOU AWAY FROM YOUR GUESTS, BUT WE HAVE AN URGENT MATTER TO LOOK INTO.
CAN IT NOT WAIT?
I WOULD NOT BOTHER YOU OTHERWISE. IT WON'T TAKE LONG...
EXCUSE ME. I'LL TRY TO BE BRIEF.
PLEASE. WE ARE FAR FROM HAVING SEEN IT ALL.
I HOPE YOU'RE NOT DISTURBING ME FOR NO REASON, JAMES.
I DON'T BELIEVE SO...

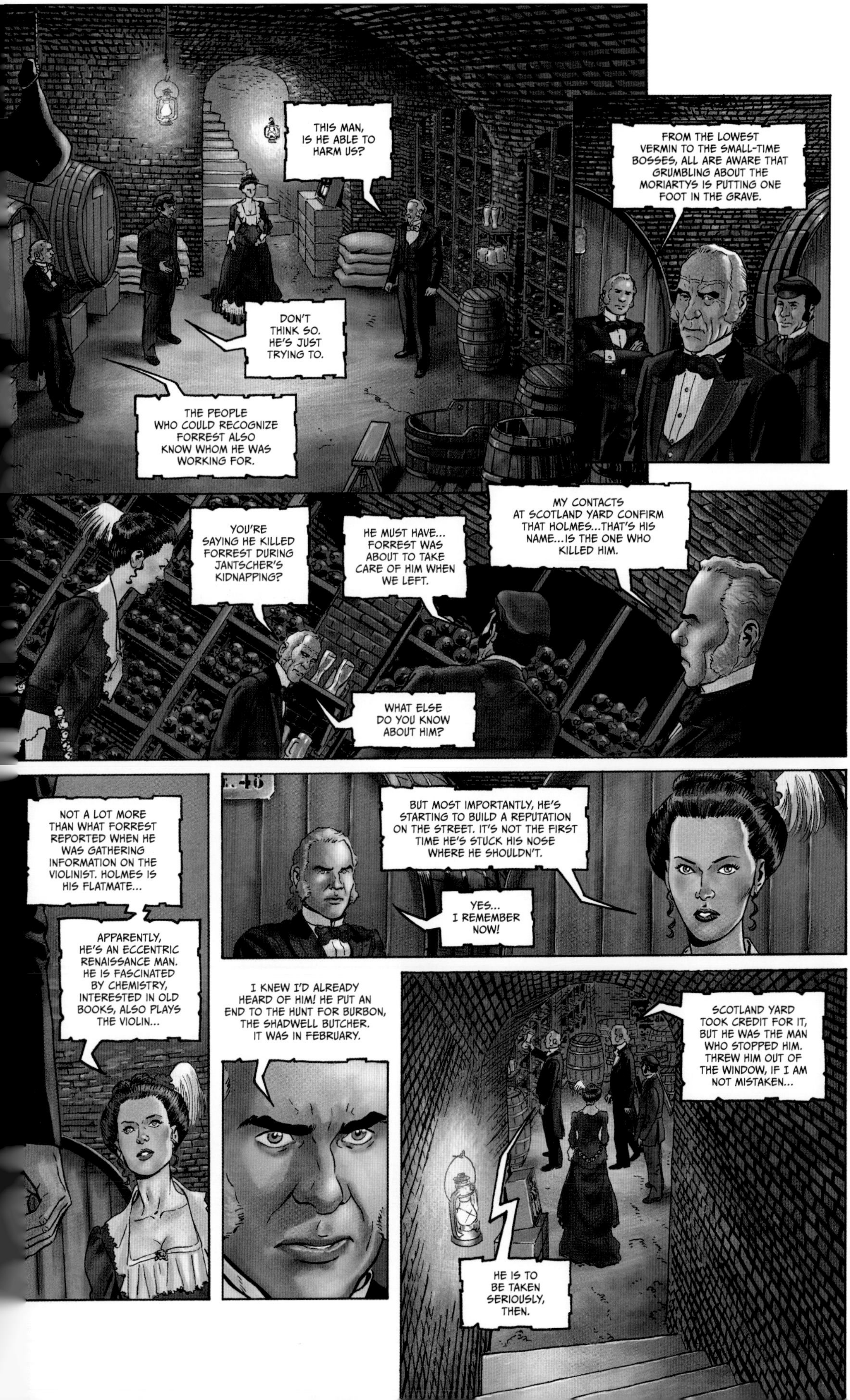
THIS MAN, IS HE ABLE TO HARM US?
DON'T THINK SO. HE'S JUST TRYING TO.
THE PEOPLE WHO COULD RECOGNIZE FORREST ALSO KNOW WHOM HE WAS WORKING FOR.
FROM THE LOWEST VERMIN TO THE SMALL-TIME BOSSES, ALL ARE AWARE THAT GRUMBLING ABOUT THE MORIARTYS IS PUTTING ONE FOOT IN THE GRAVE.
YOU'RE SAYING HE KILLED FORREST DURING JANTSCHER'S KIDNAPPING?
HE MUST HAVE... FORREST WAS ABOUT TO TAKE CARE OF HIM WHEN WE LEFT.
MY CONTACTS AT SCOTLAND YARD CONFIRM THAT HOLMES...THAT'S HIS NAME...IS THE ONE WHO KILLED HIM.
WHAT ELSE DO YOU KNOW ABOUT HIM?
NOT A LOT MORE THAN WHAT FORREST REPORTED WHEN HE WAS GATHERING INFORMATION ON THE VIOLINIST. HOLMES IS HIS FLATMATE...
APPARENTLY, HE'S AN ECCENTRIC RENAISSANCE MAN. HE IS FASCINATED BY CHEMISTRY, INTERESTED IN OLD BOOKS, ALSO PLAYS THE VIOLIN...
BUT MOST IMPORTANTLY, HE'S STARTING TO BUILD A REPUTATION ON THE STREET. IT'S NOT THE FIRST TIME HE'S STUCK HIS NOSE WHERE HE SHOULDN'T.
YES... I REMEMBER NOW!
I KNEW I'D ALREADY HEARD OF HIM! HE PUT AN END TO THE HUNT FOR BURBON, THE SHADWELL BUTCHER. IT WAS IN FEBRUARY.
SCOTLAND YARD TOOK CREDIT FOR IT, BUT HE WAS THE MAN WHO STOPPED HIM. THREW HIM OUT OF THE WINDOW, IF I AM NOT MISTAKEN...
HE IS TO BE TAKEN SERIOUSLY, THEN.

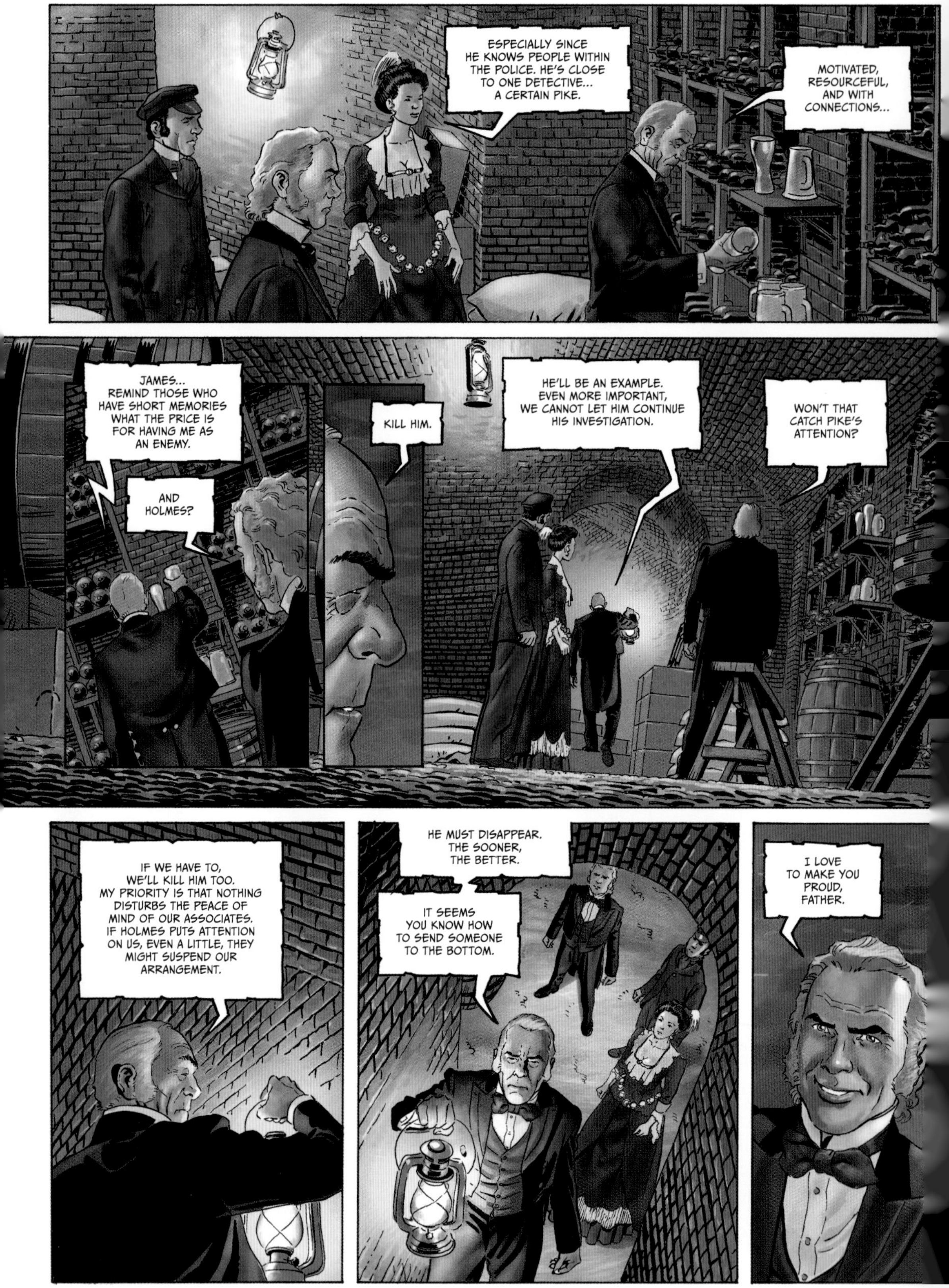
ESPECIALLY SINCE HE KNOWS PEOPLE WITHIN THE POLICE. HE'S CLOSE TO ONE DETECTIVE... A CERTAIN PIKE.
MOTIVATED, RESOURCEFUL, AND WITH CONNECTIONS...
JAMES... REMIND THOSE WHO HAVE SHORT MEMORIES WHAT THE PRICE IS FOR HAVING ME AS AN ENEMY.
AND HOLMES?
KILL HIM.
HE'LL BE AN EXAMPLE. EVEN MORE IMPORTANT, WE CANNOT LET HIM CONTINUE HIS INVESTIGATION.
WON'T THAT CATCH PIKE'S ATTENTION?
IF WE HAVE TO, WE'LL KILL HIM TOO. MY PRIORITY IS THAT NOTHING DISTURBS THE PEACE OF MIND OF OUR ASSOCIATES. IF HOLMES PUTS ATTENTION ON US, EVEN A LITTLE, THEY MIGHT SUSPEND OUR ARRANGEMENT.
HE MUST DISAPPEAR. THE SOONER, THE BETTER.
IT SEEMS YOU KNOW HOW TO SEND SOMEONE TO THE BOTTOM.
I LOVE TO MAKE YOU PROUD, FATHER.

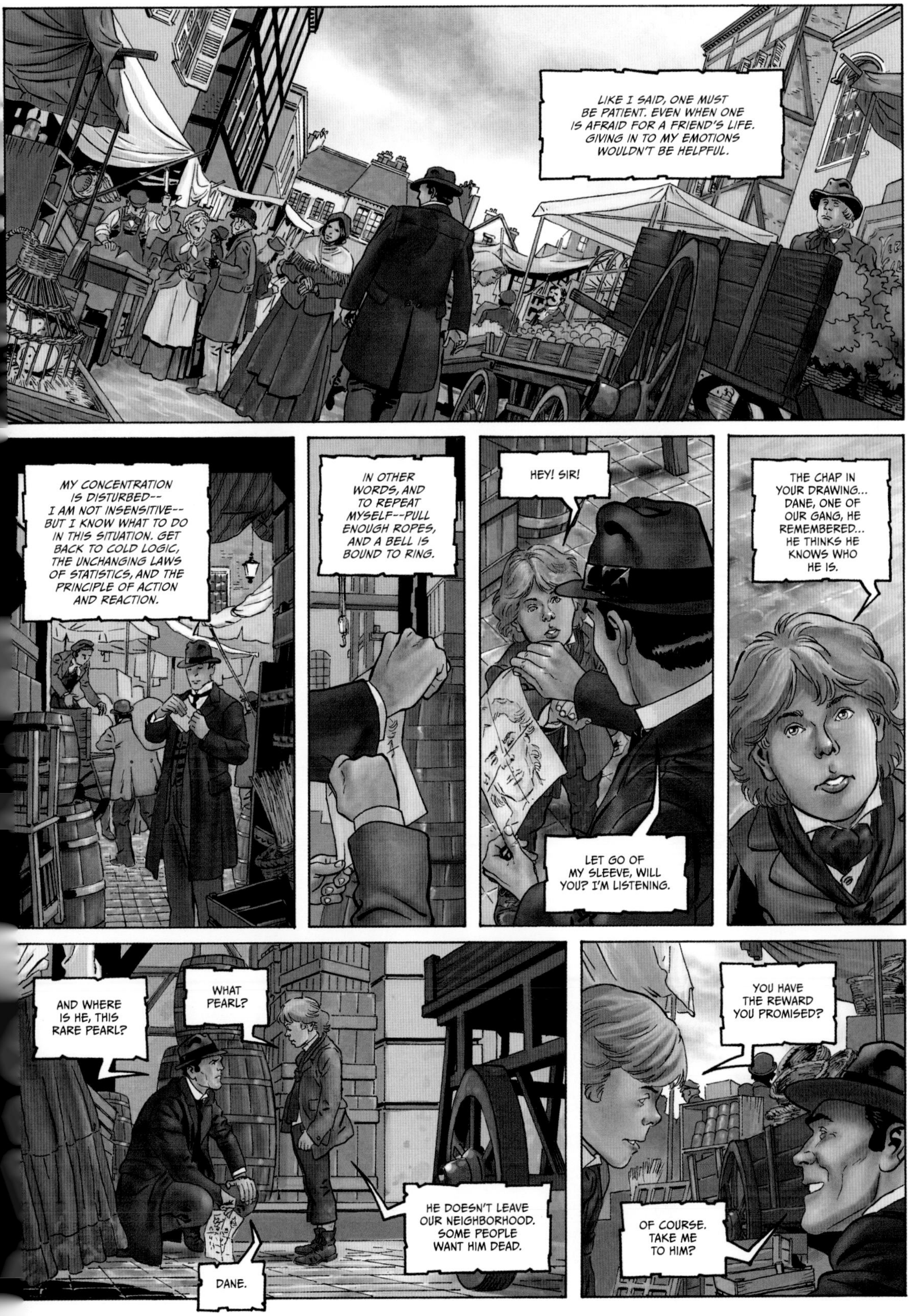
LIKE I SAID, ONE MUST BE PATIENT. EVEN WHEN ONE IS AFRAID FOR A FRIEND'S LIFE. GIVING IN TO MY EMOTIONS WOULDN'T BE HELPFUL.
MY CONCENTRATION IS DISTURBED-- I AM NOT INSENSITIVE-- BUT I KNOW WHAT TO DO IN THIS SITUATION. GET BACK TO COLD LOGIC, THE UNCHANGING LAWS OF STATISTICS, AND THE PRINCIPLE OF ACTION AND REACTION.
IN OTHER WORDS, AND TO REPEAT MYSELF--PULL ENOUGH ROPES, AND A BELL IS BOUND TO RING.
HEY! SIR!
LET GO OF MY SLEEVE, WILL YOU? I'M LISTENING.
THE CHAP IN YOUR DRAWING... DANE, ONE OF OUR GANG, HE REMEMBERED... HE THINKS HE KNOWS WHO HE IS.
AND WHERE IS HE, THIS RARE PEARL?
WHAT PEARL?
DANE.
HE DOESN'T LEAVE OUR NEIGHBORHOOD. SOME PEOPLE WANT HIM DEAD.
YOU HAVE THE REWARD YOU PROMISED?
OF COURSE. TAKE ME TO HIM?

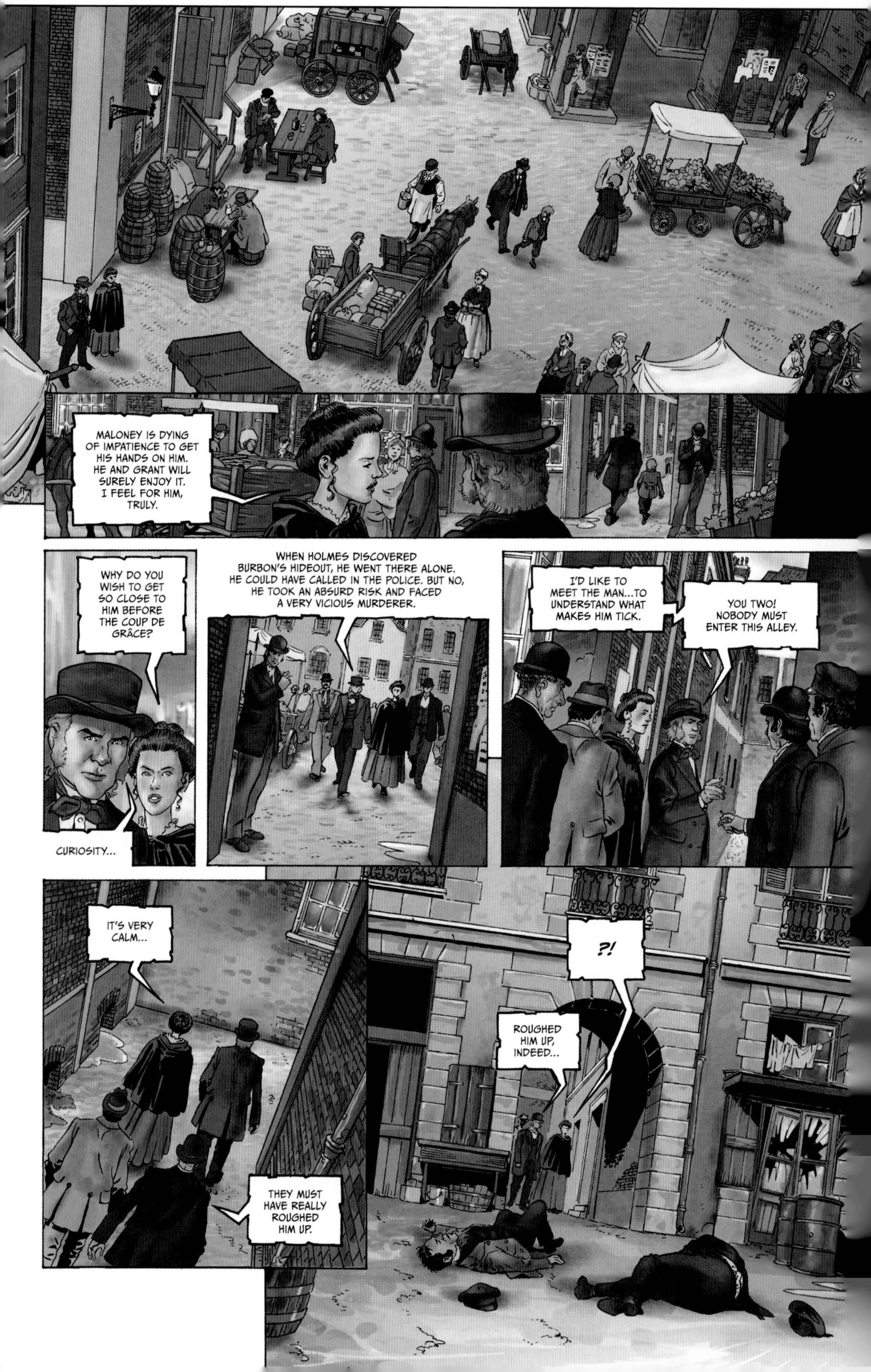
MALONEY IS DYING OF IMPATIENCE TO GET HIS HANDS ON HIM. HE AND GRANT WILL SURELY ENJOY IT. I FEEL FOR HIM, TRULY.
WHY DO YOU WISH TO GET SO CLOSE TO HIM BEFORE THE COUP DE GRÂCE?
CURIOSITY...
WHEN HOLMES DISCOVERED BURBON'S HIDEOUT, HE WENT THERE ALONE. HE COULD HAVE CALLED IN THE POLICE. BUT NO, HE TOOK AN ABSURD RISK AND FACED A VERY VICIOUS MURDERER.
I'D LIKE TO MEET THE MAN...TO UNDERSTAND WHAT MAKES HIM TICK.
YOU TWO! NOBODY MUST ENTER THIS ALLEY.
IT'S VERY CALM...
THEY MUST HAVE REALLY ROUGHED HIM UP.
?!
ROUGHED HIM UP, INDEED...

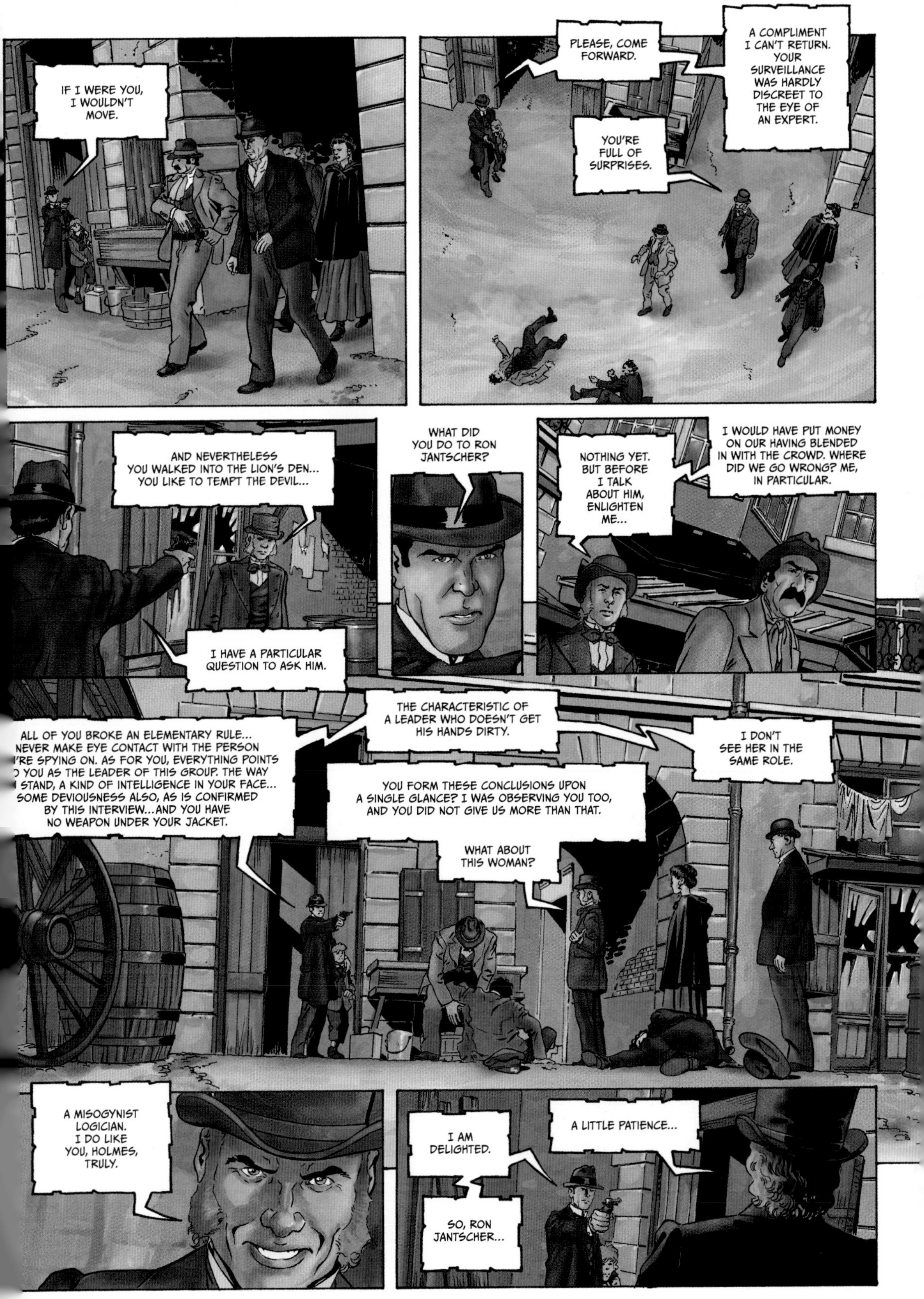
IF I WERE YOU, I WOULDN'T MOVE.
PLEASE, COME FORWARD.
A COMPLIMENT I CAN'T RETURN. YOUR SURVEILLANCE WAS HARDLY DISCREET TO THE EYE OF AN EXPERT.
YOU'RE FULL OF SURPRISES.
AND NEVERTHELESS YOU WALKED INTO THE LION'S DEN... YOU LIKE TO TEMPT THE DEVIL...
I HAVE A PARTICULAR QUESTION TO ASK HIM.
WHAT DID YOU DO TO RON JANTSCHER?
NOTHING YET. BUT BEFORE I TALK ABOUT HIM, ENLIGHTEN ME...
I WOULD HAVE PUT MONEY ON OUR HAVING BLENDED IN WITH THE CROWD. WHERE DID WE GO WRONG? ME, IN PARTICULAR.
ALL OF YOU BROKE AN ELEMENTARY RULE... NEVER MAKE EYE CONTACT WITH THE PERSON 'RE SPYING ON. AS FOR YOU, EVERYTHING POINTS O YOU AS THE LEADER OF THIS GROUP. THE WAY STAND, A KIND OF INTELLIGENCE IN YOUR FACE... SOME DEVIOUSNESS ALSO, AS IS CONFIRMED BY THIS INTERVIEW... AND YOU HAVE NO WEAPON UNDER YOUR JACKET.
THE CHARACTERISTIC OF A LEADER WHO DOESN'T GET HIS HANDS DIRTY.
YOU FORM THESE CONCLUSIONS UPON A SINGLE GLANCE? I WAS OBSERVING YOU TOO, AND YOU DID NOT GIVE US MORE THAN THAT.
I DON'T SEE HER IN THE SAME ROLE.
WHAT ABOUT THIS WOMAN?
A MISOGYNIST LOGICIAN. I DO LIKE YOU, HOLMES, TRULY.
I AM DELIGHTED.
A LITTLE PATIENCE...
SO, RON JANTSCHER...

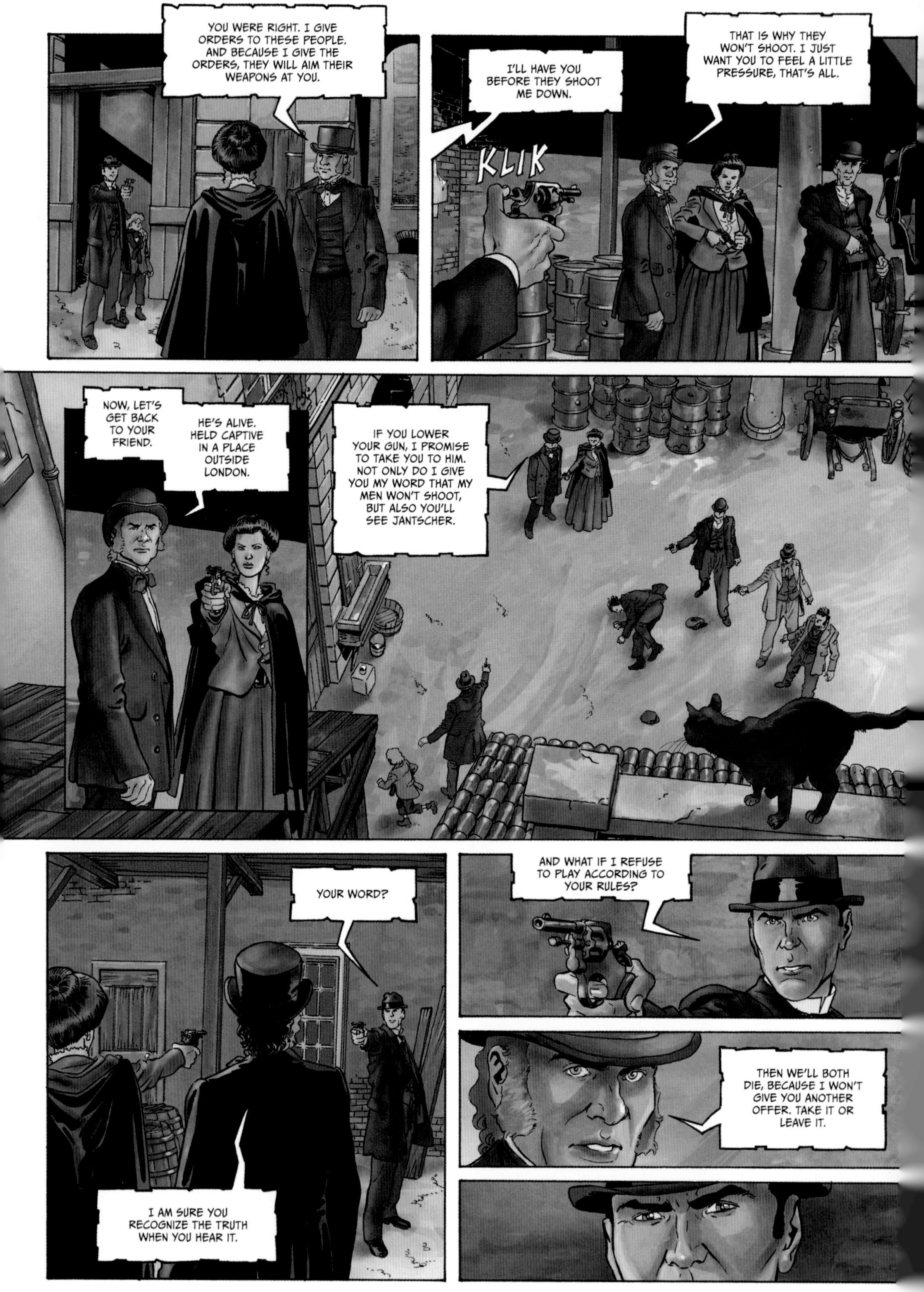
YOU WERE RIGHT. I GIVE ORDERS TO THESE PEOPLE. AND BECAUSE I GIVE THE ORDERS, THEY WILL AIM THEIR WEAPONS AT YOU.
I'LL HAVE YOU BEFORE THEY SHOOT ME DOWN.
KLIK
THAT IS WHY THEY WON'T SHOOT. I JUST WANT YOU TO FEEL A LITTLE PRESSURE, THAT'S ALL.
NOW, LET'S GET BACK TO YOUR FRIEND.
HE'S ALIVE. HELD CAPTIVE IN A PLACE OUTSIDE LONDON.
IF YOU LOWER YOUR GUN, I PROMISE TO TAKE YOU TO HIM. NOT ONLY DO I GIVE YOU MY WORD THAT MY MEN WON'T SHOOT, BUT ALSO YOU'LL SEE JANTSCHER.
YOUR WORD?
I AM SURE YOU RECOGNIZE THE TRUTH WHEN YOU HEAR IT.
AND WHAT IF I REFUSE TO PLAY ACCORDING TO YOUR RULES?
THEN WE'LL BOTH DIE, BECAUSE I WON'T GIVE YOU ANOTHER OFFER. TAKE IT OR LEAVE IT.

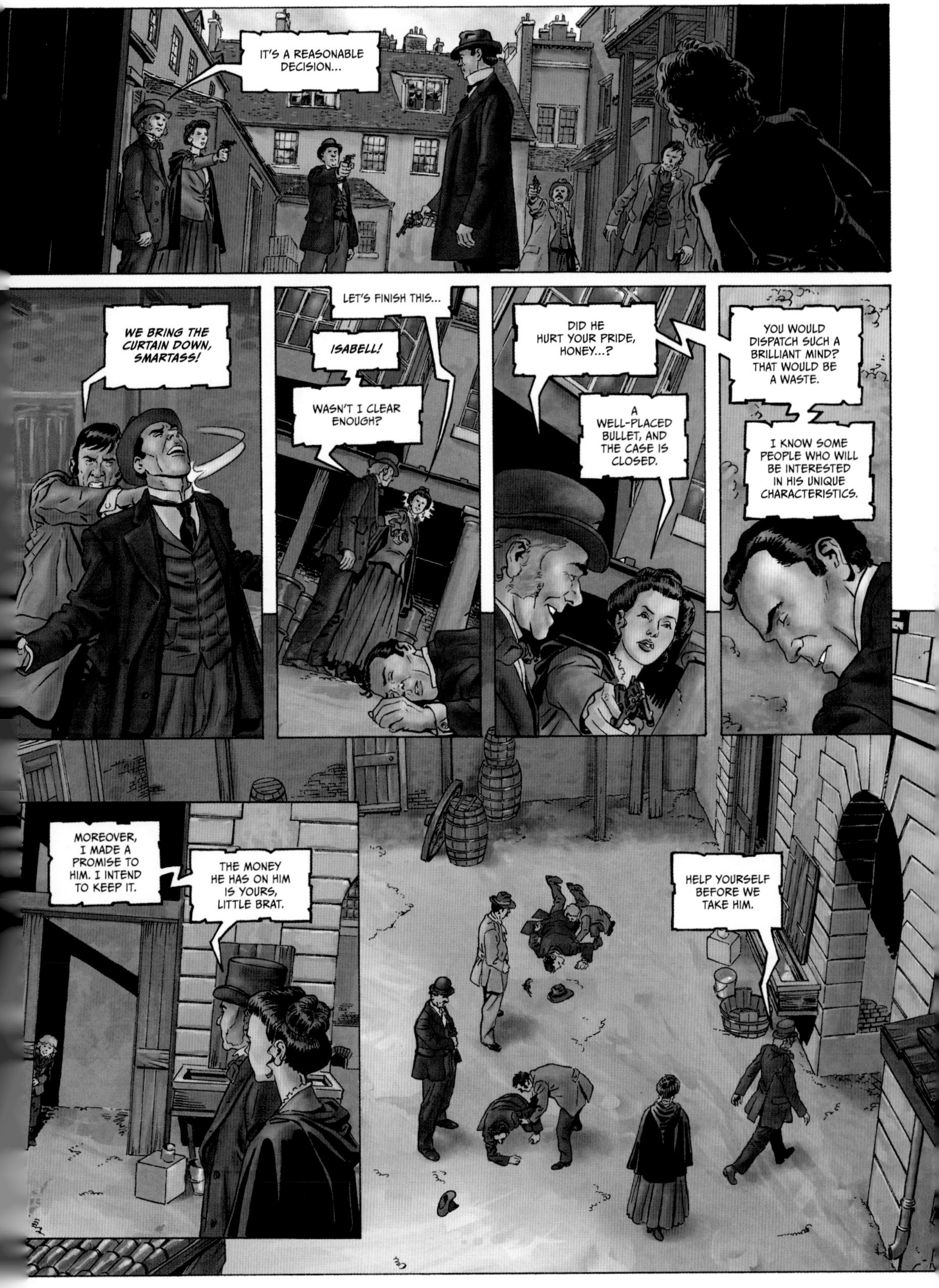
IT'S A REASONABLE DECISION...
WE BRING THE CURTAIN DOWN, SMARTASS!
LET'S FINISH THIS...
ISABELL!
WASN'T I CLEAR ENOUGH?
DID HE HURT YOUR PRIDE, HONEY...?
A WELL-PLACED BULLET, AND THE CASE IS CLOSED.
YOU WOULD DISPATCH SUCH A BRILLIANT MIND? THAT WOULD BE A WASTE.
I KNOW SOME PEOPLE WHO WILL BE INTERESTED IN HIS UNIQUE CHARACTERISTICS.
MOREOVER, I MADE A PROMISE TO HIM. I INTEND TO KEEP IT.
THE MONEY HE HAS ON HIM IS YOURS, LITTLE BRAT.
HELP YOURSELF BEFORE WE TAKE HIM.

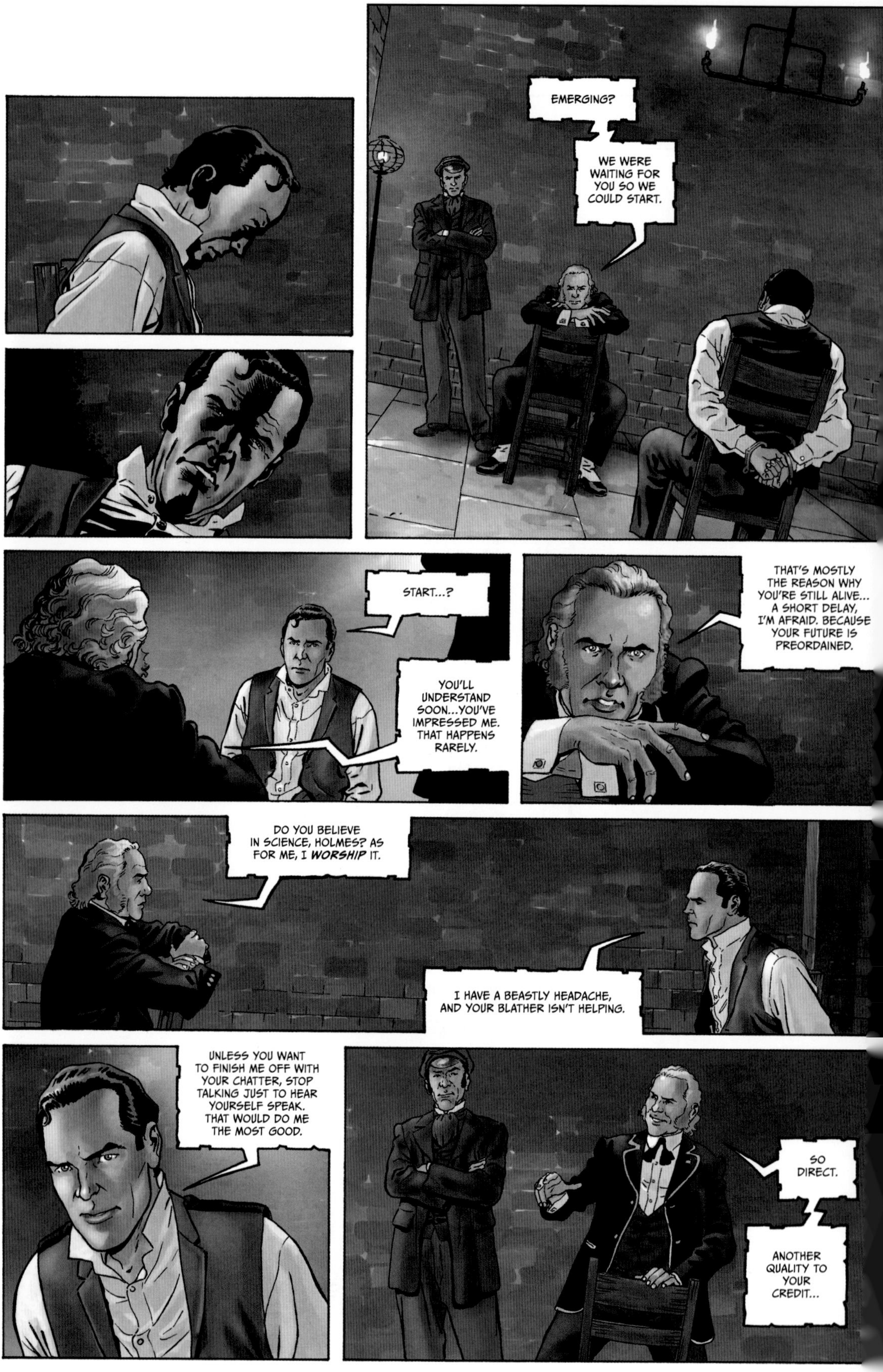
EMERGING?
WE WERE WAITING FOR YOU SO WE COULD START.
START...?
YOU'LL UNDERSTAND SOON...YOU'VE IMPRESSED ME. THAT HAPPENS RARELY.
THAT'S MOSTLY THE REASON WHY YOU'RE STILL ALIVE... A SHORT DELAY, I'M AFRAID. BECAUSE YOUR FUTURE IS PREORDAINED.
DO YOU BELIEVE IN SCIENCE, HOLMES? AS FOR ME, I *WORSHIP* IT.
I HAVE A BEASTLY HEADACHE, AND YOUR BLATHER ISN'T HELPING.
UNLESS YOU WANT TO FINISH ME OFF WITH YOUR CHATTER, STOP TALKING JUST TO HEAR YOURSELF SPEAK. THAT WOULD DO ME THE MOST GOOD.
SO DIRECT.
ANOTHER QUALITY TO YOUR CREDIT...

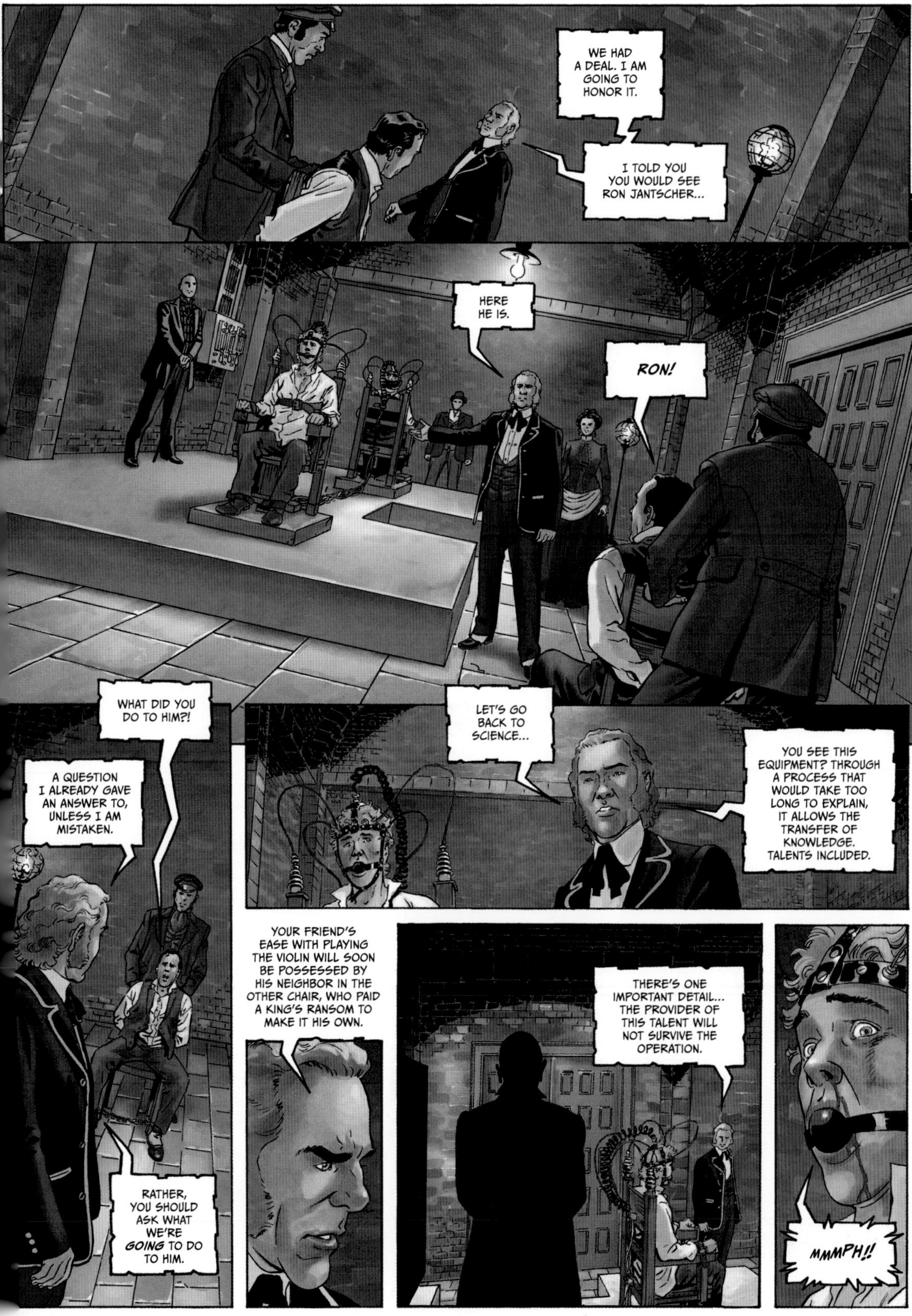

WE HAD A DEAL. I AM GOING TO HONOR IT.
I TOLD YOU YOU WOULD SEE RON JANTSCHER...
HERE HE IS.
RON!
WHAT DID YOU DO TO HIM?!
A QUESTION I ALREADY GAVE AN ANSWER TO, UNLESS I AM MISTAKEN.
RATHER, YOU SHOULD ASK WHAT WE'RE GOING TO DO TO HIM.
LET'S GO BACK TO SCIENCE...
YOU SEE THIS EQUIPMENT? THROUGH A PROCESS THAT WOULD TAKE TOO LONG TO EXPLAIN, IT ALLOWS THE TRANSFER OF KNOWLEDGE. TALENTS INCLUDED.
YOUR FRIEND'S EASE WITH PLAYING THE VIOLIN WILL SOON BE POSSESSED BY HIS NEIGHBOR IN THE OTHER CHAIR, WHO PAID A KING'S RANSOM TO MAKE IT HIS OWN.
THERE'S ONE IMPORTANT DETAIL... THE PROVIDER OF THIS TALENT WILL NOT SURVIVE THE OPERATION.
MMMPH!!

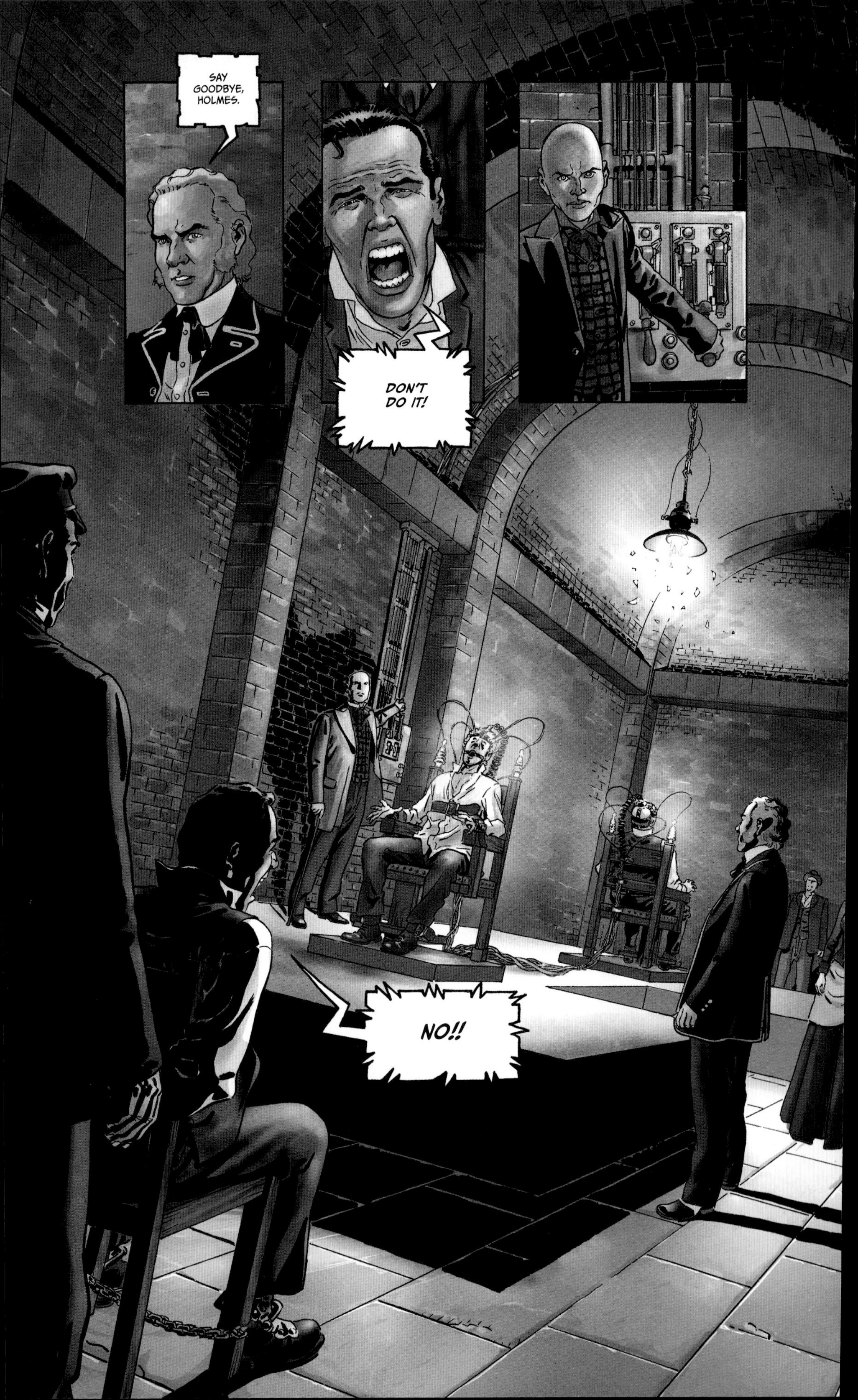
SAY GOODBYE, HOLMES.
DON'T DO IT!
NO!!

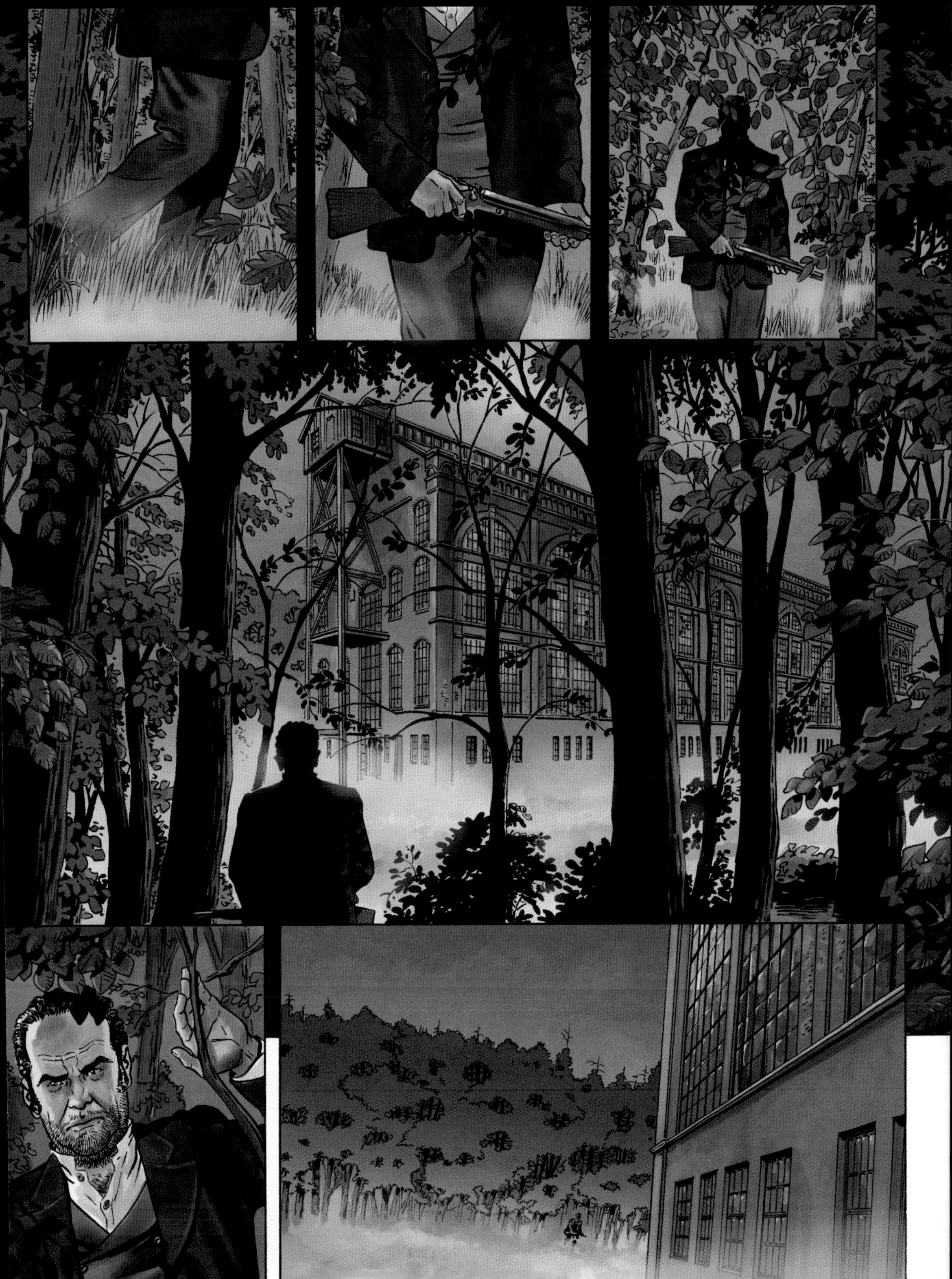

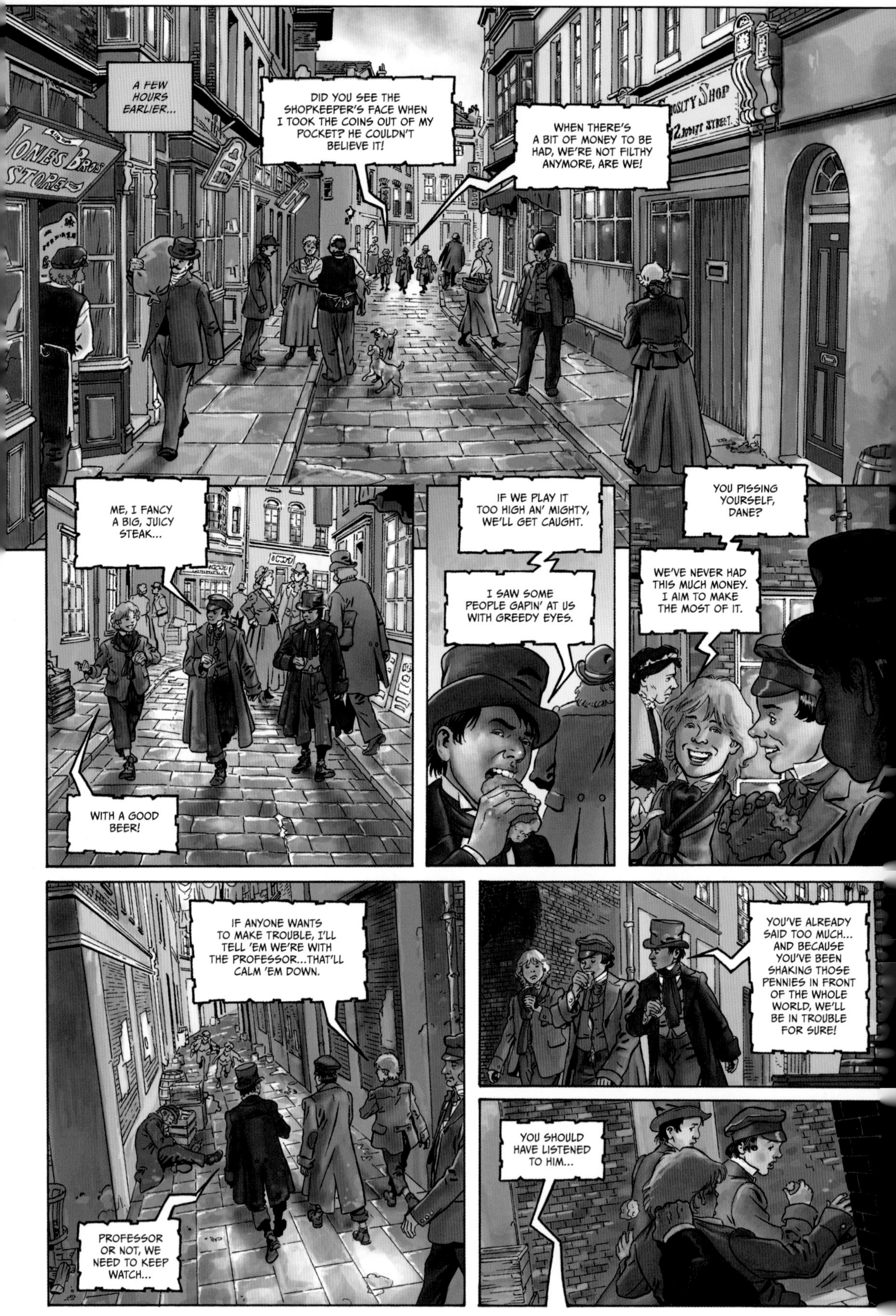
A FEW HOURS EARLIER...
JONES BROS STORE
DID YOU SEE THE SHOPKEEPER'S FACE WHEN I TOOK THE COINS OUT OF MY POCKET? HE COULDN'T BELIEVE IT!
WHEN THERE'S A BIT OF MONEY TO BE HAD, WE'RE NOT FILTHY ANYMORE, ARE WE!
ME, I FANCY A BIG, JUICY STEAK...
WITH A GOOD BEER!
IF WE PLAY IT TOO HIGH AN' MIGHTY, WE'LL GET CAUGHT.
I SAW SOME PEOPLE GAPIN' AT US WITH GREEDY EYES.
YOU PISSING YOURSELF, DANE?
WE'VE NEVER HAD THIS MUCH MONEY. I AIM TO MAKE THE MOST OF IT.
IF ANYONE WANTS TO MAKE TROUBLE, I'LL TELL 'EM WE'RE WITH THE PROFESSOR...THAT'LL CALM 'EM DOWN.
PROFESSOR OR NOT, WE NEED TO KEEP WATCH...
YOU'VE ALREADY SAID TOO MUCH... AND BECAUSE YOU'VE BEEN SHAKING THOSE PENNIES IN FRONT OF THE WHOLE WORLD, WE'LL BE IN TROUBLE FOR SURE!
YOU SHOULD HAVE LISTENED TO HIM...

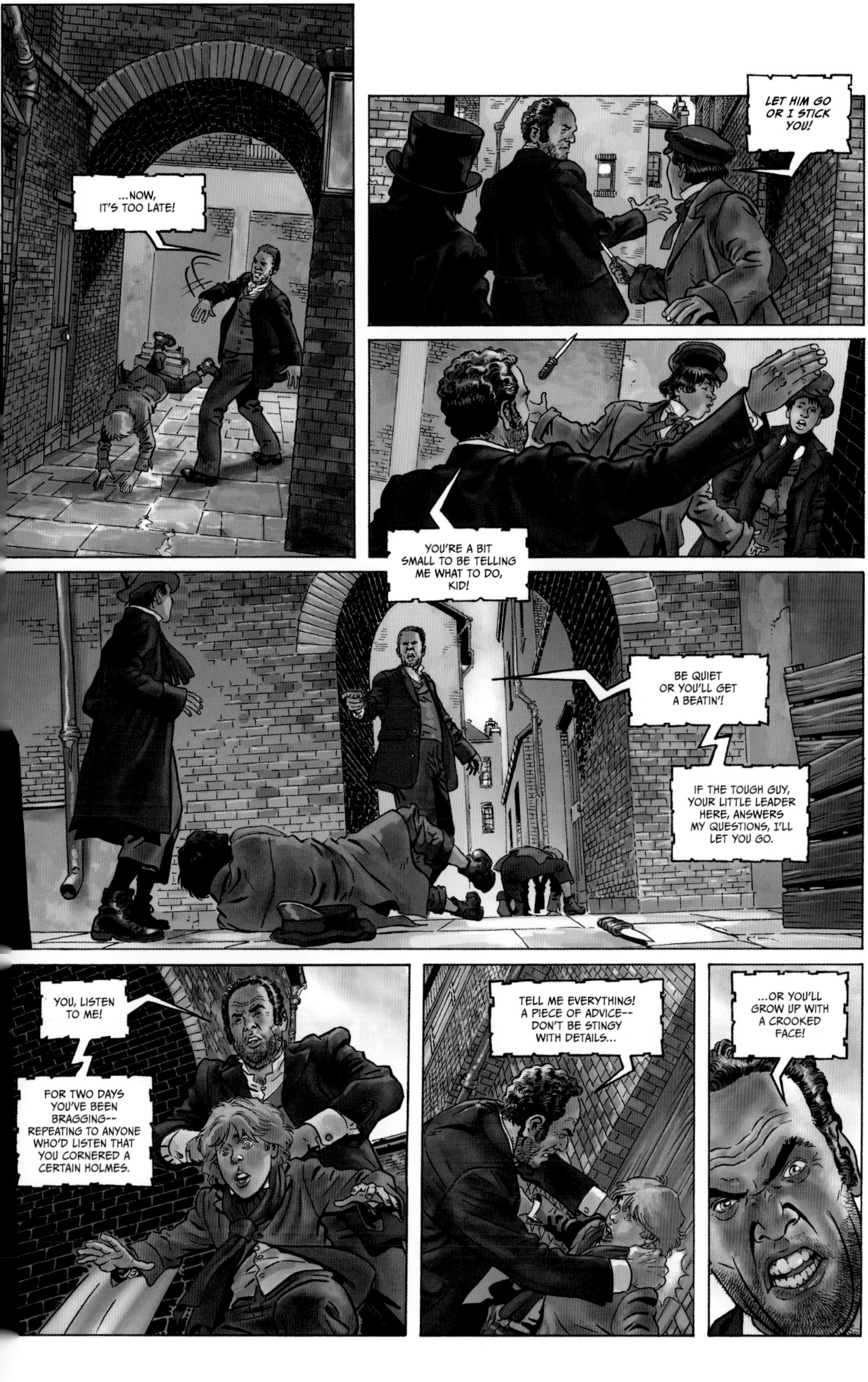
...NOW, IT'S TOO LATE!
LET HIM GO OR I STICK YOU!
YOU'RE A BIT SMALL TO BE TELLING ME WHAT TO DO, KID!
BE QUIET OR YOU'LL GET A BEATIN'!
IF THE TOUGH GUY, YOUR LITTLE LEADER HERE, ANSWERS MY QUESTIONS, I'LL LET YOU GO.
YOU, LISTEN TO ME!
FOR TWO DAYS YOU'VE BEEN BRAGGING-- REPEATING TO ANYONE WHO'D LISTEN THAT YOU CORNERED A CERTAIN HOLMES.
TELL ME EVERYTHING! A PIECE OF ADVICE-- DON'T BE STINGY WITH DETAILS...
...OR YOU'LL GROW UP WITH A CROOKED FACE!

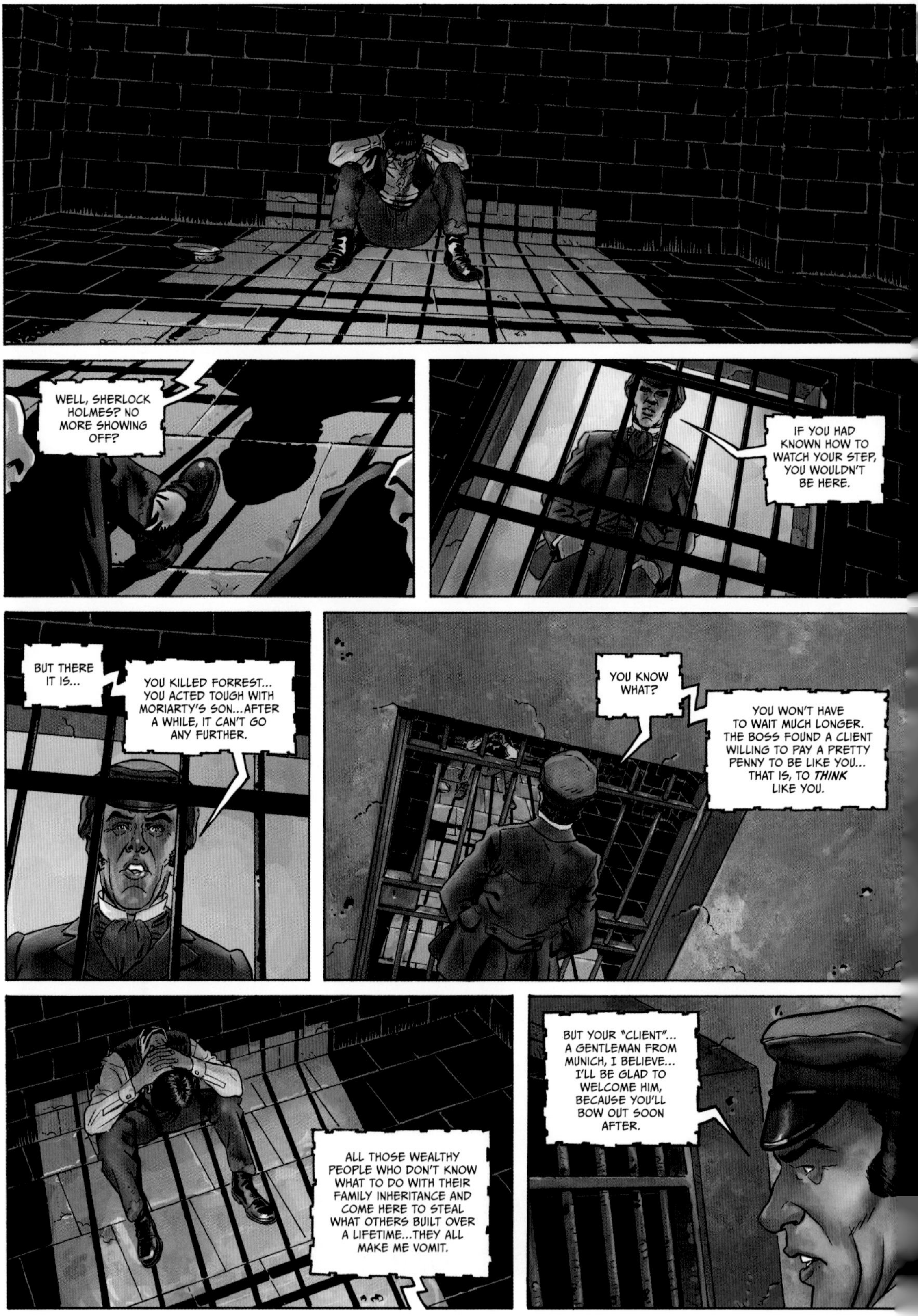
WELL, SHERLOCK HOLMES? NO MORE SHOWING OFF?
IF YOU HAD KNOWN HOW TO WATCH YOUR STEP, YOU WOULDN'T BE HERE.
BUT THERE IT IS...
YOU KILLED FORREST... YOU ACTED TOUGH WITH MORIARTY'S SON...AFTER A WHILE, IT CAN'T GO ANY FURTHER.
YOU KNOW WHAT?
YOU WON'T HAVE TO WAIT MUCH LONGER. THE BOSS FOUND A CLIENT WILLING TO PAY A PRETTY PENNY TO BE LIKE YOU... THAT IS, TO *THINK* LIKE YOU.
ALL THOSE WEALTHY PEOPLE WHO DON'T KNOW WHAT TO DO WITH THEIR FAMILY INHERITANCE AND COME HERE TO STEAL WHAT OTHERS BUILT OVER A LIFETIME...THEY ALL MAKE ME VOMIT.
BUT YOUR "CLIENT"... A GENTLEMAN FROM MUNICH, I BELIEVE... I'LL BE GLAD TO WELCOME HIM, BECAUSE YOU'LL BOW OUT SOON AFTER.

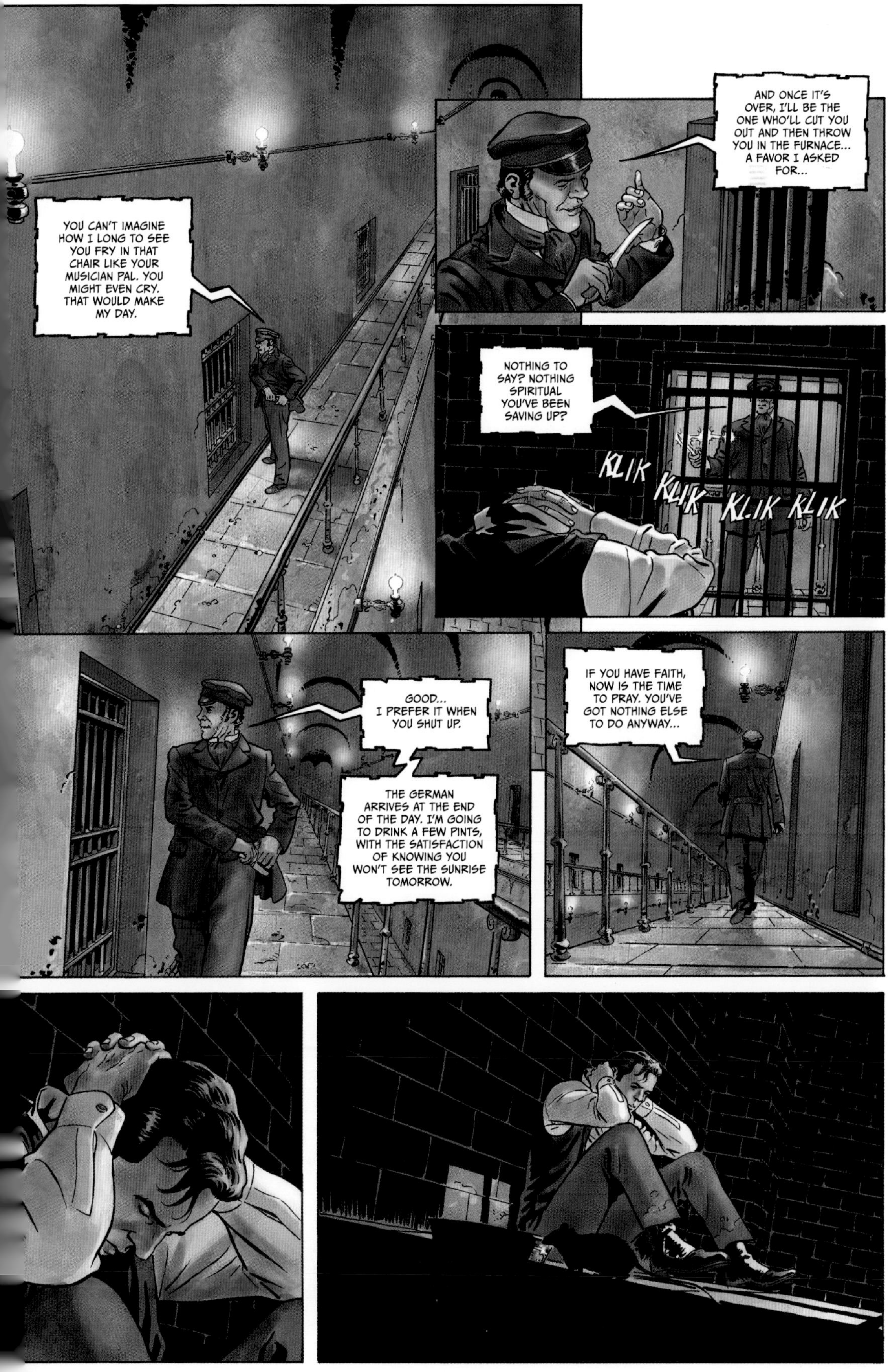
YOU CAN'T IMAGINE HOW I LONG TO SEE YOU FRY IN THAT CHAIR LIKE YOUR MUSICIAN PAL. YOU MIGHT EVEN CRY. THAT WOULD MAKE MY DAY.
AND ONCE IT'S OVER, I'LL BE THE ONE WHO'LL CUT YOU OUT AND THEN THROW YOU IN THE FURNACE... A FAVOR I ASKED FOR...
NOTHING TO SAY? NOTHING SPIRITUAL YOU'VE BEEN SAVING UP?
KLIK KLIK KLIK KLIK
GOOD... I PREFER IT WHEN YOU SHUT UP.
THE GERMAN ARRIVES AT THE END OF THE DAY. I'M GOING TO DRINK A FEW PINTS, WITH THE SATISFACTION OF KNOWING YOU WON'T SEE THE SUNRISE TOMORROW.
IF YOU HAVE FAITH, NOW IS THE TIME TO PRAY. YOU'VE GOT NOTHING ELSE TO DO ANYWAY...

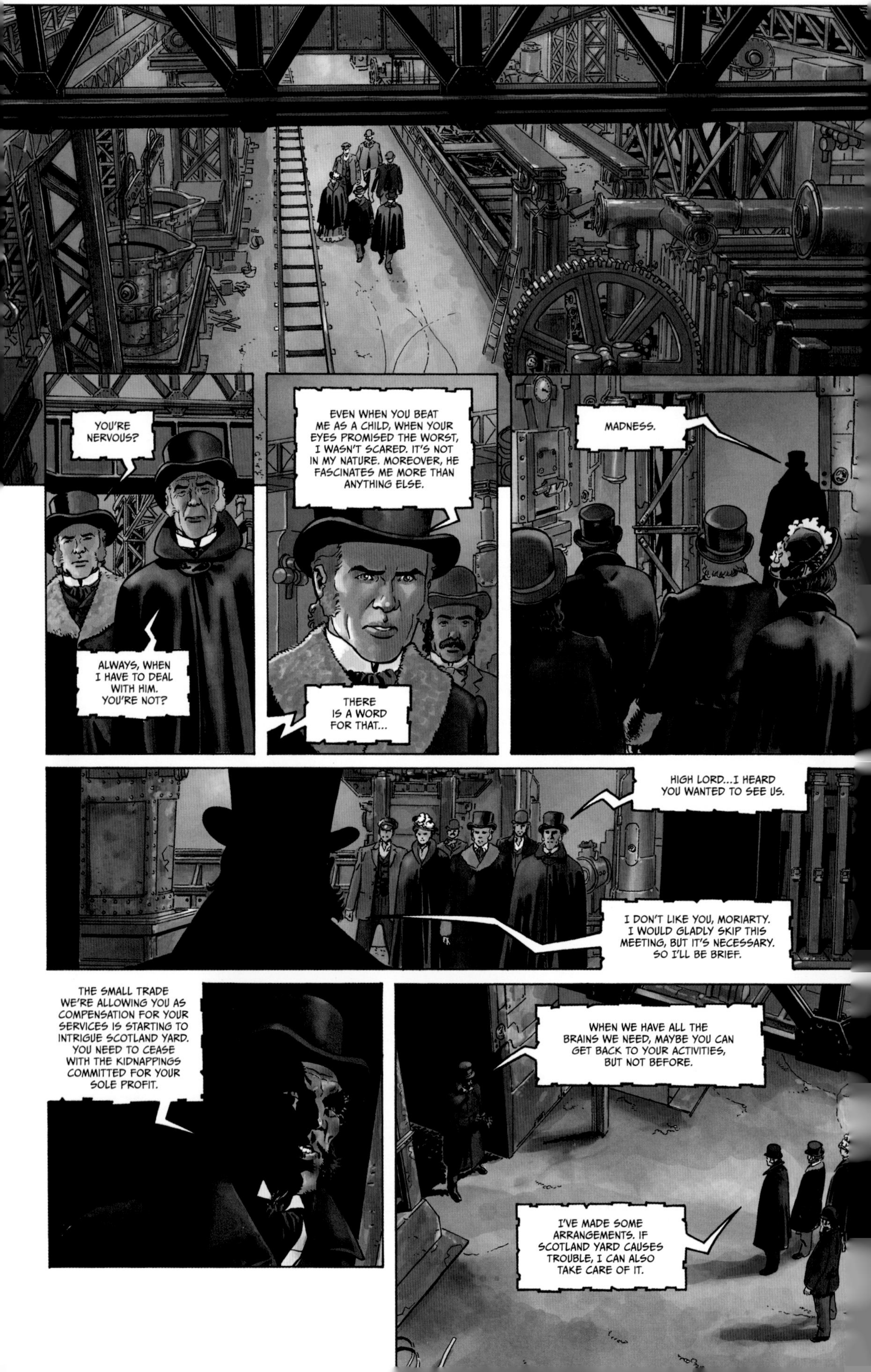

YOU'RE NERVOUS?
ALWAYS, WHEN I HAVE TO DEAL WITH HIM. YOU'RE NOT?
EVEN WHEN YOU BEAT ME AS A CHILD, WHEN YOUR EYES PROMISED THE WORST, I WASN'T SCARED. IT'S NOT IN MY NATURE. MOREOVER, HE FASCINATES ME MORE THAN ANYTHING ELSE.
THERE IS A WORD FOR THAT...
MADNESS.
HIGH LORD...I HEARD YOU WANTED TO SEE US.
I DON'T LIKE YOU, MORIARTY. I WOULD GLADLY SKIP THIS MEETING, BUT IT'S NECESSARY. SO I'LL BE BRIEF.
THE SMALL TRADE WE'RE ALLOWING YOU AS COMPENSATION FOR YOUR SERVICES IS STARTING TO INTRIGUE SCOTLAND YARD. YOU NEED TO CEASE WITH THE KIDNAPPINGS COMMITTED FOR YOUR SOLE PROFIT.
WHEN WE HAVE ALL THE BRAINS WE NEED, MAYBE YOU CAN GET BACK TO YOUR ACTIVITIES, BUT NOT BEFORE.
I'VE MADE SOME ARRANGEMENTS. IF SCOTLAND YARD CAUSES TROUBLE, I CAN ALSO TAKE CARE OF IT.

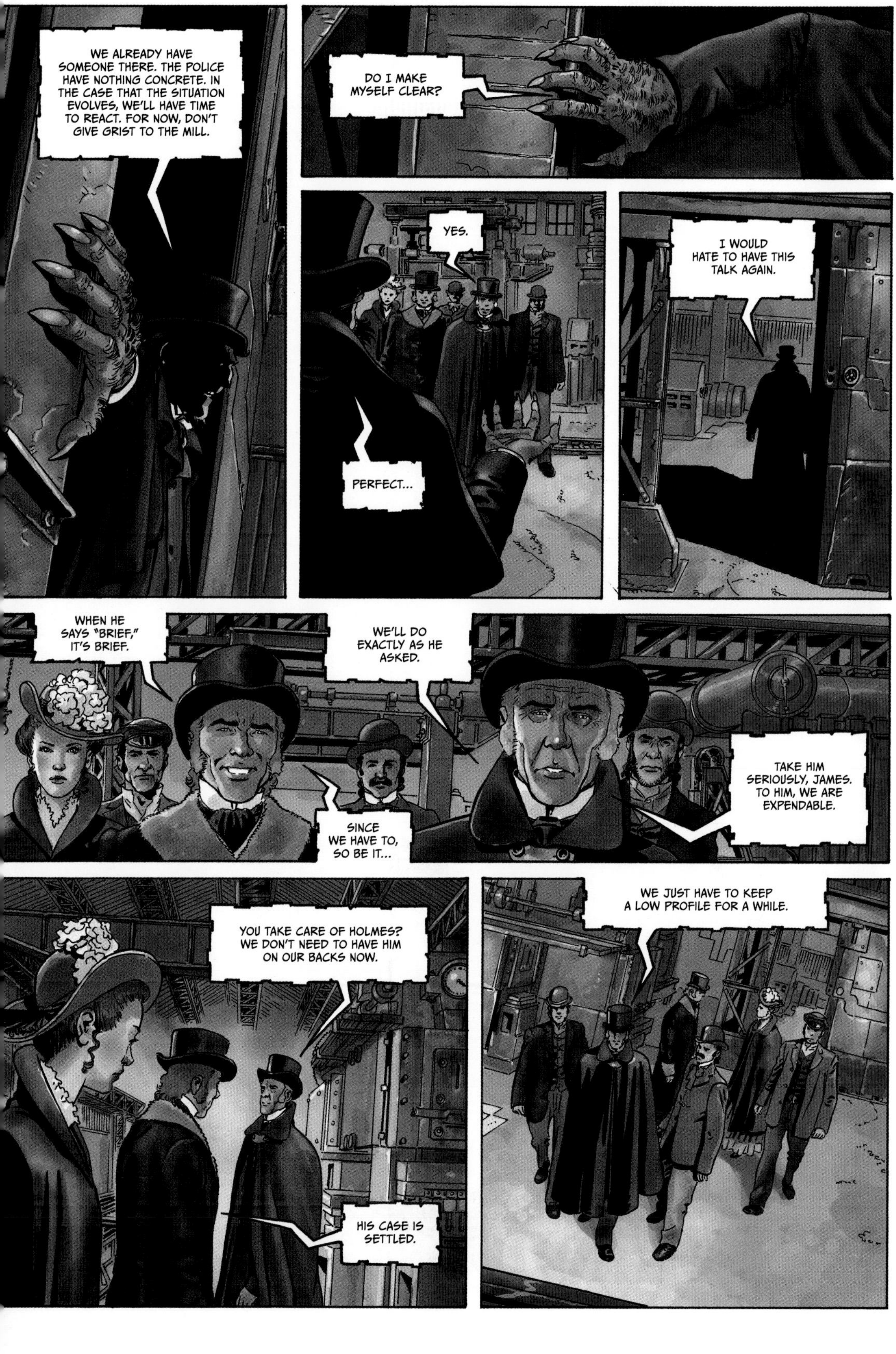
WE ALREADY HAVE SOMEONE THERE. THE POLICE HAVE NOTHING CONCRETE. IN THE CASE THAT THE SITUATION EVOLVES, WE'LL HAVE TIME TO REACT. FOR NOW, DON'T GIVE GRIST TO THE MILL.
DO I MAKE MYSELF CLEAR?
YES.
PERFECT...
I WOULD HATE TO HAVE THIS TALK AGAIN.
WHEN HE SAYS "BRIEF," IT'S BRIEF.
SINCE WE HAVE TO, SO BE IT...
WE'LL DO EXACTLY AS HE ASKED.
TAKE HIM SERIOUSLY, JAMES. TO HIM, WE ARE EXPENDABLE.
YOU TAKE CARE OF HOLMES? WE DON'T NEED TO HAVE HIM ON OUR BACKS NOW.
HIS CASE IS SETTLED.
WE JUST HAVE TO KEEP A LOW PROFILE FOR A WHILE.

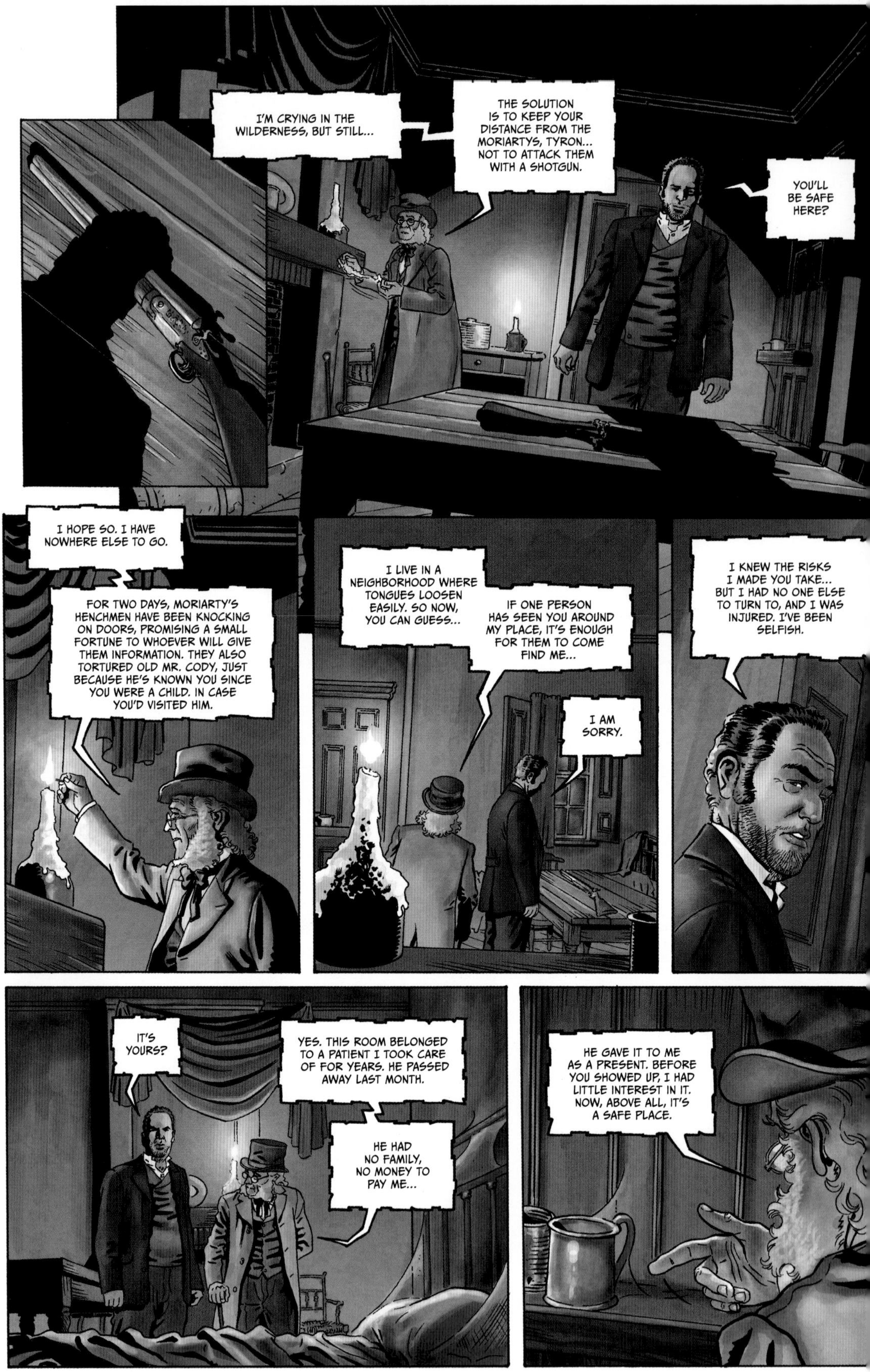
I'M CRYING IN THE WILDERNESS, BUT STILL...
THE SOLUTION IS TO KEEP YOUR DISTANCE FROM THE MORIARTYS, TYRON... NOT TO ATTACK THEM WITH A SHOTGUN.
YOU'LL BE SAFE HERE?
I HOPE SO. I HAVE NOWHERE ELSE TO GO.
FOR TWO DAYS, MORIARTY'S HENCHMEN HAVE BEEN KNOCKING ON DOORS, PROMISING A SMALL FORTUNE TO WHOEVER WILL GIVE THEM INFORMATION. THEY ALSO TORTURED OLD MR. CODY, JUST BECAUSE HE'S KNOWN YOU SINCE YOU WERE A CHILD. IN CASE YOU'D VISITED HIM.
I LIVE IN A NEIGHBORHOOD WHERE TONGUES LOOSEN EASILY. SO NOW, YOU CAN GUESS...
IF ONE PERSON HAS SEEN YOU AROUND MY PLACE, IT'S ENOUGH FOR THEM TO COME FIND ME...
I AM SORRY.
I KNEW THE RISKS I MADE YOU TAKE... BUT I HAD NO ONE ELSE TO TURN TO, AND I WAS INJURED. I'VE BEEN SELFISH.
IT'S YOURS?
YES. THIS ROOM BELONGED TO A PATIENT I TOOK CARE OF FOR YEARS. HE PASSED AWAY LAST MONTH.
HE HAD NO FAMILY, NO MONEY TO PAY ME...
HE GAVE IT TO ME AS A PRESENT. BEFORE YOU SHOWED UP, I HAD LITTLE INTEREST IN IT. NOW, ABOVE ALL, IT'S A SAFE PLACE.

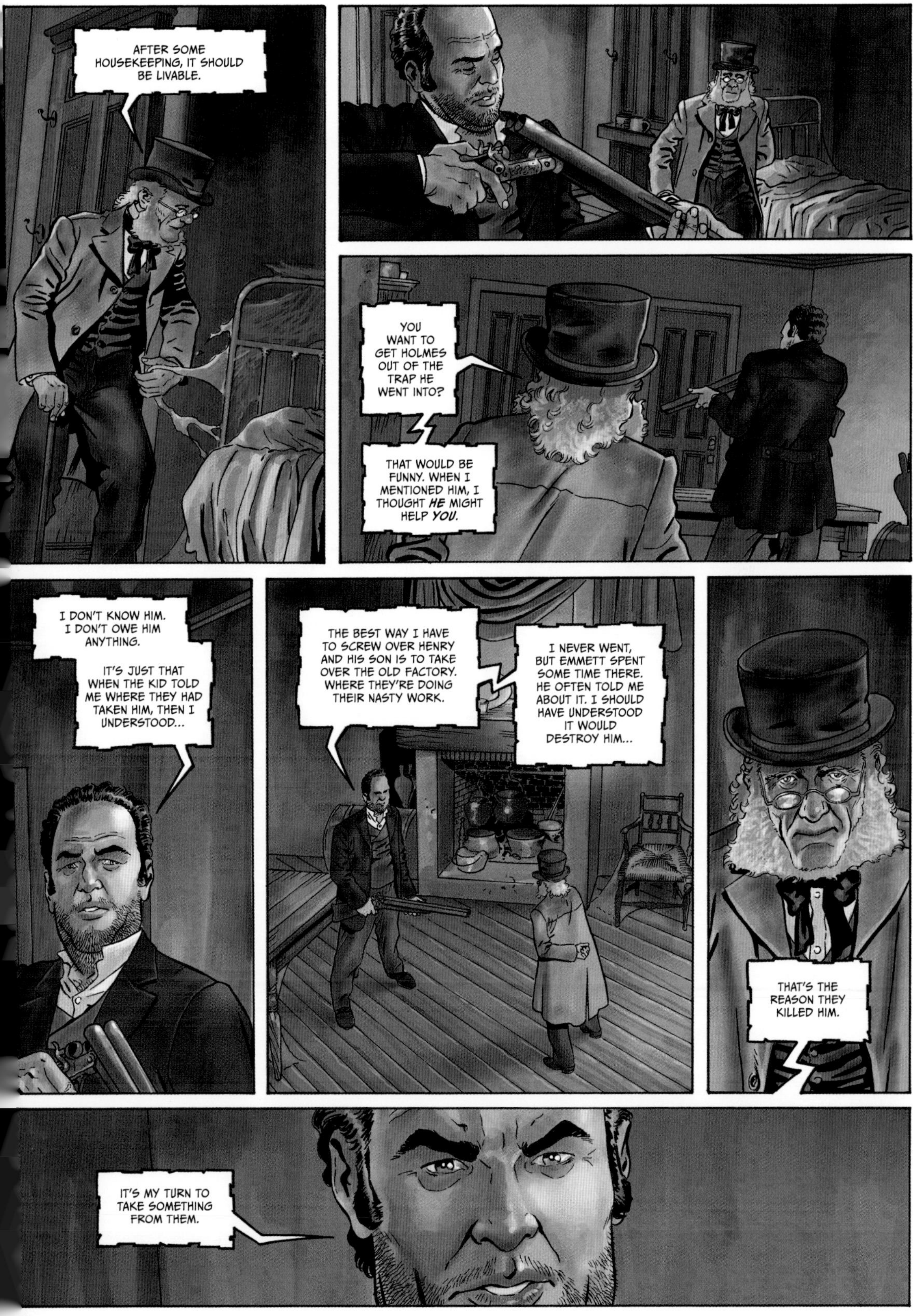
AFTER SOME HOUSEKEEPING, IT SHOULD BE LIVABLE.
YOU WANT TO GET HOLMES OUT OF THE TRAP HE WENT INTO?
THAT WOULD BE FUNNY. WHEN I MENTIONED HIM, I THOUGHT *HE* MIGHT HELP *YOU*.
I DON'T KNOW HIM. I DON'T OWE HIM ANYTHING.
IT'S JUST THAT WHEN THE KID TOLD ME WHERE THEY HAD TAKEN HIM, THEN I UNDERSTOOD...
THE BEST WAY I HAVE TO SCREW OVER HENRY AND HIS SON IS TO TAKE OVER THE OLD FACTORY. WHERE THEY'RE DOING THEIR NASTY WORK.
I NEVER WENT, BUT EMMETT SPENT SOME TIME THERE. HE OFTEN TOLD ME ABOUT IT. I SHOULD HAVE UNDERSTOOD IT WOULD DESTROY HIM...
THAT'S THE REASON THEY KILLED HIM.
IT'S MY TURN TO TAKE SOMETHING FROM THEM.

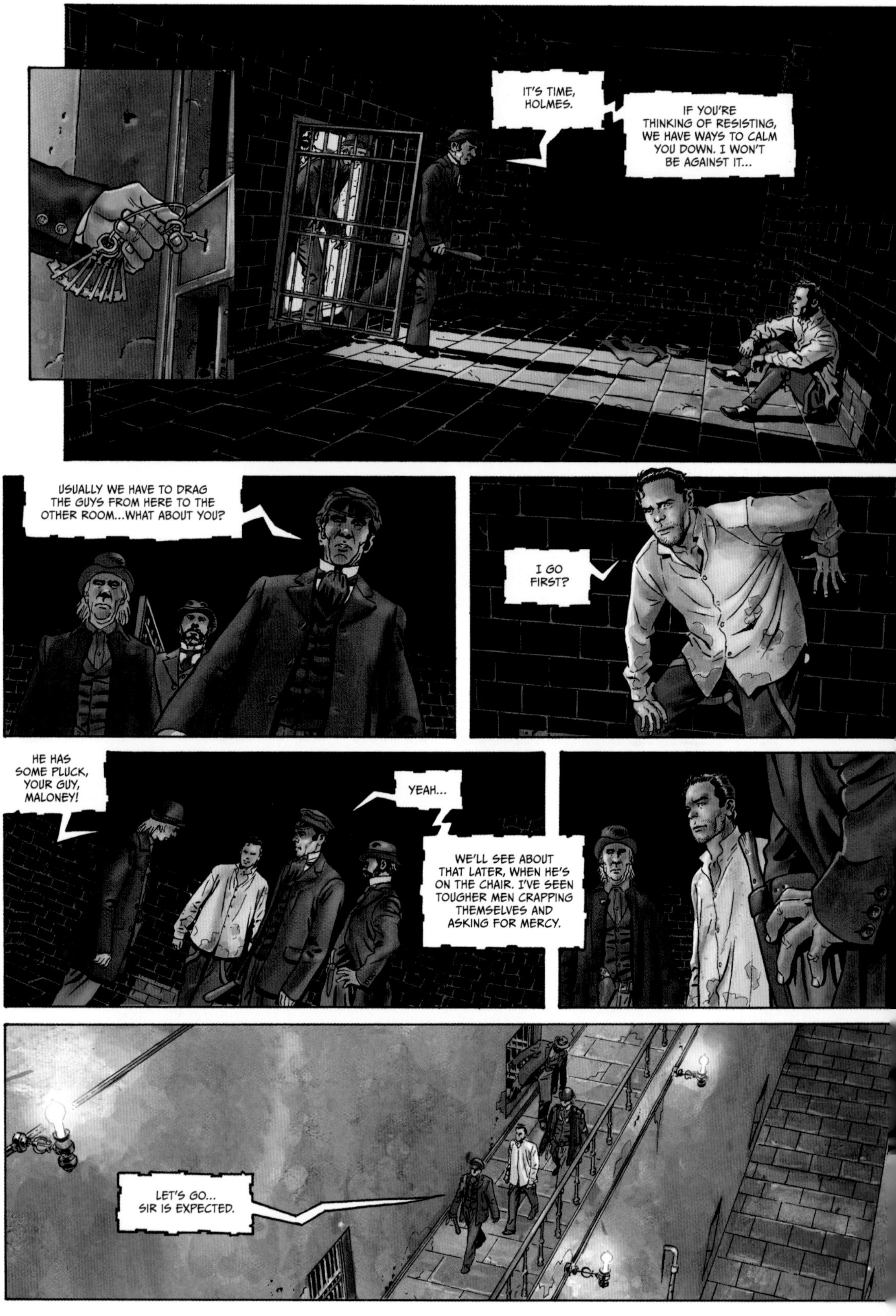
IT'S TIME, HOLMES.
IF YOU'RE THINKING OF RESISTING, WE HAVE WAYS TO CALM YOU DOWN. I WON'T BE AGAINST IT...
USUALLY WE HAVE TO DRAG THE GUYS FROM HERE TO THE OTHER ROOM...WHAT ABOUT YOU?
I GO FIRST?
HE HAS SOME PLUCK, YOUR GUY, MALONEY!
YEAH...
WE'LL SEE ABOUT THAT LATER, WHEN HE'S ON THE CHAIR. I'VE SEEN TOUGHER MEN CRAPPING THEMSELVES AND ASKING FOR MERCY.
LET'S GO... SIR IS EXPECTED.

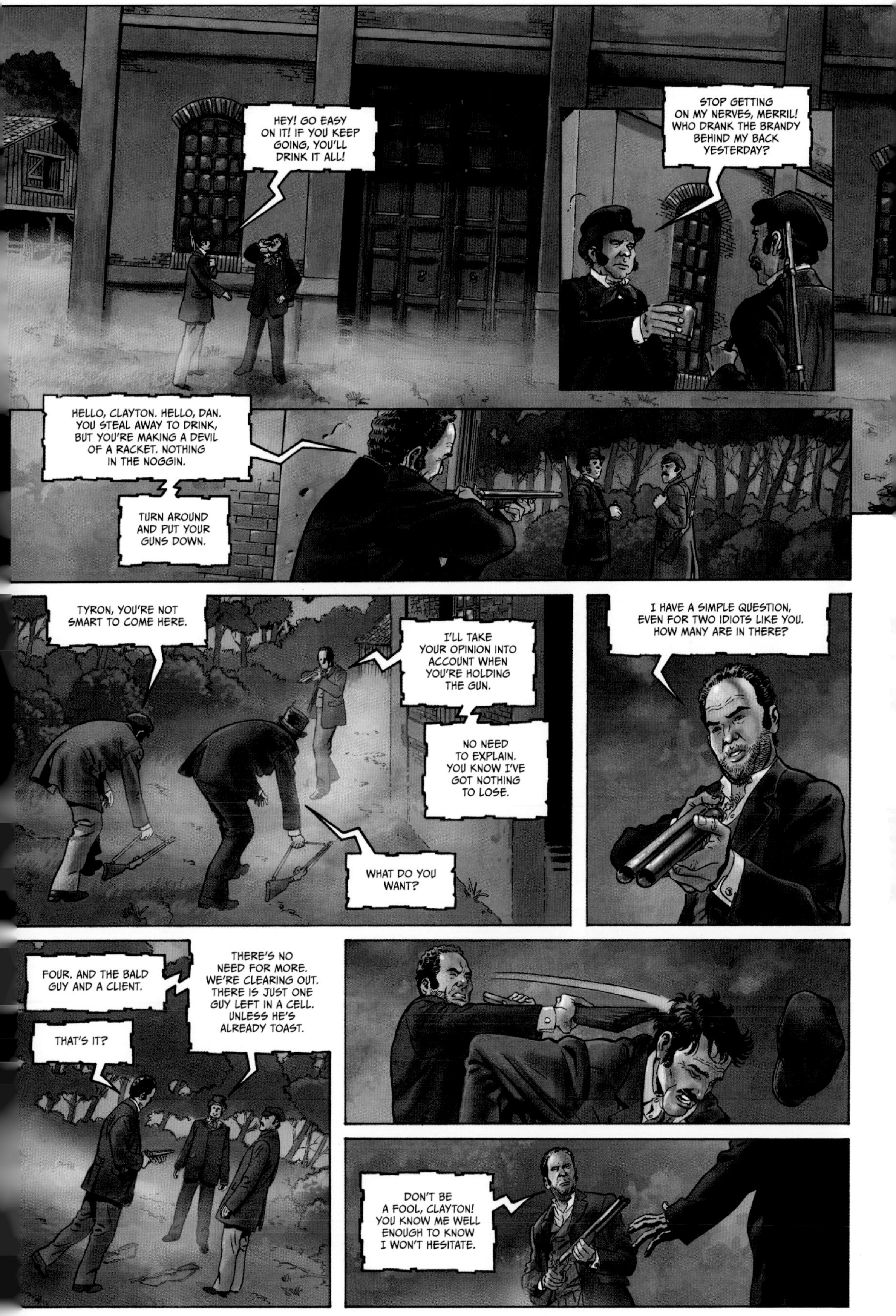
HEY! GO EASY ON IT! IF YOU KEEP GOING, YOU'LL DRINK IT ALL!
STOP GETTING ON MY NERVES, MERRIL! WHO DRANK THE BRANDY BEHIND MY BACK YESTERDAY?
HELLO, CLAYTON. HELLO, DAN. YOU STEAL AWAY TO DRINK, BUT YOU'RE MAKING A DEVIL OF A RACKET. NOTHING IN THE NOGGIN.
TURN AROUND AND PUT YOUR GUNS DOWN.
TYRON, YOU'RE NOT SMART TO COME HERE.
I'LL TAKE YOUR OPINION INTO ACCOUNT WHEN YOU'RE HOLDING THE GUN.
NO NEED TO EXPLAIN. YOU KNOW I'VE GOT NOTHING TO LOSE.
WHAT DO YOU WANT?
I HAVE A SIMPLE QUESTION, EVEN FOR TWO IDIOTS LIKE YOU. HOW MANY ARE IN THERE?
FOUR. AND THE BALD GUY AND A CLIENT.
THAT'S IT?
THERE'S NO NEED FOR MORE. WE'RE CLEARING OUT. THERE IS JUST ONE GUY LEFT IN A CELL. UNLESS HE'S ALREADY TOAST.
DON'T BE A FOOL, CLAYTON! YOU KNOW ME WELL ENOUGH TO KNOW I WON'T HESITATE.

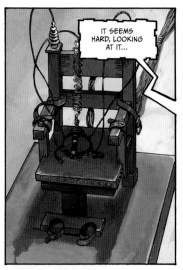

IT SEEMS HARD, LOOKING AT IT...

...BUT YOU'LL SEE. YOU'LL FEEL GOOD ONCE YOU'RE SETTLED IN.

EDWARD IS MAD AT YOU. IT'S NORMAL...BECAUSE OF YOU, HE'LL HAVE LESS WORK IN THE COMING WEEKS... AND HE LIKES HIS JOB.

DEAF AND DUMB?

HOW DO YOU KNOW?

THE INTENSITY IN HIS EYES... HE NEVER LOOKS AWAY WHEN SOMEONE'S SPEAKING... AND OTHER DETAILS.

EVEN NOW, YOU CAN'T HELP ANALYZING EVERYTHING.

WELL...THAT WAY THE CLIENT SEES WHAT HE'S INVESTING IN.

I'LL MAKE GOOD USE OF YOUR TALENTS, YOUNG MAN.

SHERLOCK HOLMES. THAT'S MY NAME. REMEMBER IT. I WANT YOU TO THINK ABOUT IT EVERY TIME YOU USE THEM.

I...I...

IF YOU DON'T WANT A BALL IN YOUR MOUTH LIKE THE VIOLINIST, DON'T TALK TO THE CLIENT.

THAT WOULD BE A SHAME... IF THERE IS A SMALL CHANCE TO HEAR YOU SCREAM, I WOULDN'T MISS IT.

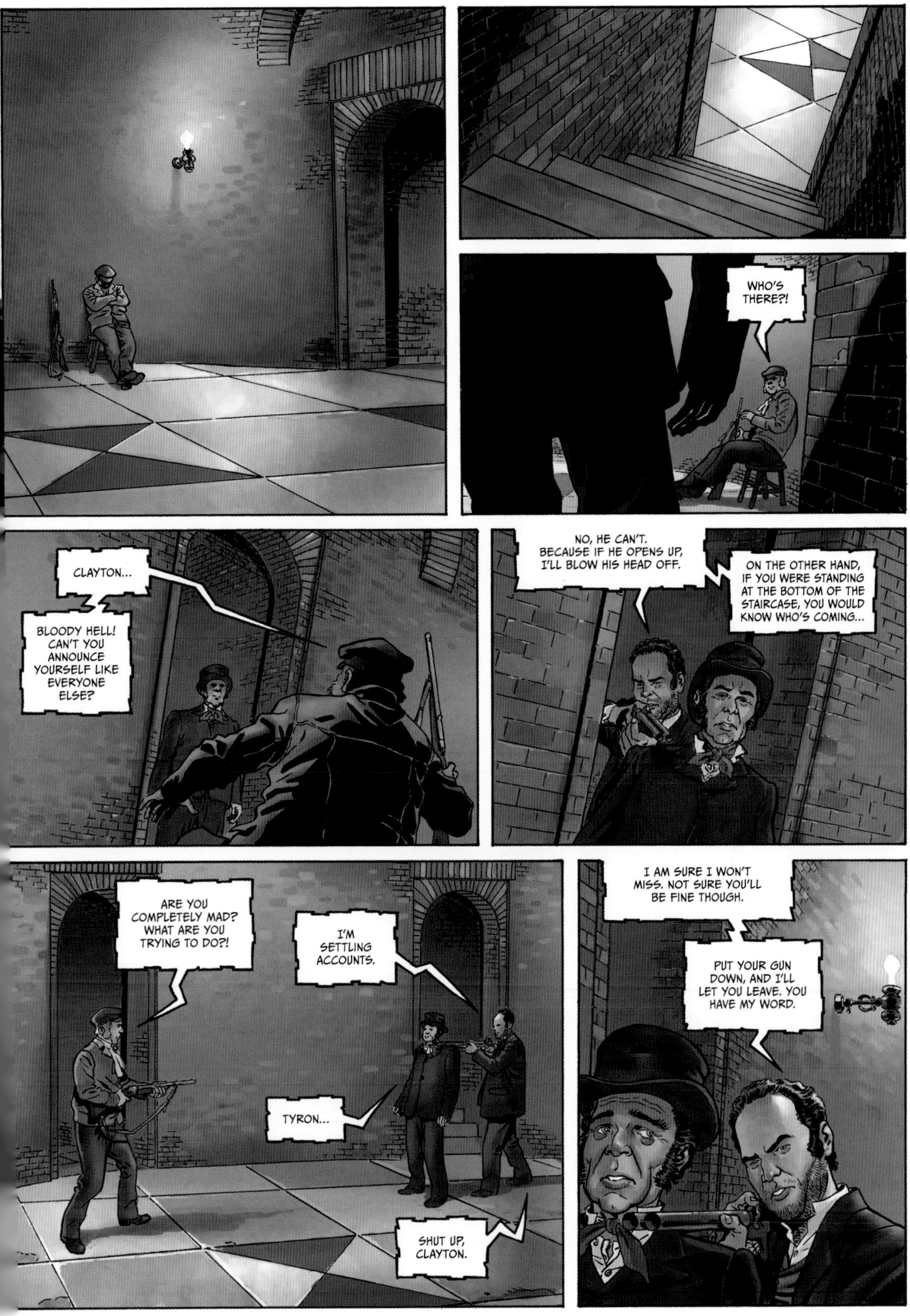
WHO'S THERE?!
CLAYTON...
BLOODY HELL! CAN'T YOU ANNOUNCE YOURSELF LIKE EVERYONE ELSE?
NO, HE CAN'T. BECAUSE IF HE OPENS UP, I'LL BLOW HIS HEAD OFF.
ON THE OTHER HAND, IF YOU WERE STANDING AT THE BOTTOM OF THE STAIRCASE, YOU WOULD KNOW WHO'S COMING...
ARE YOU COMPLETELY MAD? WHAT ARE YOU TRYING TO DO?!
I'M SETTLING ACCOUNTS.
TYRON...
SHUT UP, CLAYTON.
I AM SURE I WON'T MISS. NOT SURE YOU'LL BE FINE THOUGH.
PUT YOUR GUN DOWN, AND I'LL LET YOU LEAVE. YOU HAVE MY WORD.

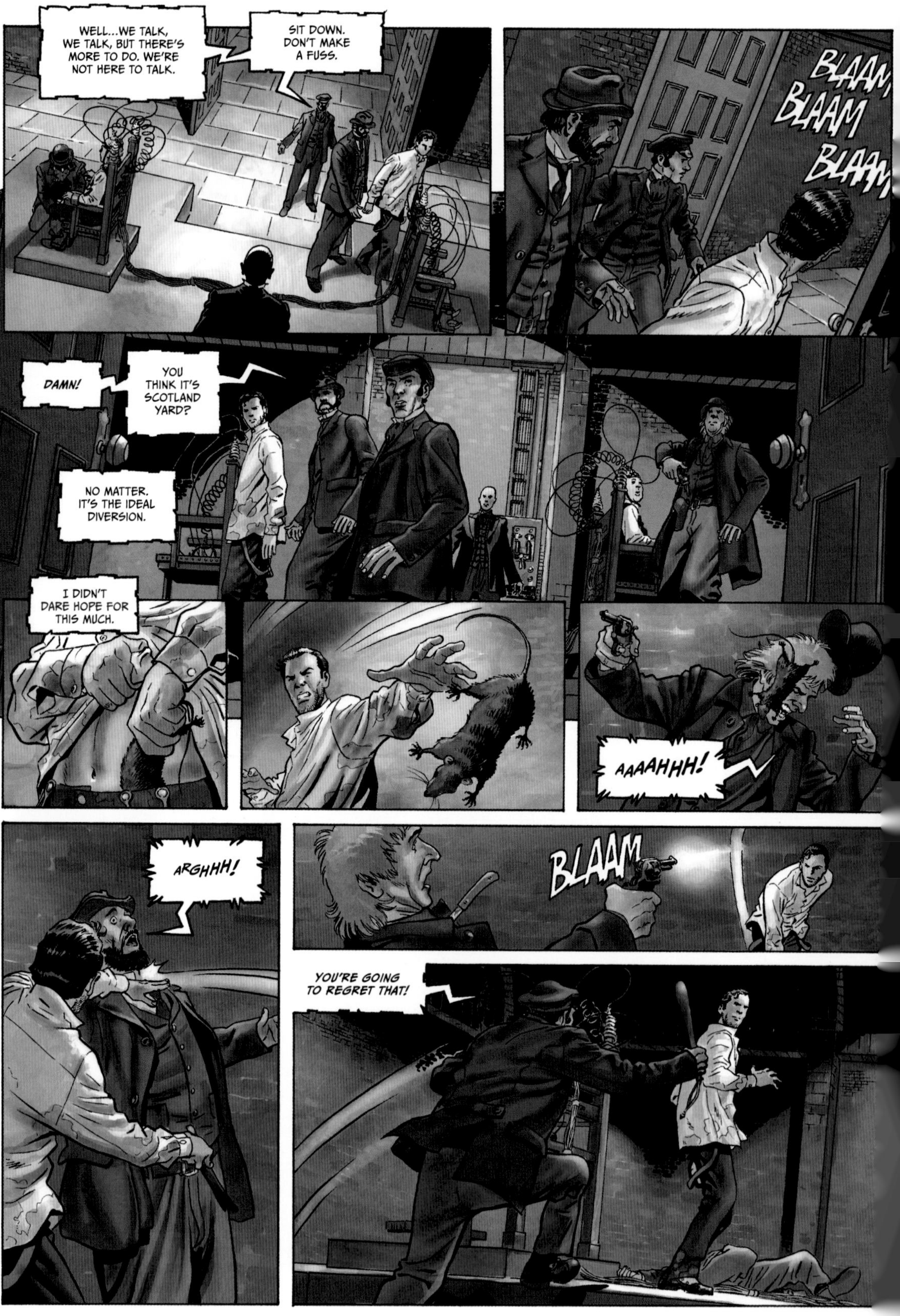

WELL...WE TALK, WE TALK, BUT THERE'S MORE TO DO. WE'RE NOT HERE TO TALK.
SIT DOWN. DON'T MAKE A FUSS.
BLAAM, BLAAM BLAAM
DAMN!
YOU THINK IT'S SCOTLAND YARD?
NO MATTER. IT'S THE IDEAL DIVERSION.
I DIDN'T DARE HOPE FOR THIS MUCH.
AAAAHHH!
ARGHHH!
BLAAM
YOU'RE GOING TO REGRET THAT!

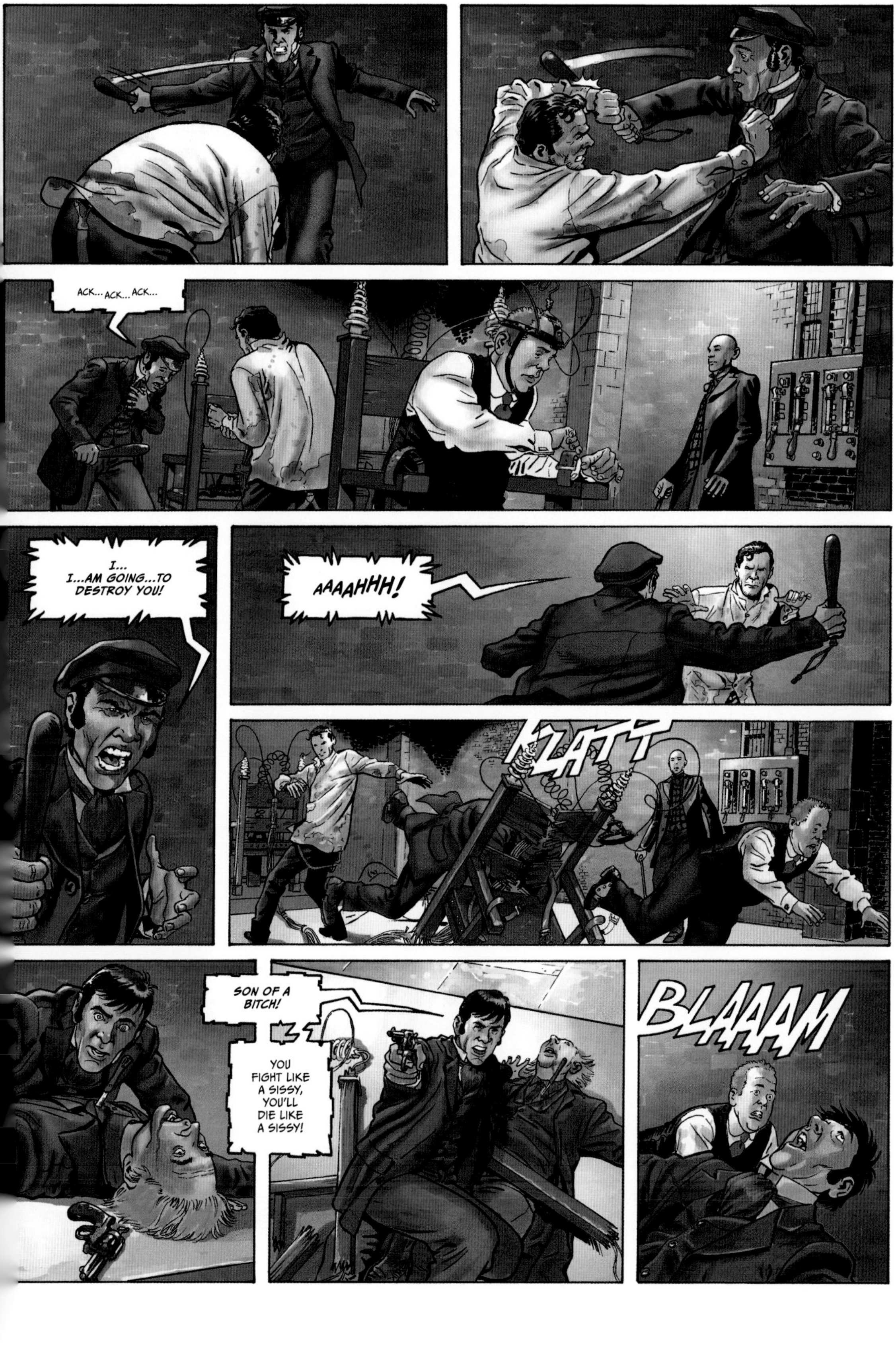
ACK... ACK... ACK...
I... I...AM GOING...TO DESTROY YOU!
AAAAHHH!
KZATT
SON OF A BITCH!
YOU FIGHT LIKE A SISSY, YOU'LL DIE LIKE A SISSY!
BLAAAM

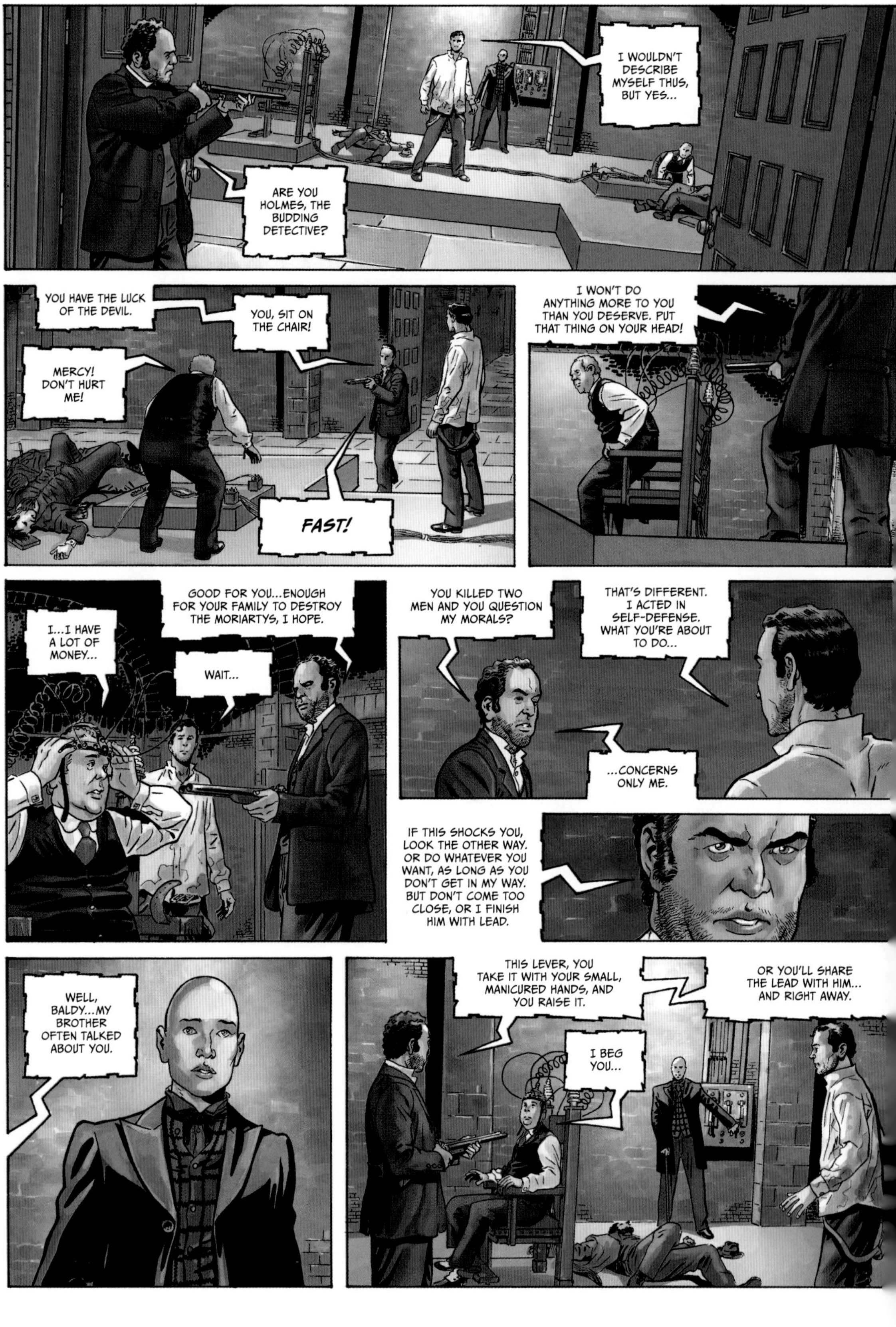

ARE YOU HOLMES, THE BUDDING DETECTIVE?
I WOULDN'T DESCRIBE MYSELF THUS, BUT YES...
YOU HAVE THE LUCK OF THE DEVIL.
YOU, SIT ON THE CHAIR!
MERCY! DON'T HURT ME!
FAST!
I WON'T DO ANYTHING MORE TO YOU THAN YOU DESERVE. PUT THAT THING ON YOUR HEAD!
I...I HAVE A LOT OF MONEY...
GOOD FOR YOU...ENOUGH FOR YOUR FAMILY TO DESTROY THE MORIARTYS, I HOPE.
WAIT...
YOU KILLED TWO MEN AND YOU QUESTION MY MORALS?
THAT'S DIFFERENT. I ACTED IN SELF-DEFENSE. WHAT YOU'RE ABOUT TO DO...
...CONCERNS ONLY ME.
IF THIS SHOCKS YOU, LOOK THE OTHER WAY. OR DO WHATEVER YOU WANT, AS LONG AS YOU DON'T GET IN MY WAY. BUT DON'T COME TOO CLOSE, OR I FINISH HIM WITH LEAD.
WELL, BALDY...MY BROTHER OFTEN TALKED ABOUT YOU.
THIS LEVER, YOU TAKE IT WITH YOUR SMALL, MANICURED HANDS, AND YOU RAISE IT.
I BEG YOU...
OR YOU'LL SHARE THE LEAD WITH HIM... AND RIGHT AWAY.

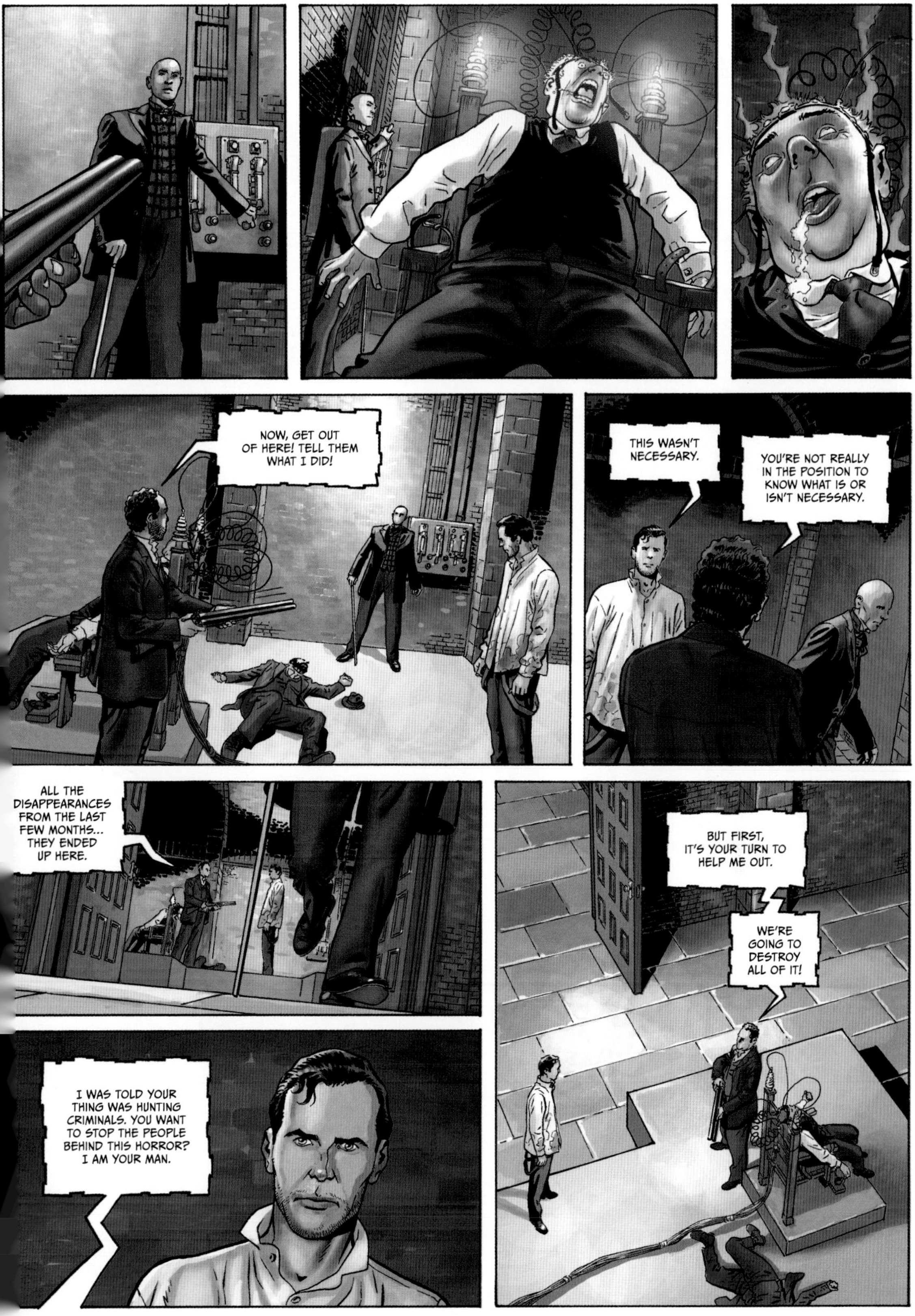
NOW, GET OUT OF HERE! TELL THEM WHAT I DID!
THIS WASN'T NECESSARY.
YOU'RE NOT REALLY IN THE POSITION TO KNOW WHAT IS OR ISN'T NECESSARY.
ALL THE DISAPPEARANCES FROM THE LAST FEW MONTHS... THEY ENDED UP HERE.
I WAS TOLD YOUR THING WAS HUNTING CRIMINALS. YOU WANT TO STOP THE PEOPLE BEHIND THIS HORROR? I AM YOUR MAN.
BUT FIRST, IT'S YOUR TURN TO HELP ME OUT.
WE'RE GOING TO DESTROY ALL OF IT!

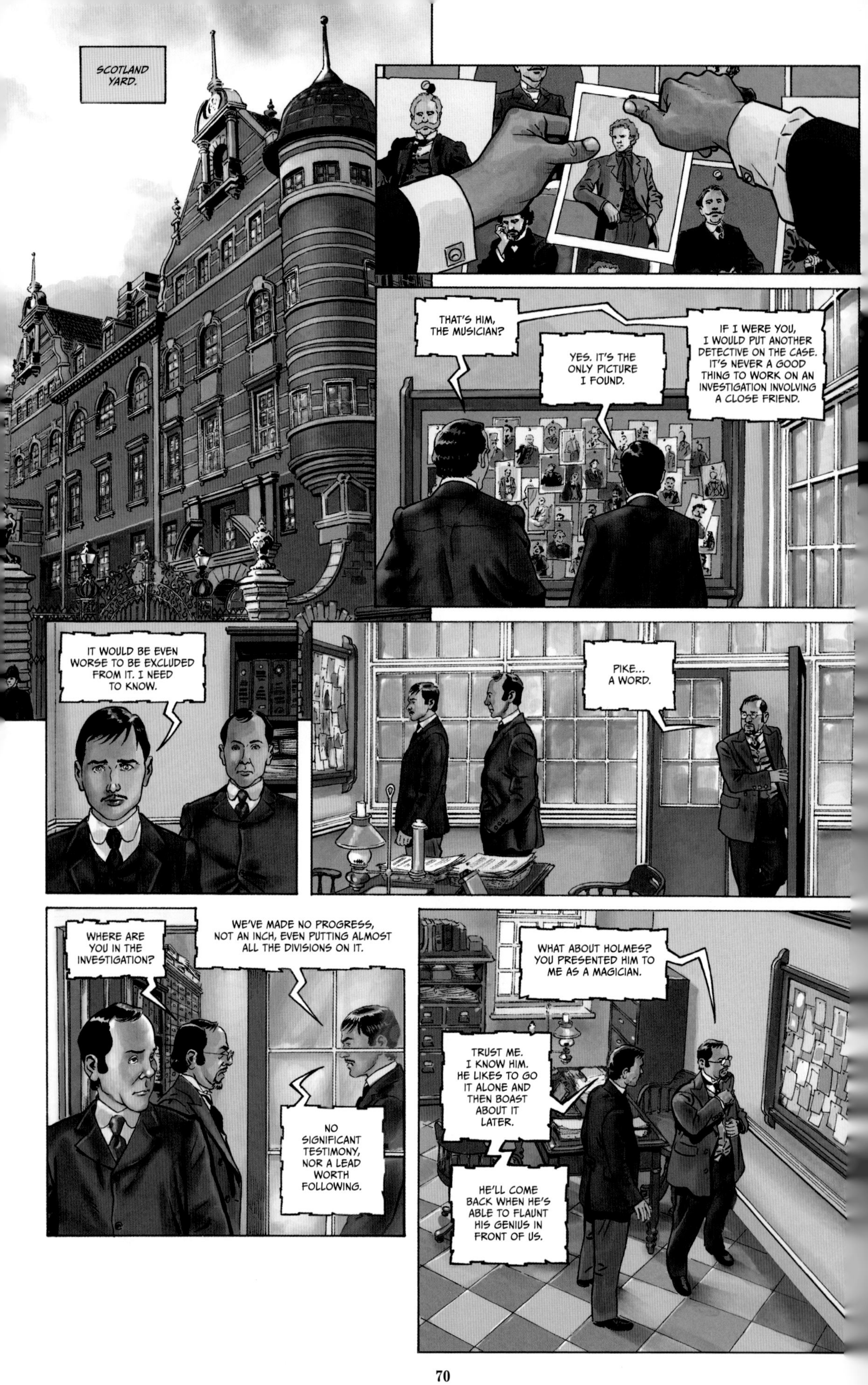
SCOTLAND YARD.
THAT'S HIM, THE MUSICIAN?
YES. IT'S THE ONLY PICTURE I FOUND.
IF I WERE YOU, I WOULD PUT ANOTHER DETECTIVE ON THE CASE. IT'S NEVER A GOOD THING TO WORK ON AN INVESTIGATION INVOLVING A CLOSE FRIEND.
IT WOULD BE EVEN WORSE TO BE EXCLUDED FROM IT. I NEED TO KNOW.
PIKE... A WORD.
WHERE ARE YOU IN THE INVESTIGATION?
WE'VE MADE NO PROGRESS, NOT AN INCH, EVEN PUTTING ALMOST ALL THE DIVISIONS ON IT.
NO SIGNIFICANT TESTIMONY, NOR A LEAD WORTH FOLLOWING.
WHAT ABOUT HOLMES? YOU PRESENTED HIM TO ME AS A MAGICIAN.
TRUST ME. I KNOW HIM. HE LIKES TO GO IT ALONE AND THEN BOAST ABOUT IT LATER.
HE'LL COME BACK WHEN HE'S ABLE TO FLAUNT HIS GENIUS IN FRONT OF US.

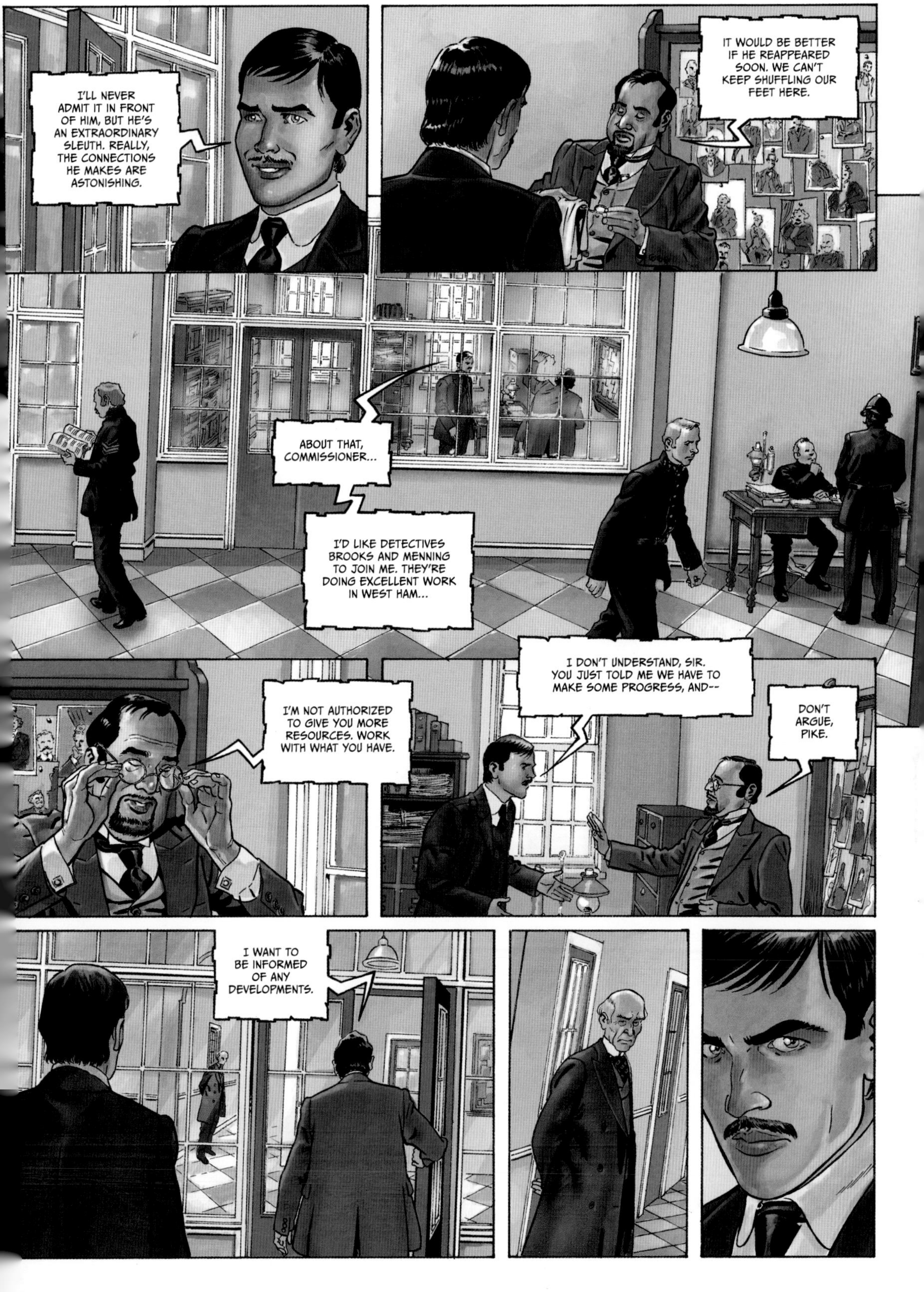
I'LL NEVER ADMIT IT IN FRONT OF HIM, BUT HE'S AN EXTRAORDINARY SLEUTH. REALLY, THE CONNECTIONS HE MAKES ARE ASTONISHING.
IT WOULD BE BETTER IF HE REAPPEARED SOON. WE CAN'T KEEP SHUFFLING OUR FEET HERE.
ABOUT THAT, COMMISSIONER...
I'D LIKE DETECTIVES BROOKS AND MENNING TO JOIN ME. THEY'RE DOING EXCELLENT WORK IN WEST HAM...
I'M NOT AUTHORIZED TO GIVE YOU MORE RESOURCES. WORK WITH WHAT YOU HAVE.
I DON'T UNDERSTAND, SIR. YOU JUST TOLD ME WE HAVE TO MAKE SOME PROGRESS, AND--
DON'T ARGUE, PIKE.
I WANT TO BE INFORMED OF ANY DEVELOPMENTS.

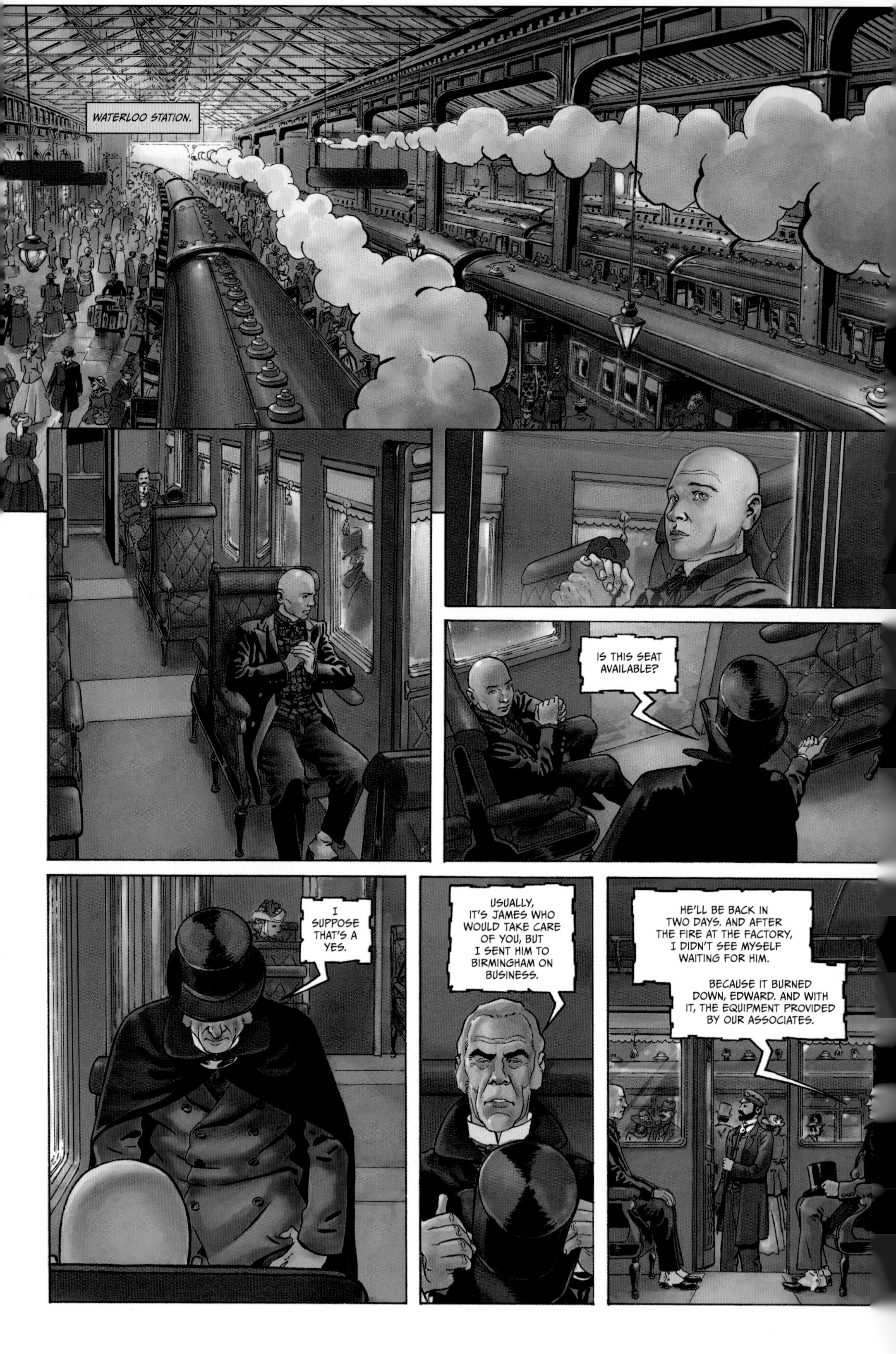
WATERLOO STATION.
IS THIS SEAT AVAILABLE?
I SUPPOSE THAT'S A YES.
USUALLY, IT'S JAMES WHO WOULD TAKE CARE OF YOU, BUT I SENT HIM TO BIRMINGHAM ON BUSINESS.
HE'LL BE BACK IN TWO DAYS. AND AFTER THE FIRE AT THE FACTORY, I DIDN'T SEE MYSELF WAITING FOR HIM.
BECAUSE IT BURNED DOWN, EDWARD. AND WITH IT, THE EQUIPMENT PROVIDED BY OUR ASSOCIATES.

THE FLAMES WERE SO HIGH THAT THEY WERE SEEN FROM ALL THE NEARBY VILLAGES. YOU CAN IMAGINE MY SURPRISE WHEN I FOUND OUT...

THE ENORMOUS FINANCIAL LOSS AND THE PROBLEMS THAT WILL FOLLOW... I'D RATHER NOT THINK ABOUT THAT RIGHT NOW.

I'M INTERESTED IN ONLY ONE THING. WHY AND HOW?

I WAS THINKING ABOUT THAT WHEN I WAS TOLD YOU WERE ABOUT TO LEAVE TOWN, LOOKING GUILTY.

YOU WERE IN CHARGE OF THE PLACE AND SEEM TO KNOW ABOUT THE INCIDENT, AND YOU FLEE INSTEAD OF COMING TO ME.

WITHOUT HAVING THE PRESENCE OF MIND TO THINK THAT THE STATIONS WOULD BE UNDER MY SURVEILLANCE, IN CASE PATERSON SHOULD SHOW UP.

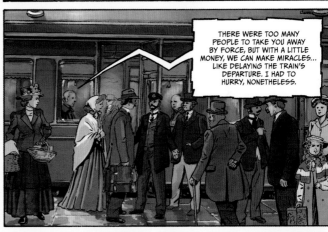

THERE WERE TOO MANY PEOPLE TO TAKE YOU AWAY BY FORCE, BUT WITH A LITTLE MONEY, WE CAN MAKE MIRACLES... LIKE DELAYING THE TRAIN'S DEPARTURE. I HAD TO HURRY, NONETHELESS.

WHATEVER YOU MAY HAVE DONE, I UNDERSTAND YOU WANT TO GO AWAY. YOU'RE SCARED. HOWEVER, NO DISTANCE CAN REMOVE YOU FROM MY SHADOW.

HERE IS WHAT WE'RE GOING TO DO. WE LEAVE THIS CAR TOGETHER, AND YOU TELL ME WHAT YOU KNOW. OR MY MEN WILL FOLLOW YOU AND KIDNAP YOU AT THE FIRST CHANCE...AND THEN TORTURE YOU.

DECIDE QUICKLY.

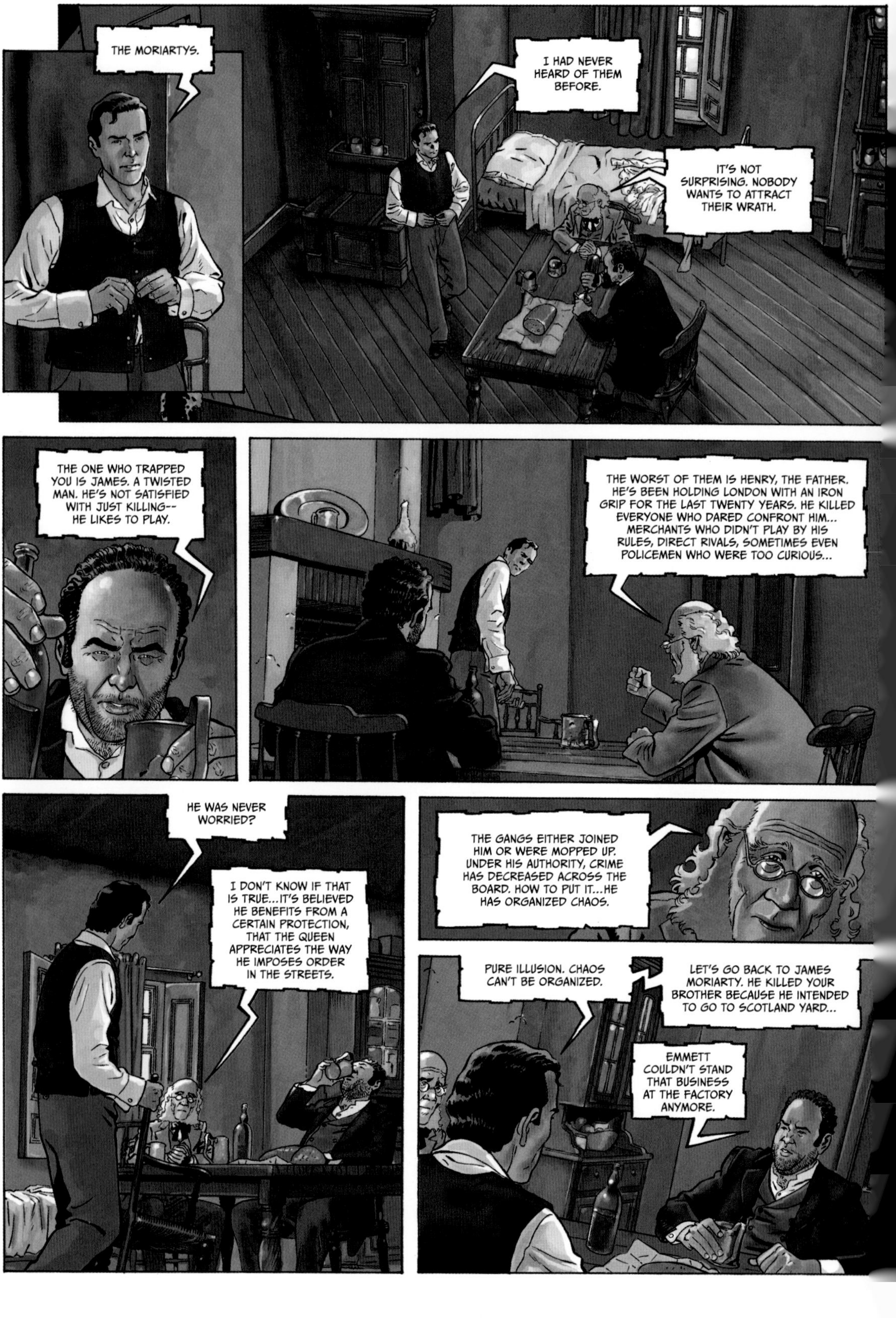
THE MORIARTYS.
I HAD NEVER HEARD OF THEM BEFORE.
IT'S NOT SURPRISING. NOBODY WANTS TO ATTRACT THEIR WRATH.
THE ONE WHO TRAPPED YOU IS JAMES. A TWISTED MAN. HE'S NOT SATISFIED WITH JUST KILLING-- HE LIKES TO PLAY.
THE WORST OF THEM IS HENRY, THE FATHER. HE'S BEEN HOLDING LONDON WITH AN IRON GRIP FOR THE LAST TWENTY YEARS. HE KILLED EVERYONE WHO DARED CONFRONT HIM... MERCHANTS WHO DIDN'T PLAY BY HIS RULES, DIRECT RIVALS, SOMETIMES EVEN POLICEMEN WHO WERE TOO CURIOUS...
HE WAS NEVER WORRIED?
I DON'T KNOW IF THAT IS TRUE...IT'S BELIEVED HE BENEFITS FROM A CERTAIN PROTECTION, THAT THE QUEEN APPRECIATES THE WAY HE IMPOSES ORDER IN THE STREETS.
THE GANGS EITHER JOINED HIM OR WERE MOPPED UP. UNDER HIS AUTHORITY, CRIME HAS DECREASED ACROSS THE BOARD. HOW TO PUT IT...HE HAS ORGANIZED CHAOS.
PURE ILLUSION. CHAOS CAN'T BE ORGANIZED.
LET'S GO BACK TO JAMES MORIARTY. HE KILLED YOUR BROTHER BECAUSE HE INTENDED TO GO TO SCOTLAND YARD...
EMMETT COULDN'T STAND THAT BUSINESS AT THE FACTORY ANYMORE.

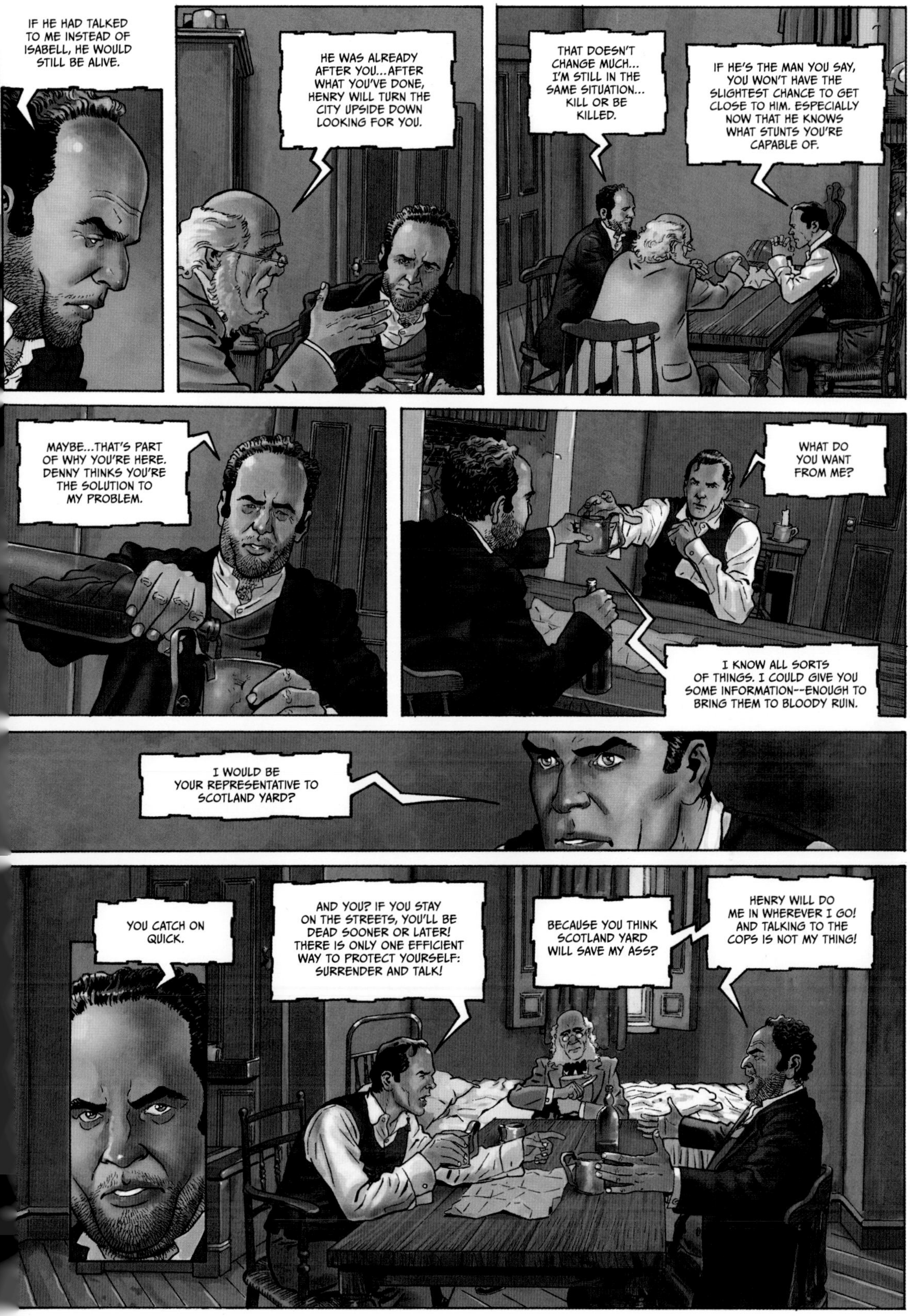
IF HE HAD TALKED TO ME INSTEAD OF ISABELL, HE WOULD STILL BE ALIVE.
HE WAS ALREADY AFTER YOU...AFTER WHAT YOU'VE DONE, HENRY WILL TURN THE CITY UPSIDE DOWN LOOKING FOR YOU.
THAT DOESN'T CHANGE MUCH... I'M STILL IN THE SAME SITUATION... KILL OR BE KILLED.
IF HE'S THE MAN YOU SAY, YOU WON'T HAVE THE SLIGHTEST CHANCE TO GET CLOSE TO HIM. ESPECIALLY NOW THAT HE KNOWS WHAT STUNTS YOU'RE CAPABLE OF.
MAYBE...THAT'S PART OF WHY YOU'RE HERE. DENNY THINKS YOU'RE THE SOLUTION TO MY PROBLEM.
WHAT DO YOU WANT FROM ME?
I KNOW ALL SORTS OF THINGS. I COULD GIVE YOU SOME INFORMATION--ENOUGH TO BRING THEM TO BLOODY RUIN.
I WOULD BE YOUR REPRESENTATIVE TO SCOTLAND YARD?
YOU CATCH ON QUICK.
AND YOU? IF YOU STAY ON THE STREETS, YOU'LL BE DEAD SOONER OR LATER! THERE IS ONLY ONE EFFICIENT WAY TO PROTECT YOURSELF: SURRENDER AND TALK!
BECAUSE YOU THINK SCOTLAND YARD WILL SAVE MY ASS?
HENRY WILL DO ME IN WHEREVER I GO! AND TALKING TO THE COPS IS NOT MY THING!

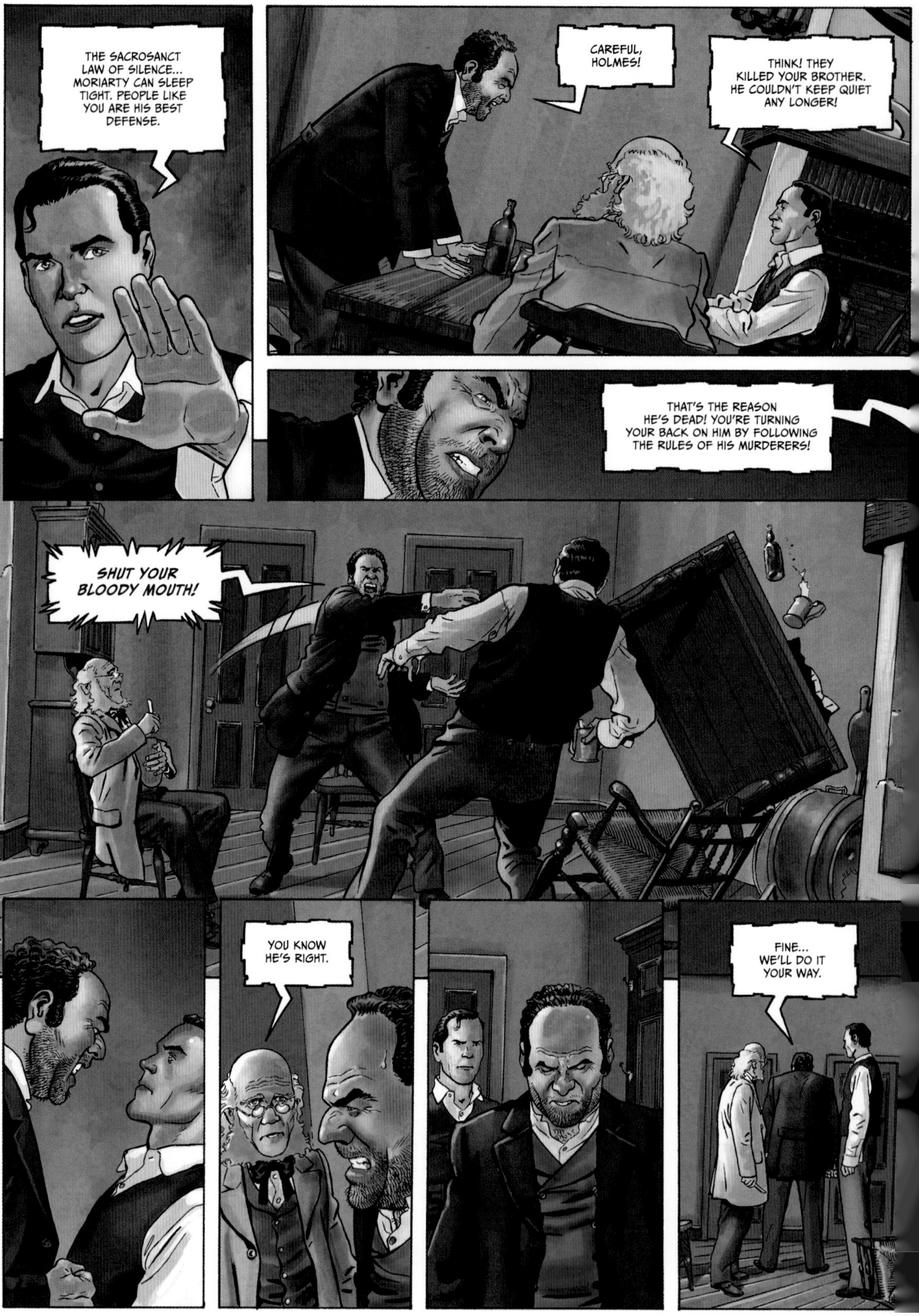
THE SACROSANCT LAW OF SILENCE... MORIARTY CAN SLEEP TIGHT. PEOPLE LIKE YOU ARE HIS BEST DEFENSE.
CAREFUL, HOLMES!
THINK! THEY KILLED YOUR BROTHER. HE COULDN'T KEEP QUIET ANY LONGER!
THAT'S THE REASON HE'S DEAD! YOU'RE TURNING YOUR BACK ON HIM BY FOLLOWING THE RULES OF HIS MURDERERS!
SHUT YOUR BLOODY MOUTH!
YOU KNOW HE'S RIGHT.
FINE... WE'LL DO IT YOUR WAY.

HOLMES!

I SEE YOU GOT MY MESSAGE...

WHERE HAVE YOU BEEN, FOR CHRIST'S SAKE? I'VE BEEN LOOKING FOR YOU FOR DAYS!

OUTWARDLY I STAYED CALM, BUT I WAS STARTING TO GET SERIOUSLY WORRIED.

I AM TOUCHED.

THE TRUTH IS I WAS ALMOST TAKEN FROM YOU FOR GOOD.

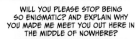

WILL YOU PLEASE STOP BEING SO ENIGMATIC? AND EXPLAIN WHY YOU MADE ME MEET YOU OUT HERE IN THE MIDDLE OF NOWHERE?

RON IS DEAD, COLIN.

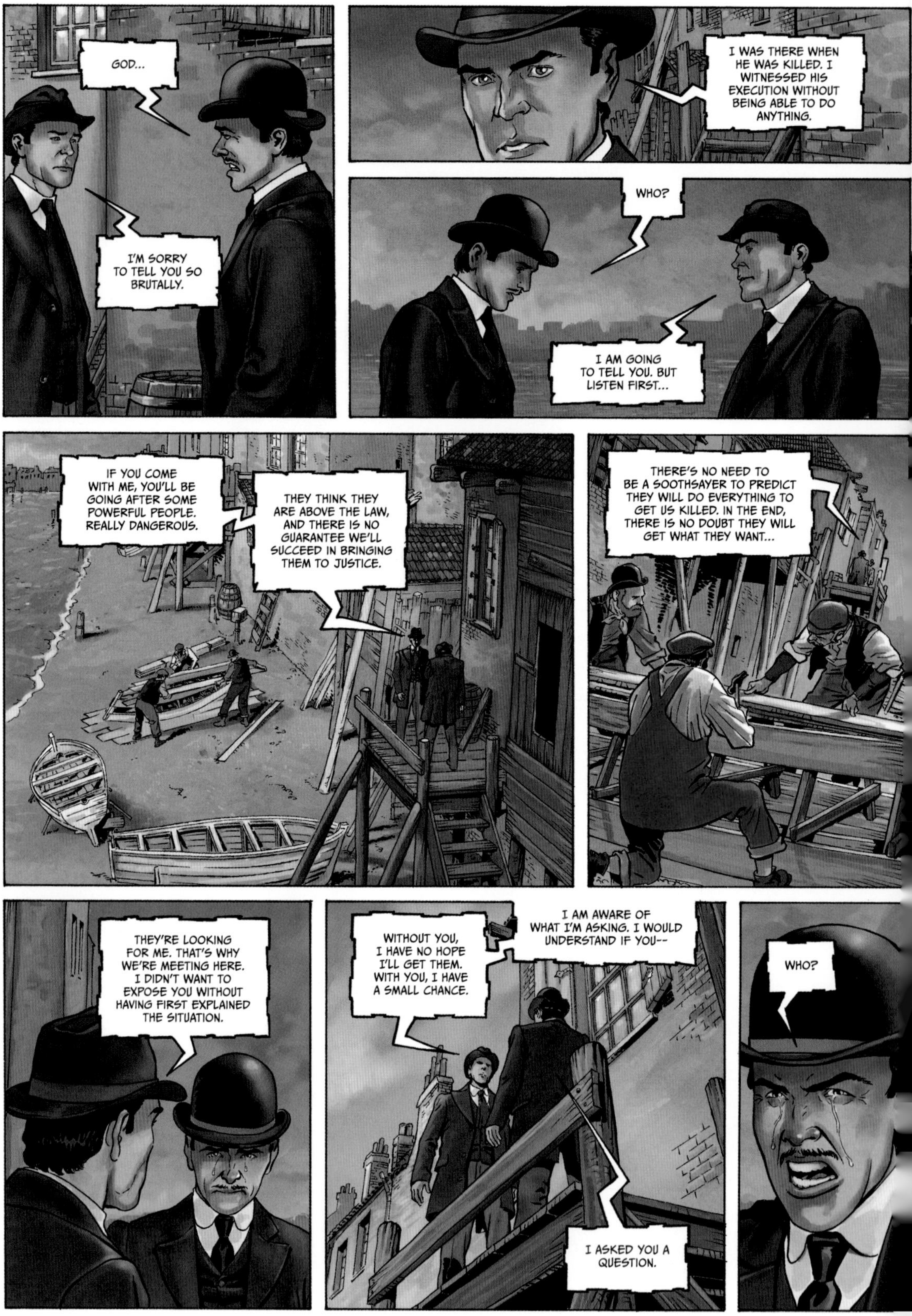
GOD...
I'M SORRY TO TELL YOU SO BRUTALLY.
I WAS THERE WHEN HE WAS KILLED. I WITNESSED HIS EXECUTION WITHOUT BEING ABLE TO DO ANYTHING.
WHO?
I AM GOING TO TELL YOU. BUT LISTEN FIRST...
IF YOU COME WITH ME, YOU'LL BE GOING AFTER SOME POWERFUL PEOPLE. REALLY DANGEROUS.
THEY THINK THEY ARE ABOVE THE LAW, AND THERE IS NO GUARANTEE WE'LL SUCCEED IN BRINGING THEM TO JUSTICE.
THERE'S NO NEED TO BE A SOOTHSAYER TO PREDICT THEY WILL DO EVERYTHING TO GET US KILLED. IN THE END, THERE IS NO DOUBT THEY WILL GET WHAT THEY WANT...
THEY'RE LOOKING FOR ME. THAT'S WHY WE'RE MEETING HERE. I DIDN'T WANT TO EXPOSE YOU WITHOUT HAVING FIRST EXPLAINED THE SITUATION.
WITHOUT YOU, I HAVE NO HOPE I'LL GET THEM. WITH YOU, I HAVE A SMALL CHANCE.
I AM AWARE OF WHAT I'M ASKING. I WOULD UNDERSTAND IF YOU--
I ASKED YOU A QUESTION.
WHO?

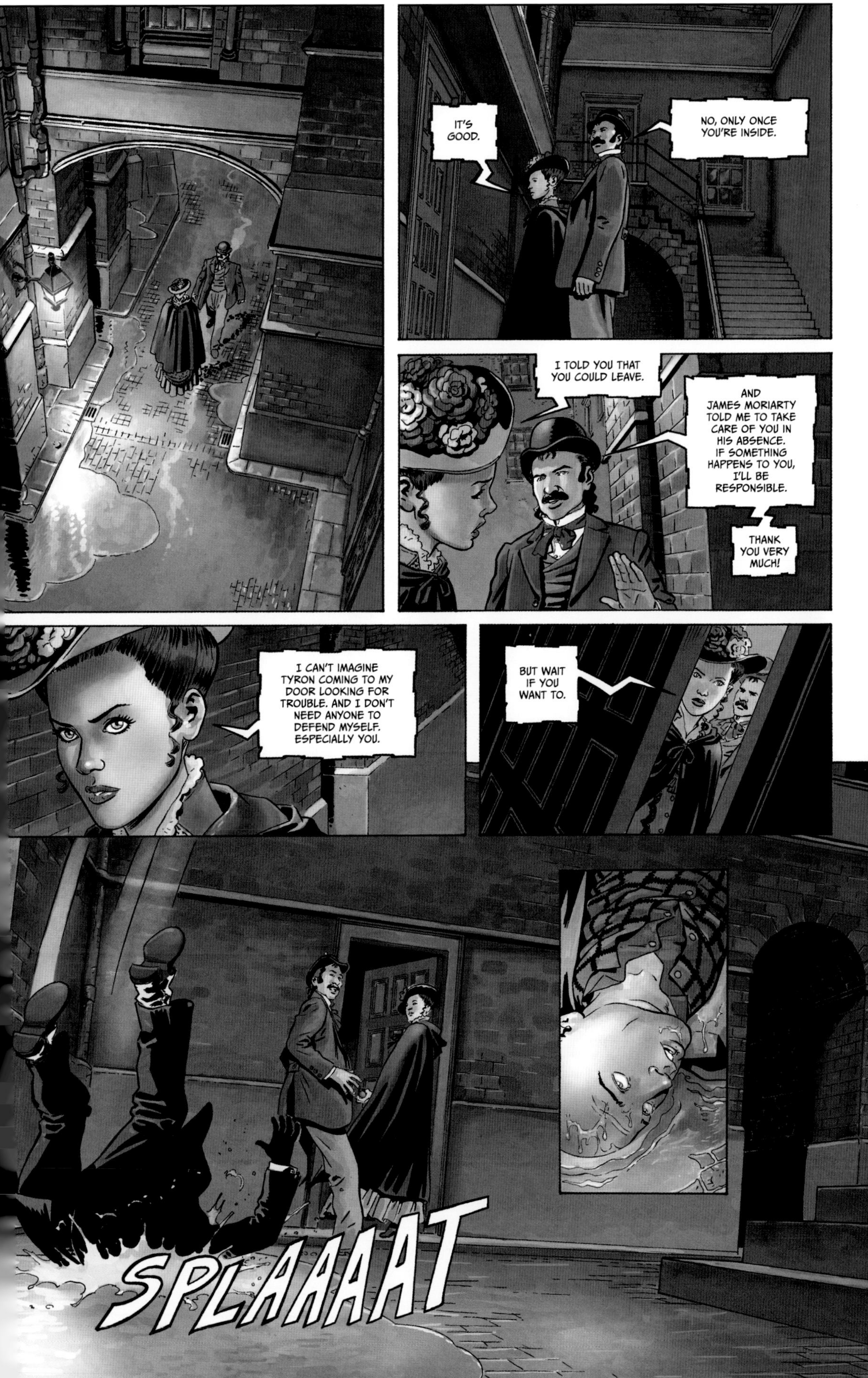
IT'S GOOD.
NO, ONLY ONCE YOU'RE INSIDE.
I TOLD YOU THAT YOU COULD LEAVE.
AND JAMES MORIARTY TOLD ME TO TAKE CARE OF YOU IN HIS ABSENCE. IF SOMETHING HAPPENS TO YOU, I'LL BE RESPONSIBLE.
THANK YOU VERY MUCH!
I CAN'T IMAGINE TYRON COMING TO MY DOOR LOOKING FOR TROUBLE. AND I DON'T NEED ANYONE TO DEFEND MYSELF. ESPECIALLY YOU.
BUT WAIT IF YOU WANT TO.
SPLAAAAT

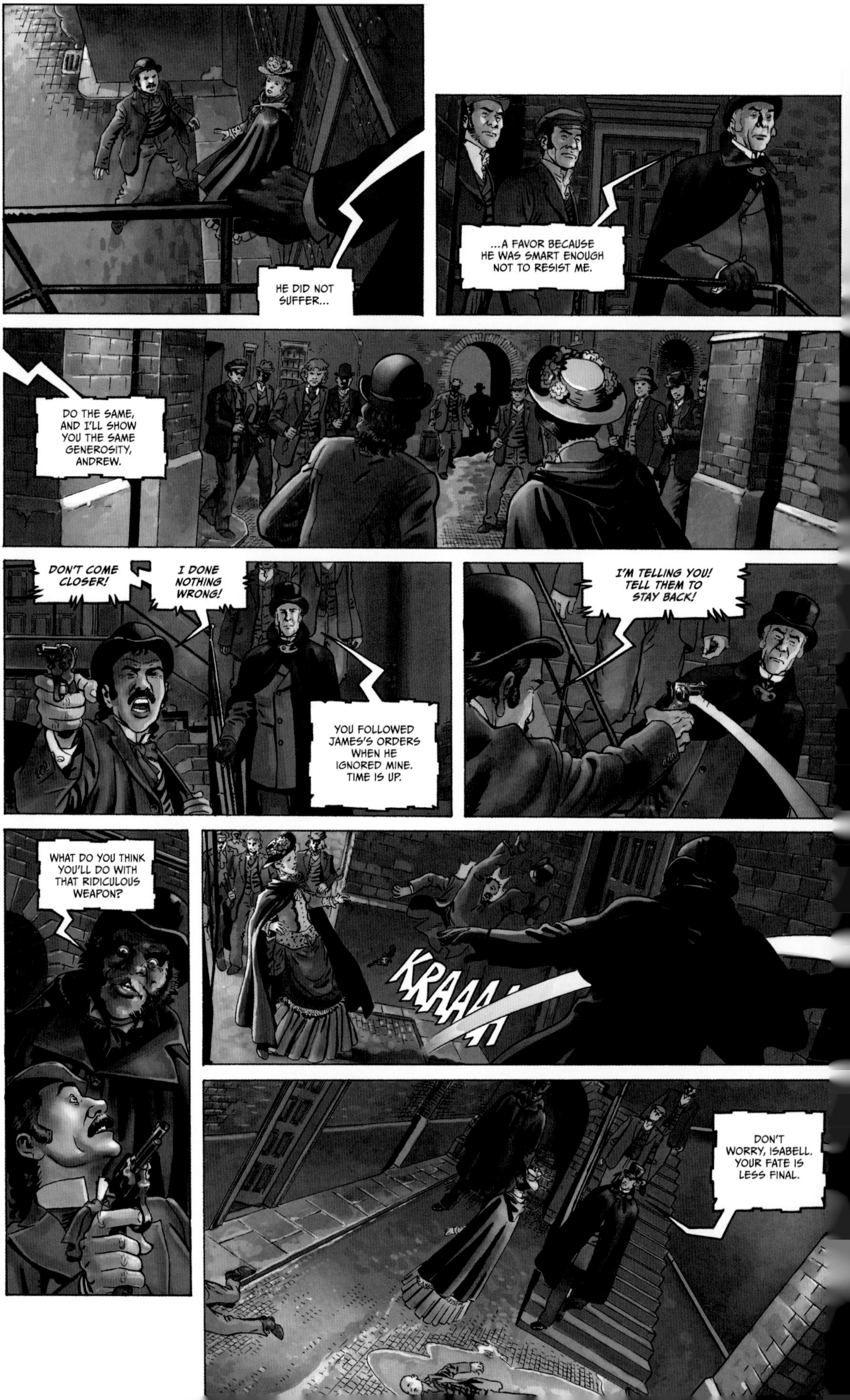
HE DID NOT SUFFER...
...A FAVOR BECAUSE HE WAS SMART ENOUGH NOT TO RESIST ME.
DO THE SAME, AND I'LL SHOW YOU THE SAME GENEROSITY, ANDREW.
DON'T COME CLOSER!
I DONE NOTHING WRONG!
YOU FOLLOWED JAMES'S ORDERS WHEN HE IGNORED MINE. TIME IS UP.
I'M TELLING YOU! TELL THEM TO STAY BACK!
WHAT DO YOU THINK YOU'LL DO WITH THAT RIDICULOUS WEAPON?
KRAAA
DON'T WORRY, ISABELL. YOUR FATE IS LESS FINAL.

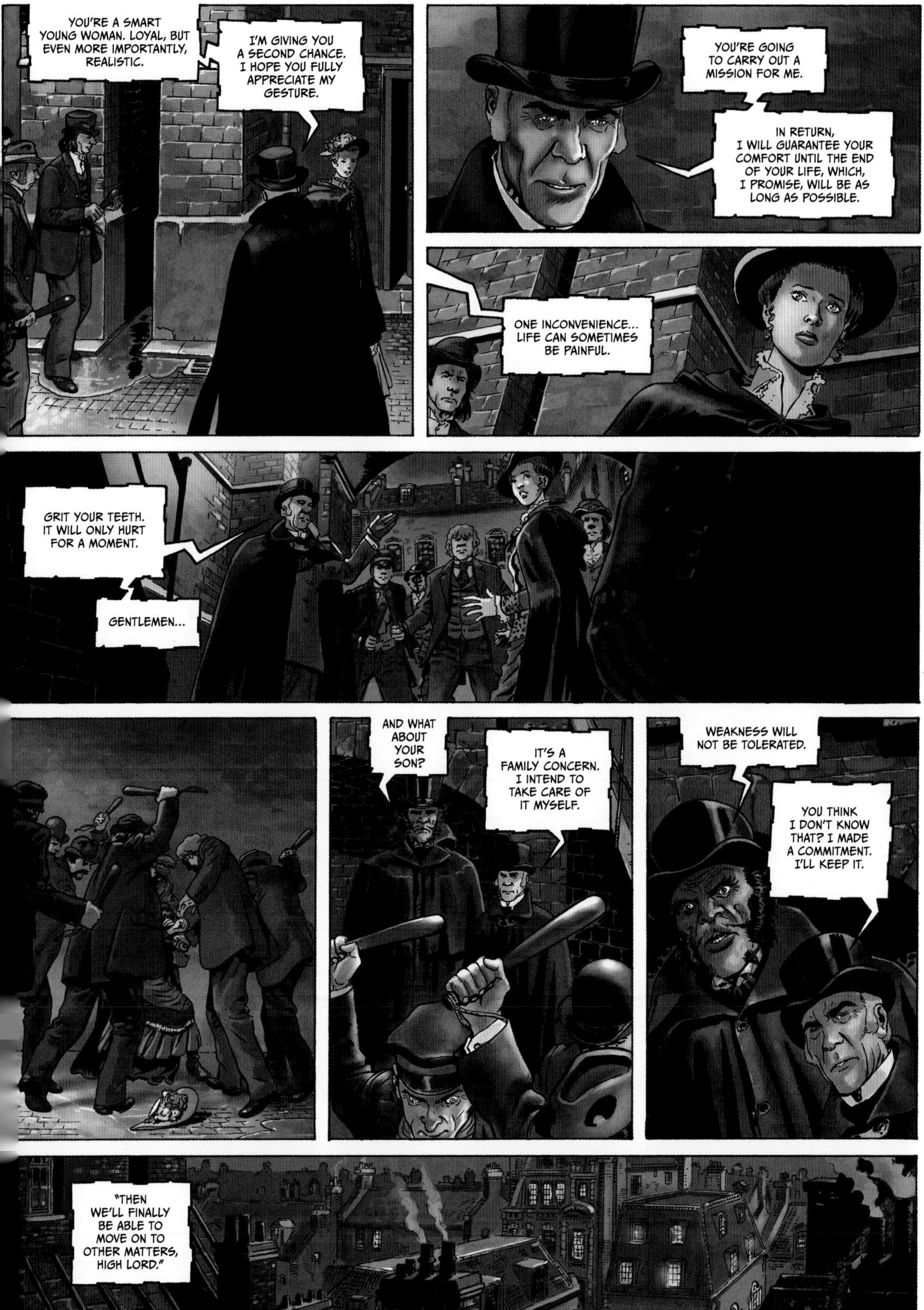
YOU'RE A SMART YOUNG WOMAN. LOYAL, BUT EVEN MORE IMPORTANTLY, REALISTIC.
I'M GIVING YOU A SECOND CHANCE. I HOPE YOU FULLY APPRECIATE MY GESTURE.
YOU'RE GOING TO CARRY OUT A MISSION FOR ME.
IN RETURN, I WILL GUARANTEE YOUR COMFORT UNTIL THE END OF YOUR LIFE, WHICH, I PROMISE, WILL BE AS LONG AS POSSIBLE.
ONE INCONVENIENCE... LIFE CAN SOMETIMES BE PAINFUL.
GRIT YOUR TEETH. IT WILL ONLY HURT FOR A MOMENT.
GENTLEMEN...
AND WHAT ABOUT YOUR SON?
IT'S A FAMILY CONCERN. I INTEND TO TAKE CARE OF IT MYSELF.
WEAKNESS WILL NOT BE TOLERATED.
YOU THINK I DON'T KNOW THAT? I MADE A COMMITMENT. I'LL KEEP IT.
"THEN WE'LL FINALLY BE ABLE TO MOVE ON TO OTHER MATTERS, HIGH LORD."

A POLICE ESCORT JUST FOR ME. EMMETT WOULDN'T BELIEVE IT.

IT'S MUCH MORE THAN THAT. ALL OF SCOTLAND YARD HAS BEEN CALLED OUT FOR YOU.

I'M FLATTERED...

YOU SHOULD BE. NO ONE'S HAD SUCH FAVOR BEFORE.

WHEN I EXPLAINED YOUR IMPORTANCE TO THE ASSISTANT COMMISSIONER, HE DECIDED TO DO THINGS BIG.

HE SURPRISED ME. EVEN IF HE DOESN'T MENTION IT, I THINK HE'S UNDER PRESSURE.

CERTAINLY.

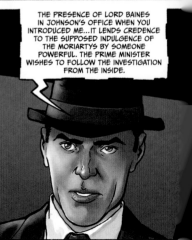

THE PRESENCE OF LORD BAINES IN JOHNSON'S OFFICE WHEN YOU INTRODUCED ME...IT LENDS CREDENCE TO THE SUPPOSED INDULGENCE OF THE MORIARTYS BY SOMEONE POWERFUL. THE PRIME MINISTER WISHES TO FOLLOW THE INVESTIGATION FROM THE INSIDE.

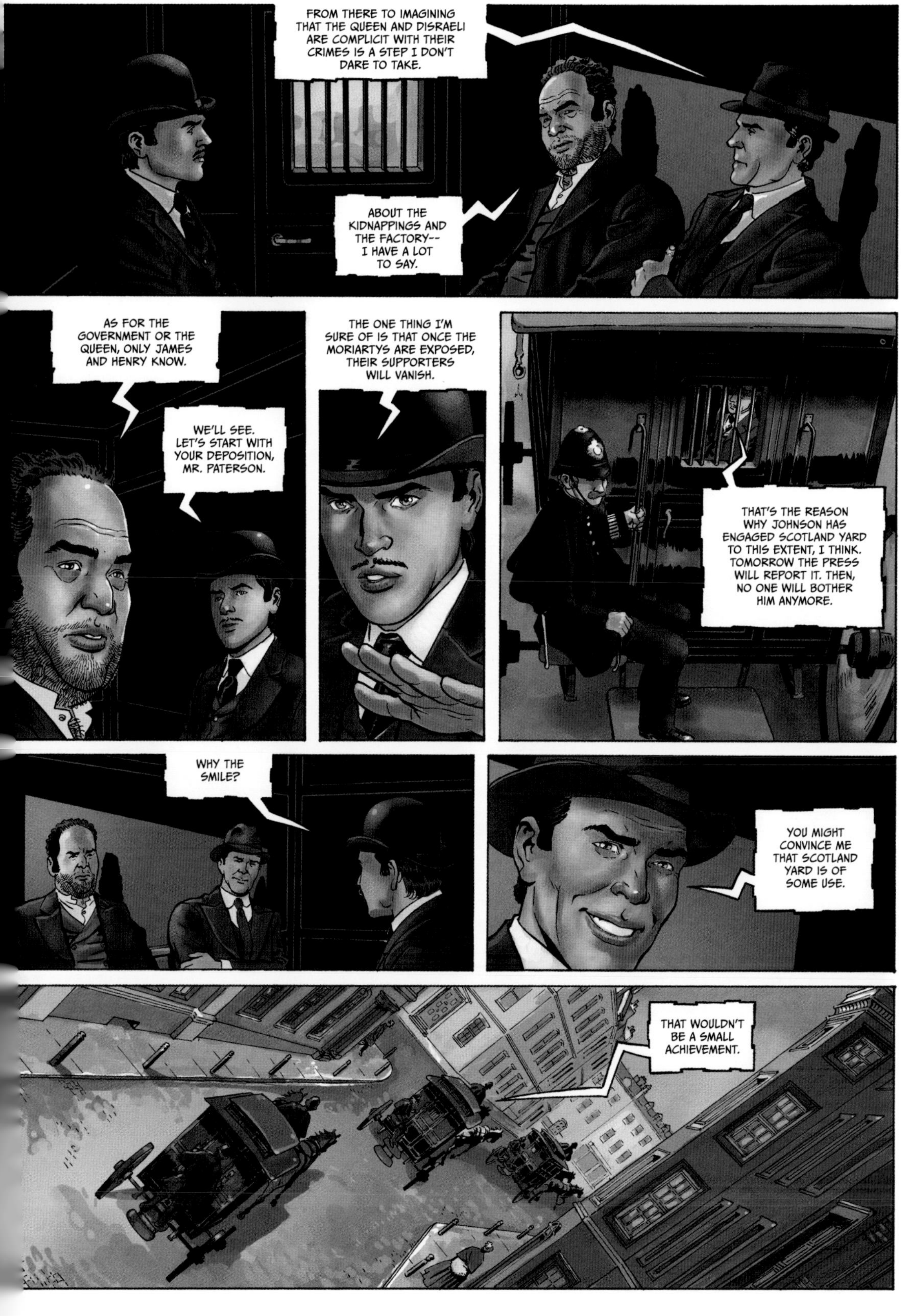
FROM THERE TO IMAGINING THAT THE QUEEN AND DISRAELI ARE COMPLICIT WITH THEIR CRIMES IS A STEP I DON'T DARE TO TAKE.
ABOUT THE KIDNAPPINGS AND THE FACTORY-- I HAVE A LOT TO SAY.
AS FOR THE GOVERNMENT OR THE QUEEN, ONLY JAMES AND HENRY KNOW.
WE'LL SEE. LET'S START WITH YOUR DEPOSITION, MR. PATERSON.
THE ONE THING I'M SURE OF IS THAT ONCE THE MORIARTYS ARE EXPOSED, THEIR SUPPORTERS WILL VANISH.
THAT'S THE REASON WHY JOHNSON HAS ENGAGED SCOTLAND YARD TO THIS EXTENT, I THINK. TOMORROW THE PRESS WILL REPORT IT. THEN, NO ONE WILL BOTHER HIM ANYMORE.
WHY THE SMILE?
YOU MIGHT CONVINCE ME THAT SCOTLAND YARD IS OF SOME USE.
THAT WOULDN'T BE A SMALL ACHIEVEMENT.

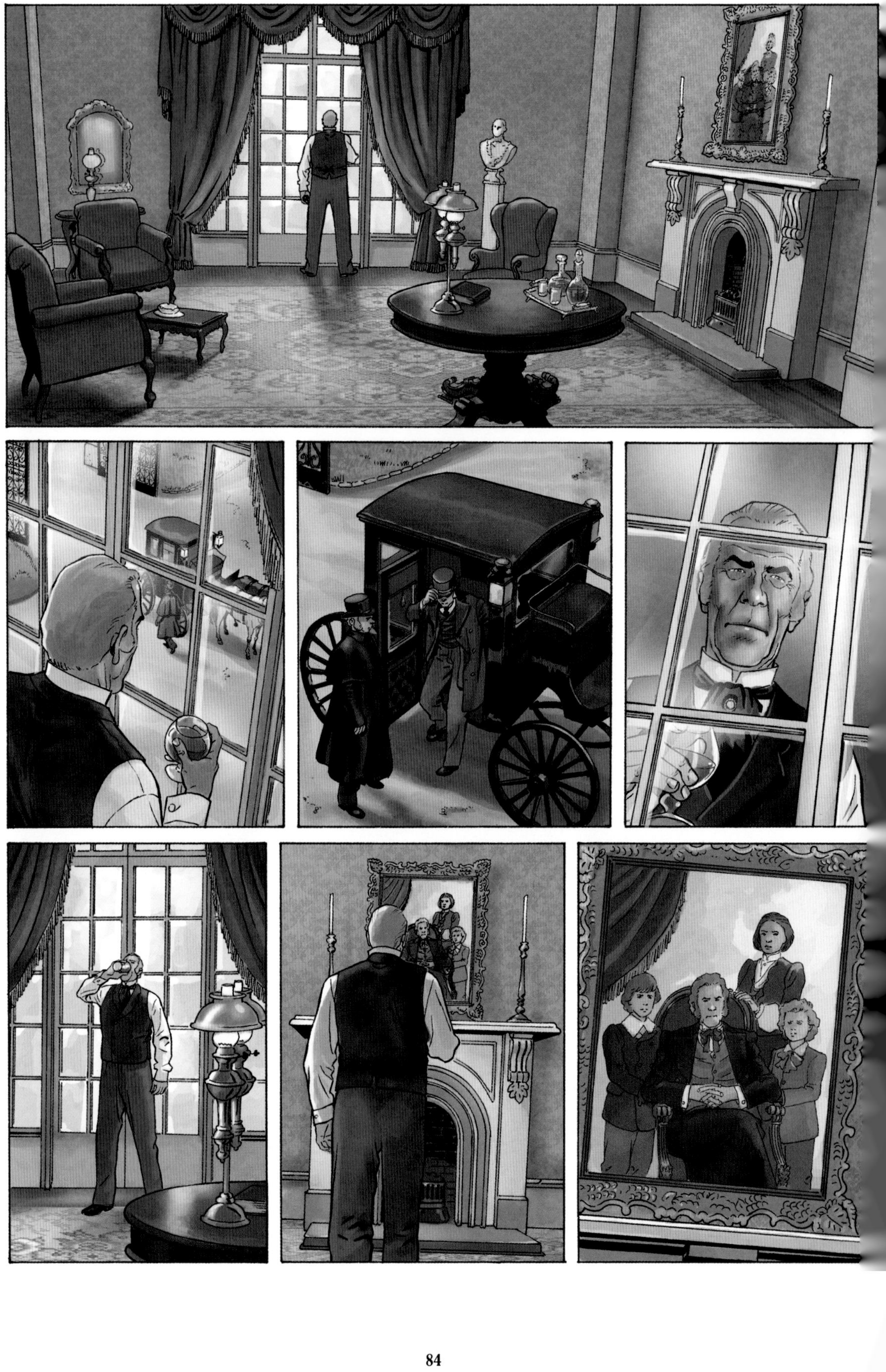

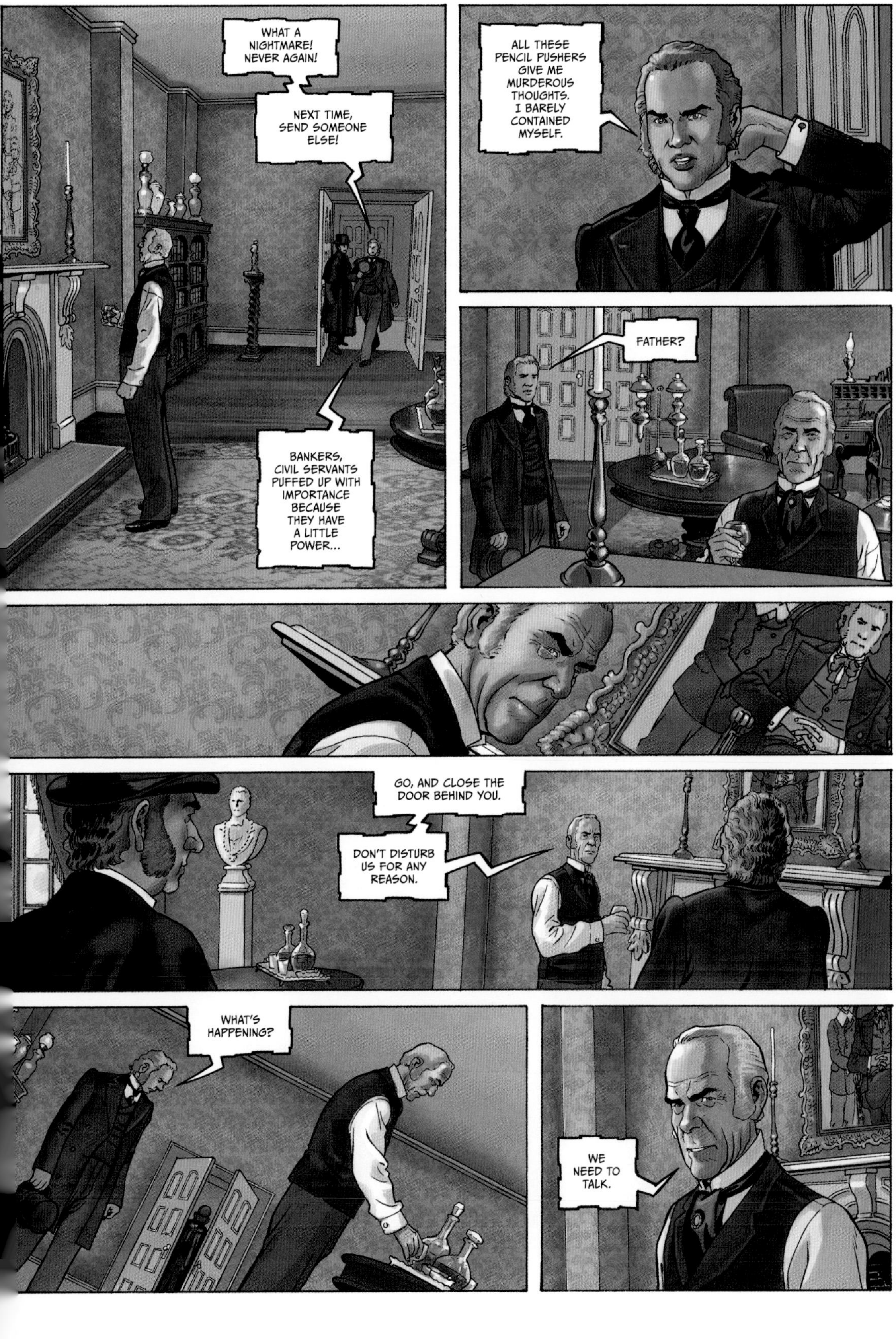
WHAT A NIGHTMARE! NEVER AGAIN!
NEXT TIME, SEND SOMEONE ELSE!
BANKERS, CIVIL SERVANTS PUFFED UP WITH IMPORTANCE BECAUSE THEY HAVE A LITTLE POWER...
ALL THESE PENCIL PUSHERS GIVE ME MURDEROUS THOUGHTS. I BARELY CONTAINED MYSELF.
FATHER?
GO, AND CLOSE THE DOOR BEHIND YOU.
DON'T DISTURB US FOR ANY REASON.
WHAT'S HAPPENING?
WE NEED TO TALK.

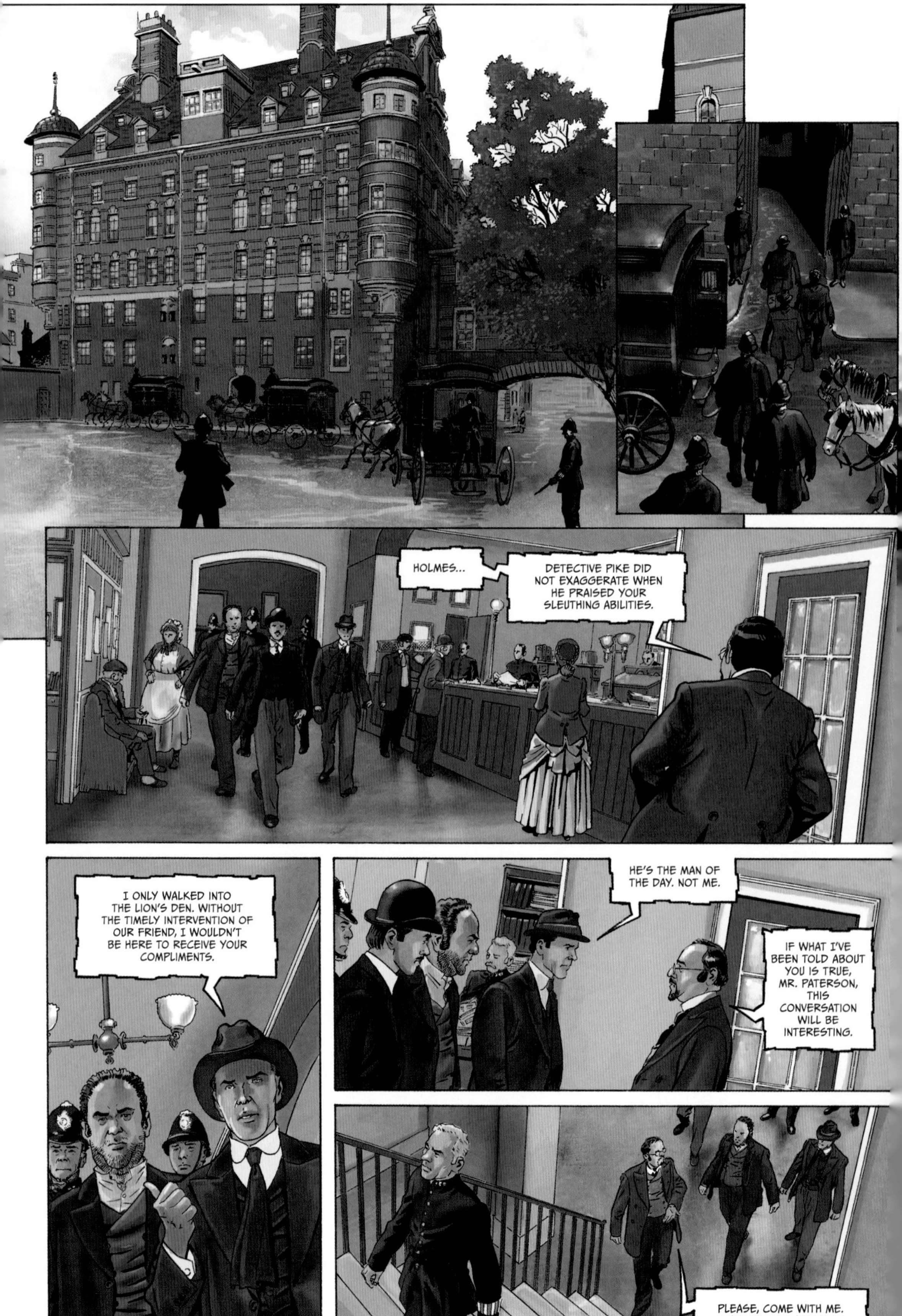
HOLMES...
DETECTIVE PIKE DID NOT EXAGGERATE WHEN HE PRAISED YOUR SLEUTHING ABILITIES.
I ONLY WALKED INTO THE LION'S DEN. WITHOUT THE TIMELY INTERVENTION OF OUR FRIEND, I WOULDN'T BE HERE TO RECEIVE YOUR COMPLIMENTS.
HE'S THE MAN OF THE DAY. NOT ME.
IF WHAT I'VE BEEN TOLD ABOUT YOU IS TRUE, MR. PATERSON, THIS CONVERSATION WILL BE INTERESTING.
PLEASE, COME WITH ME. MY OFFICE IS UPSTAIRS.

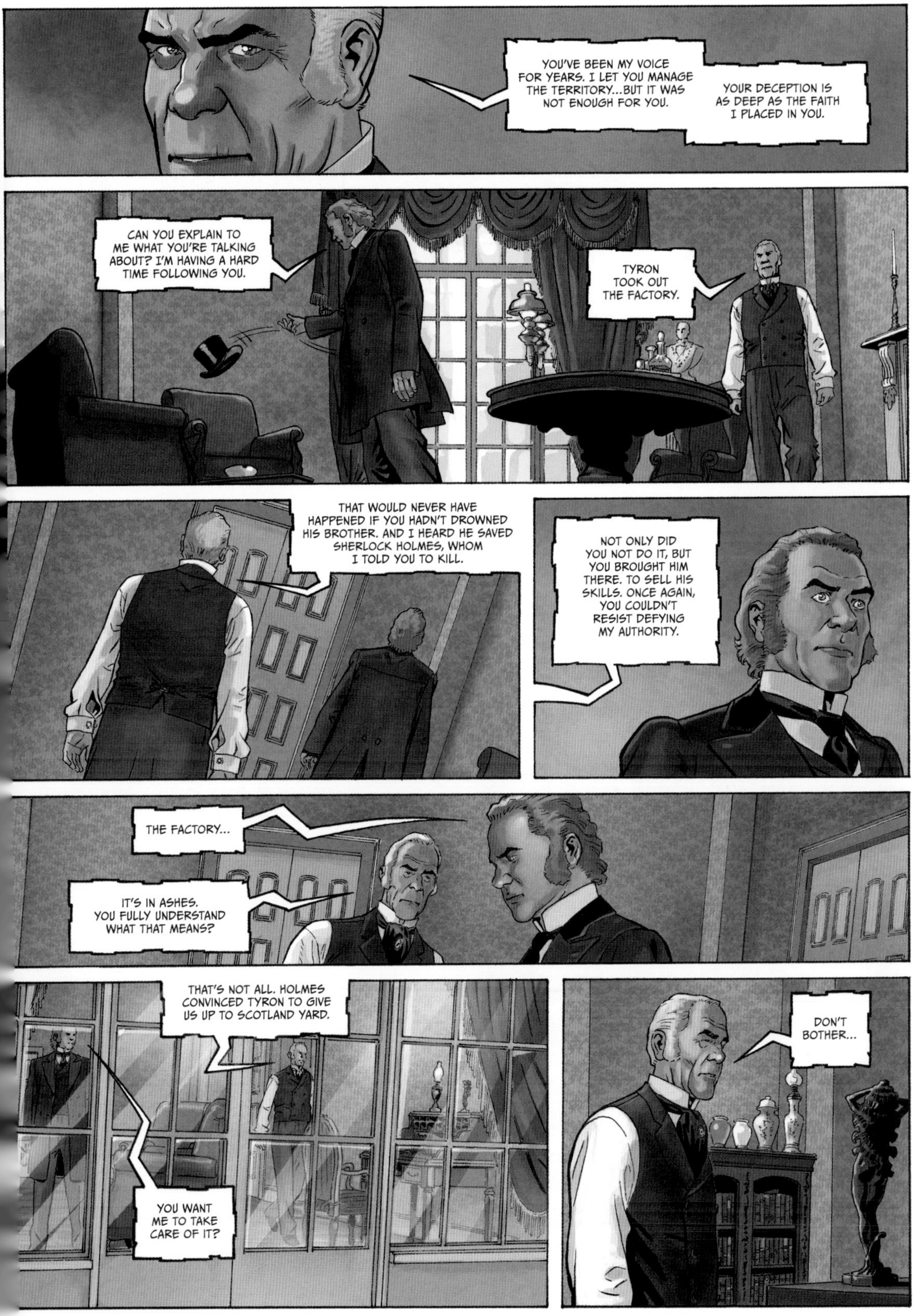
YOU'VE BEEN MY VOICE FOR YEARS. I LET YOU MANAGE THE TERRITORY...BUT IT WAS NOT ENOUGH FOR YOU.
YOUR DECEPTION IS AS DEEP AS THE FAITH I PLACED IN YOU.
CAN YOU EXPLAIN TO ME WHAT YOU'RE TALKING ABOUT? I'M HAVING A HARD TIME FOLLOWING YOU.
TYRON TOOK OUT THE FACTORY.
THAT WOULD NEVER HAVE HAPPENED IF YOU HADN'T DROWNED HIS BROTHER. AND I HEARD HE SAVED SHERLOCK HOLMES, WHOM I TOLD YOU TO KILL.
NOT ONLY DID YOU NOT DO IT, BUT YOU BROUGHT HIM THERE. TO SELL HIS SKILLS. ONCE AGAIN, YOU COULDN'T RESIST DEFYING MY AUTHORITY.
THE FACTORY...
IT'S IN ASHES. YOU FULLY UNDERSTAND WHAT THAT MEANS?
THAT'S NOT ALL. HOLMES CONVINCED TYRON TO GIVE US UP TO SCOTLAND YARD.
YOU WANT ME TO TAKE CARE OF IT?
DON'T BOTHER...

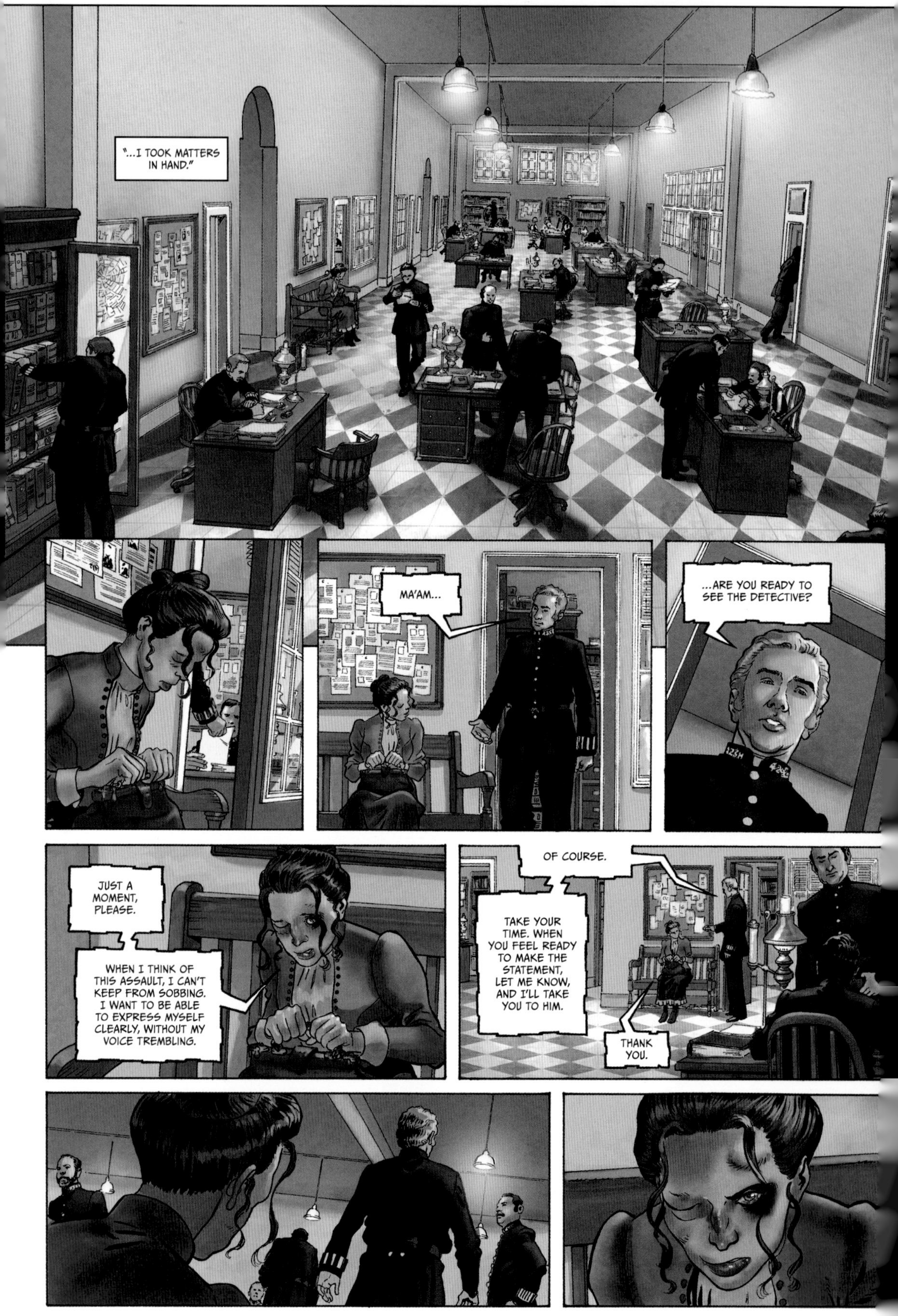
"...I TOOK MATTERS IN HAND."
MA'AM...
...ARE YOU READY TO SEE THE DETECTIVE?
JUST A MOMENT, PLEASE.
WHEN I THINK OF THIS ASSAULT, I CAN'T KEEP FROM SOBBING. I WANT TO BE ABLE TO EXPRESS MYSELF CLEARLY, WITHOUT MY VOICE TREMBLING.
OF COURSE.
TAKE YOUR TIME. WHEN YOU FEEL READY TO MAKE THE STATEMENT, LET ME KNOW, AND I'LL TAKE YOU TO HIM.
THANK YOU.

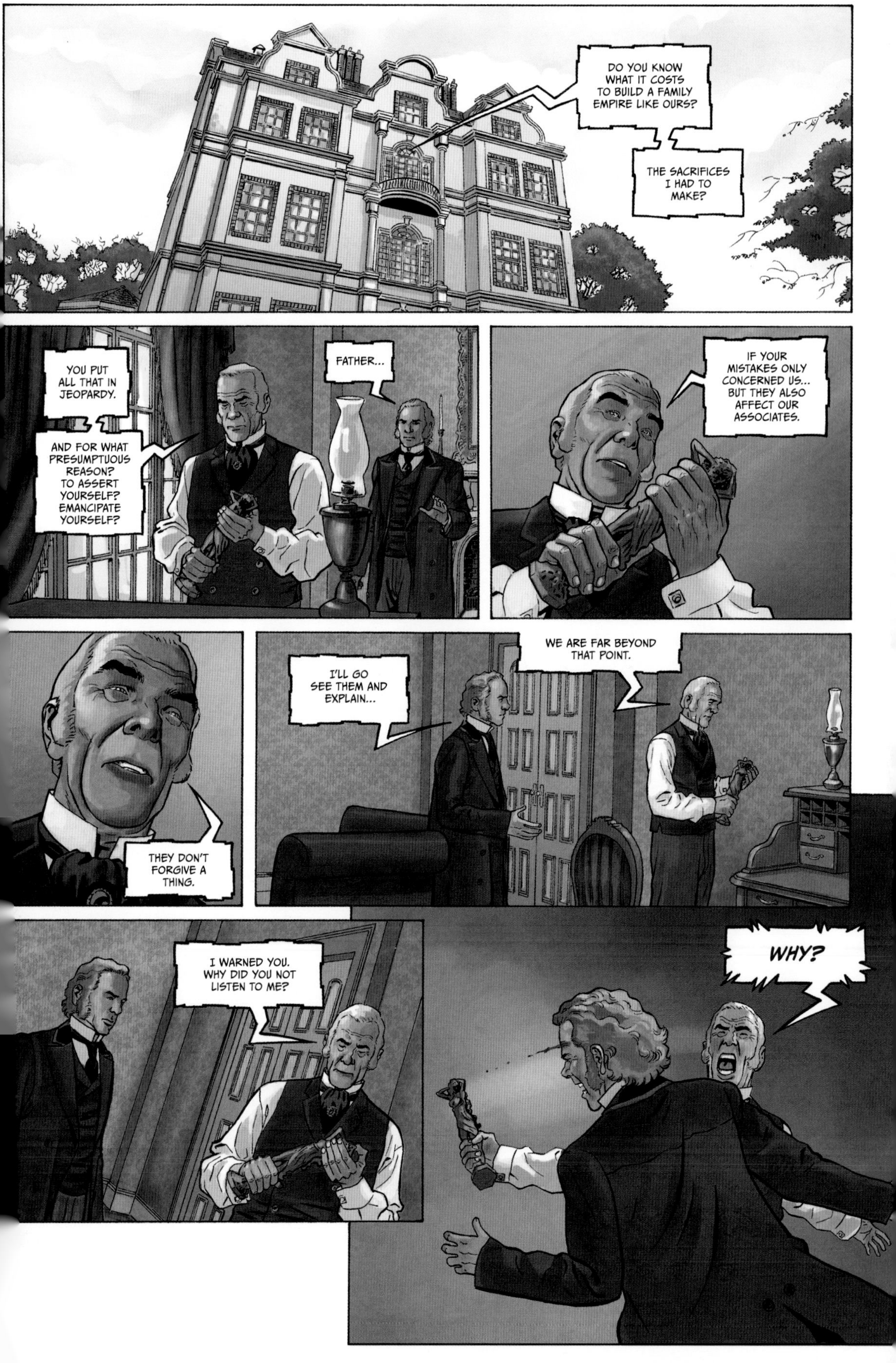
DO YOU KNOW WHAT IT COSTS TO BUILD A FAMILY EMPIRE LIKE OURS?
THE SACRIFICES I HAD TO MAKE?
YOU PUT ALL THAT IN JEOPARDY.
AND FOR WHAT PRESUMPTUOUS REASON? TO ASSERT YOURSELF? EMANCIPATE YOURSELF?
FATHER...
IF YOUR MISTAKES ONLY CONCERNED US... BUT THEY ALSO AFFECT OUR ASSOCIATES.
THEY DON'T FORGIVE A THING.
I'LL GO SEE THEM AND EXPLAIN...
WE ARE FAR BEYOND THAT POINT.
I WARNED YOU. WHY DID YOU NOT LISTEN TO ME?
WHY?

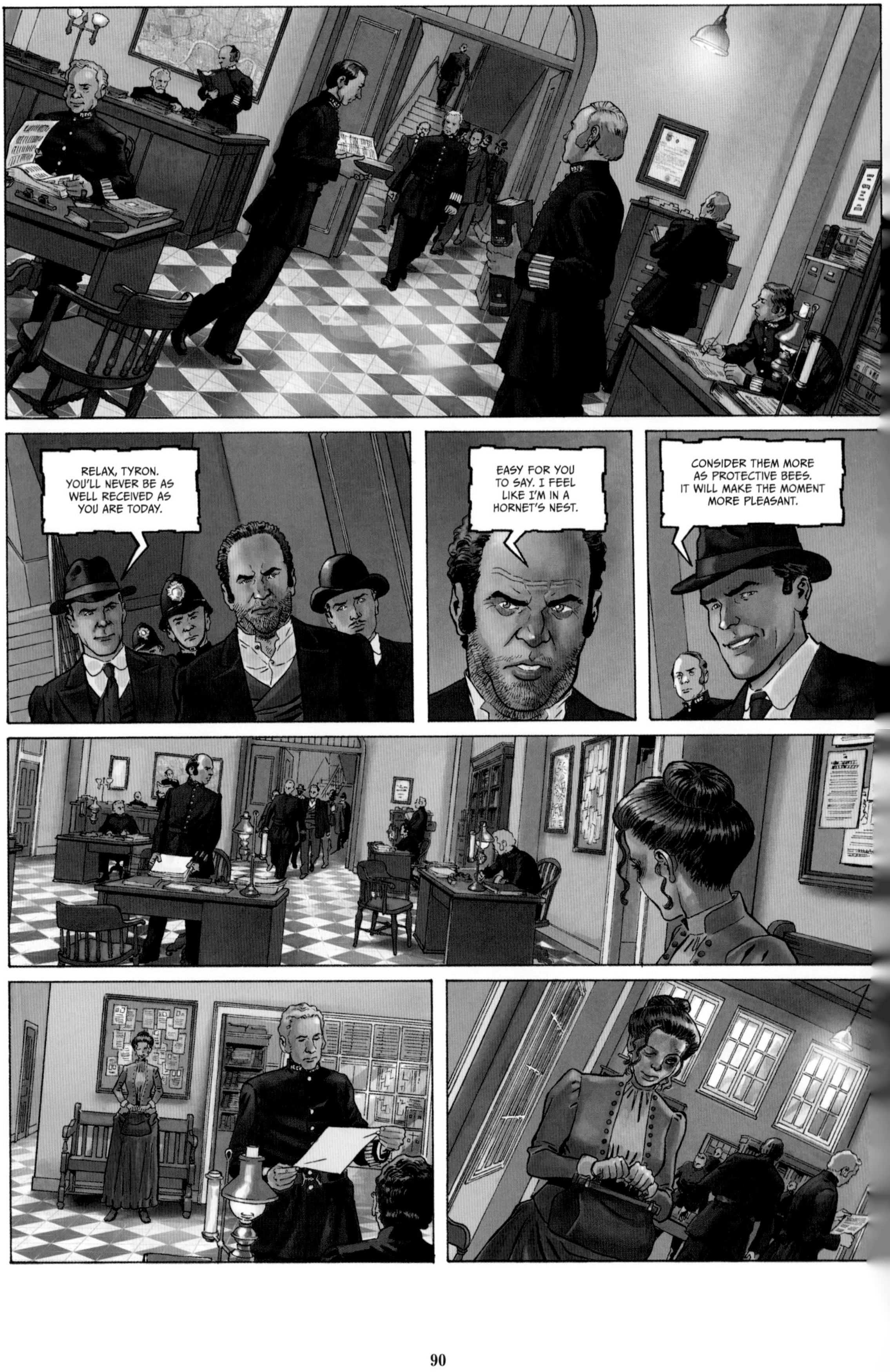
RELAX, TYRON. YOU'LL NEVER BE AS WELL RECEIVED AS YOU ARE TODAY.
EASY FOR YOU TO SAY. I FEEL LIKE I'M IN A HORNET'S NEST.
CONSIDER THEM MORE AS PROTECTIVE BEES. IT WILL MAKE THE MOMENT MORE PLEASANT.

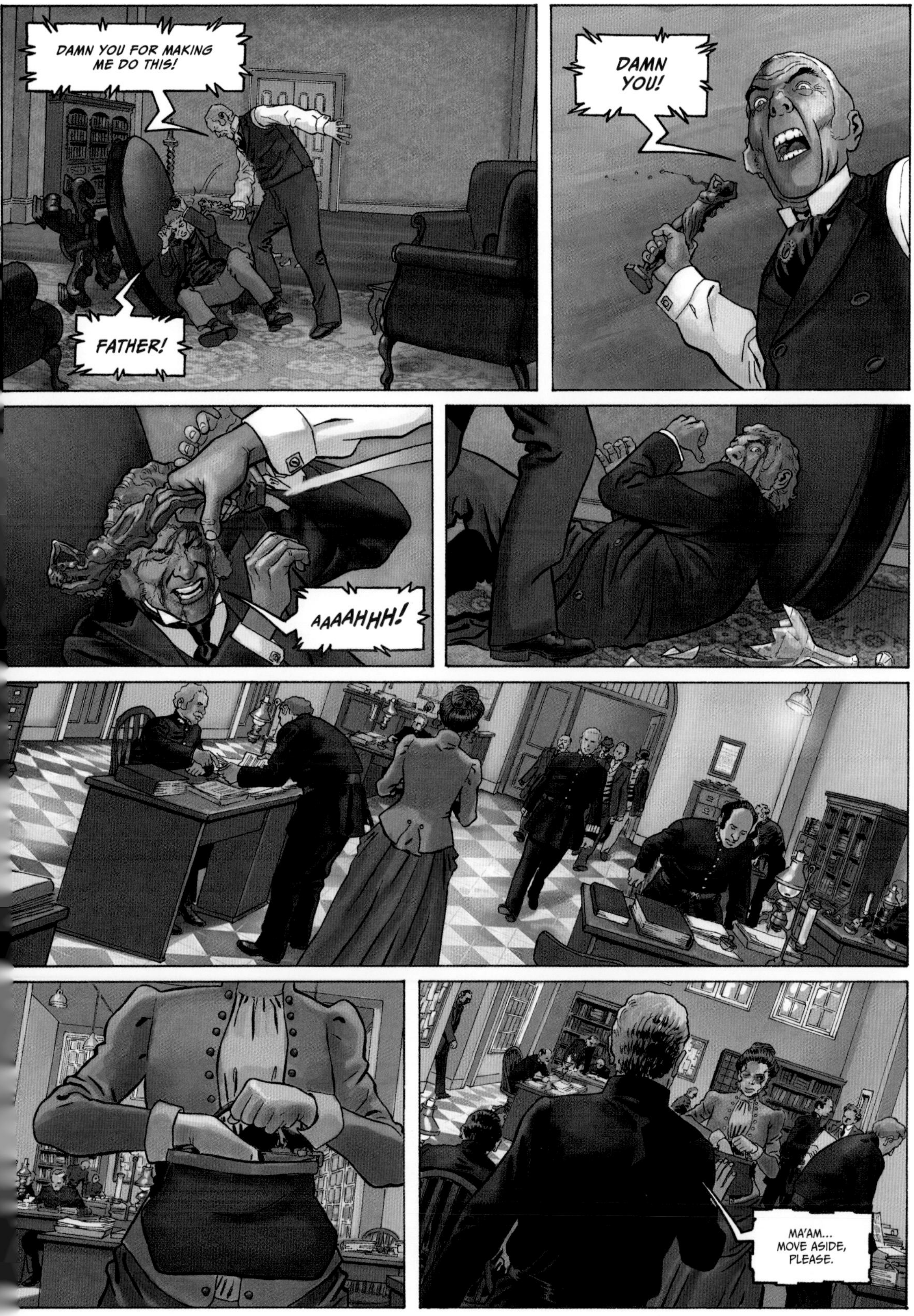
DAMN YOU FOR MAKING ME DO THIS!
FATHER!
DAMN YOU!
AAAAHHH!
MA'AM... MOVE ASIDE, PLEASE.

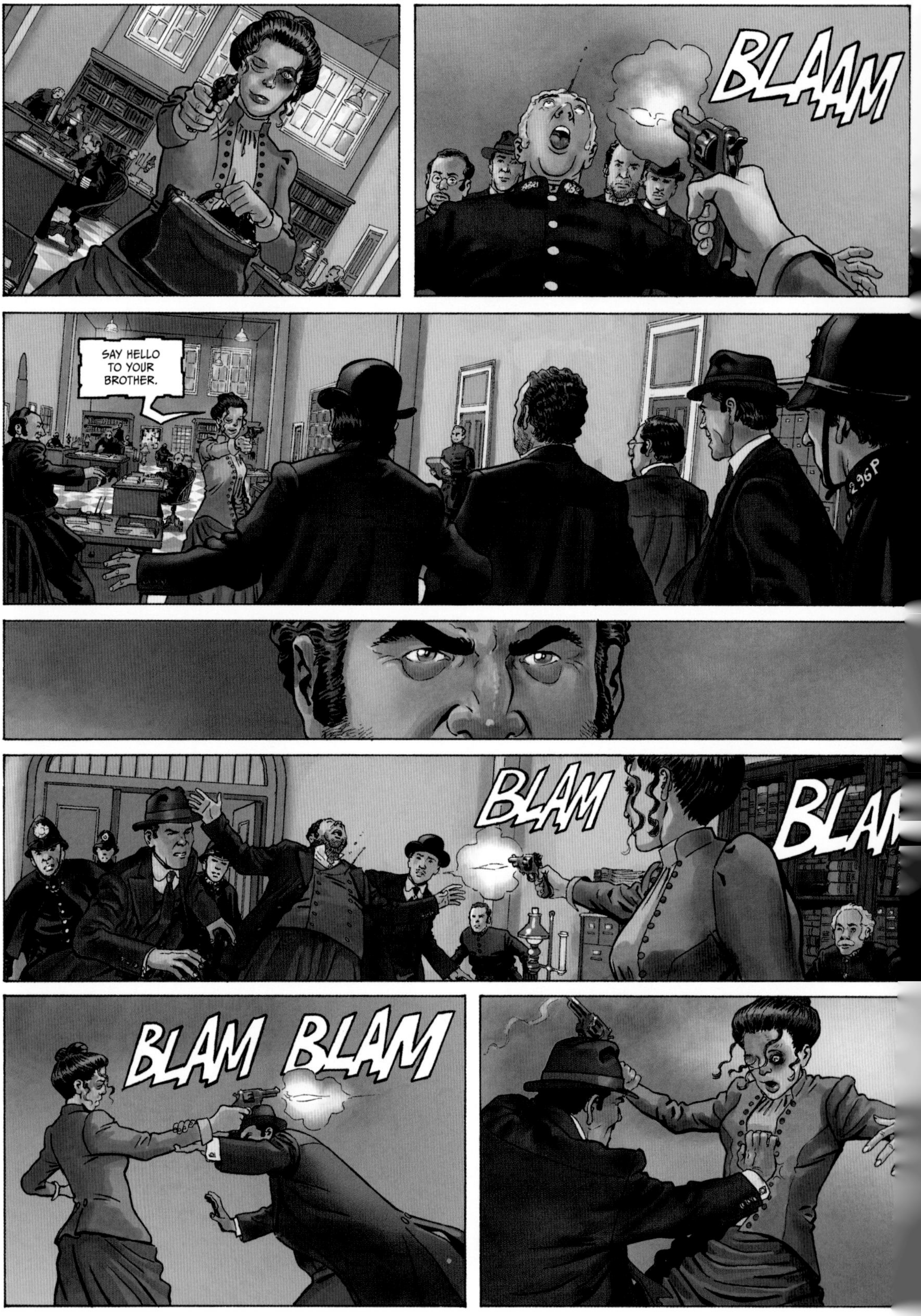
BLAAM
SAY HELLO TO YOUR BROTHER.
BLAM
BLAM
BLAM BLAM

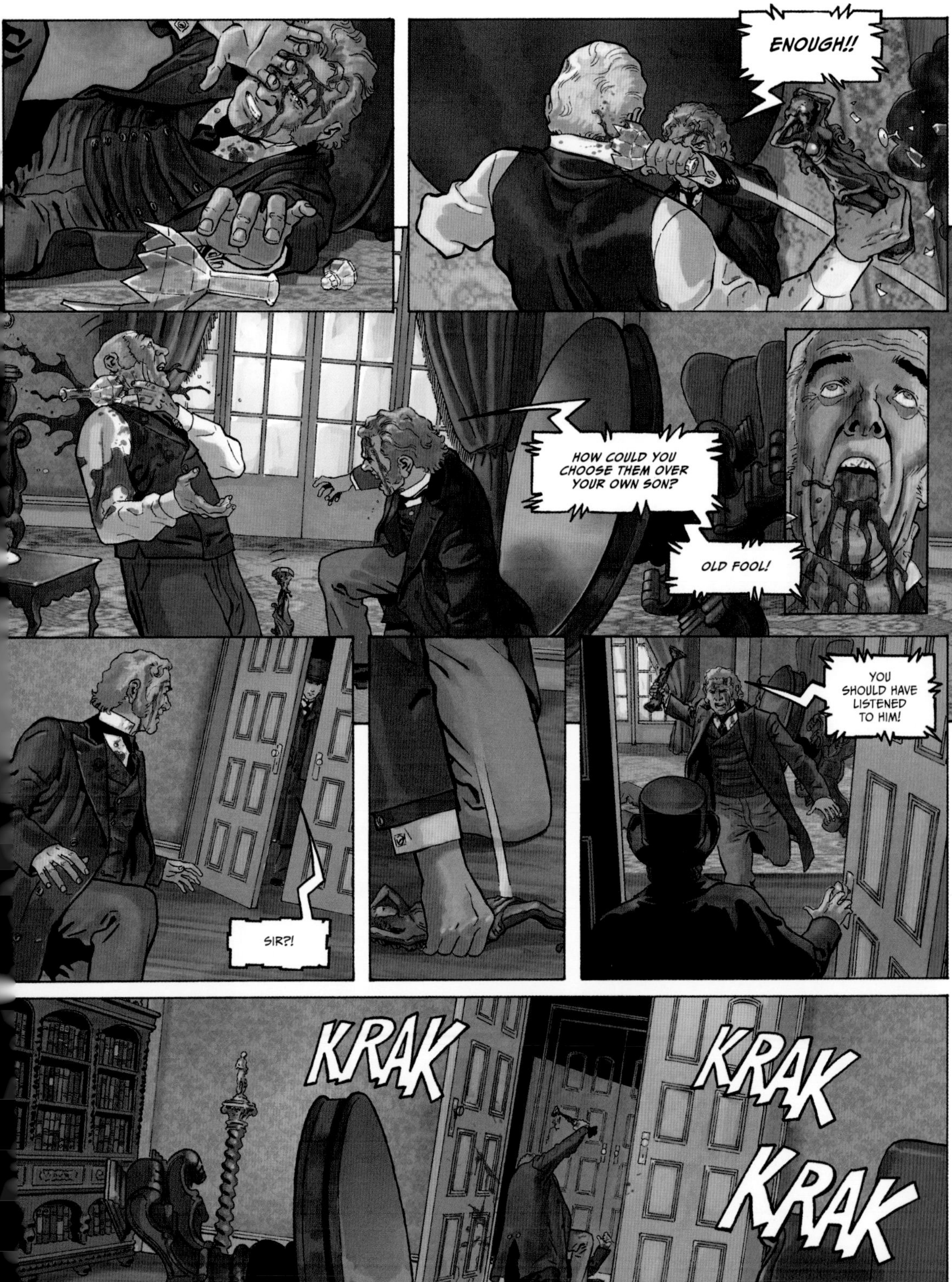
ENOUGH!!
HOW COULD YOU CHOOSE THEM OVER YOUR OWN SON?
OLD FOOL!
SIR?!
YOU SHOULD HAVE LISTENED TO HIM!
KRAK
KRAK
KRAK

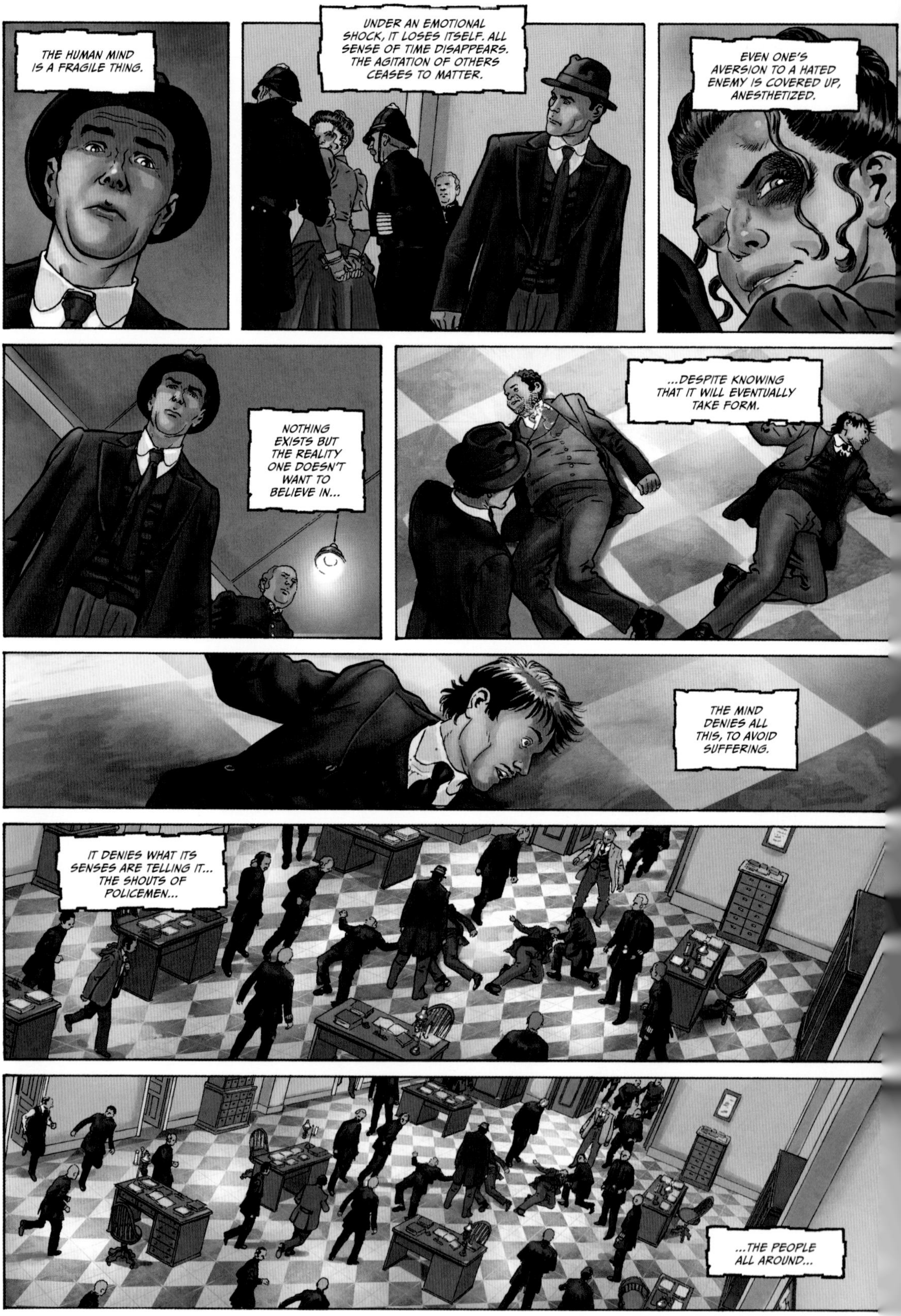
THE HUMAN MIND IS A FRAGILE THING.
UNDER AN EMOTIONAL SHOCK, IT LOSES ITSELF. ALL SENSE OF TIME DISAPPEARS. THE AGITATION OF OTHERS CEASES TO MATTER.
EVEN ONE'S AVERSION TO A HATED ENEMY IS COVERED UP, ANESTHETIZED.
NOTHING EXISTS BUT THE REALITY ONE DOESN'T WANT TO BELIEVE IN...
...DESPITE KNOWING THAT IT WILL EVENTUALLY TAKE FORM.
THE MIND DENIES ALL THIS, TO AVOID SUFFERING.
IT DENIES WHAT ITS SENSES ARE TELLING IT... THE SHOUTS OF POLICEMEN...
...THE PEOPLE ALL AROUND...

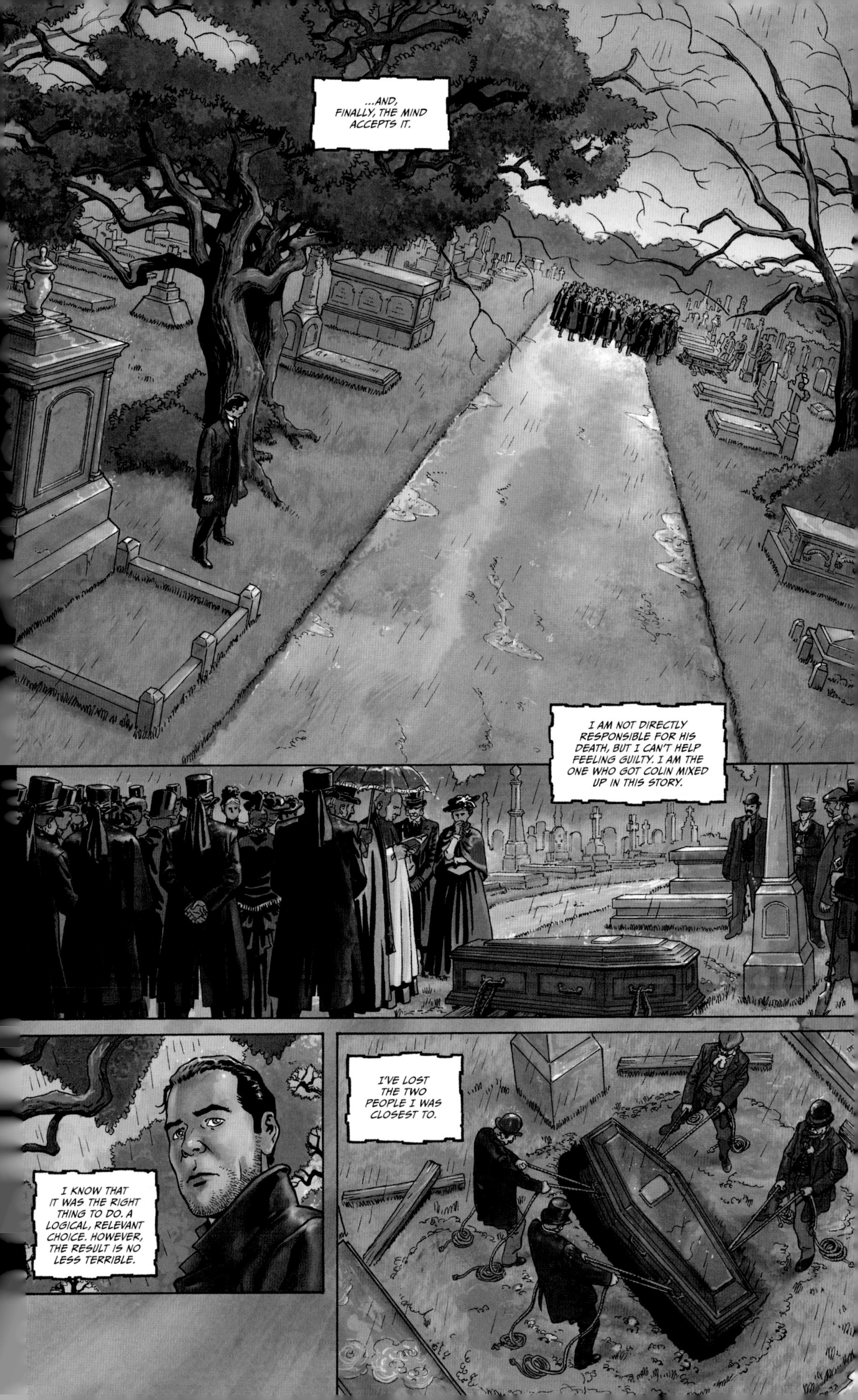
...AND, FINALLY, THE MIND ACCEPTS IT.
I AM NOT DIRECTLY RESPONSIBLE FOR HIS DEATH, BUT I CAN'T HELP FEELING GUILTY. I AM THE ONE WHO GOT COLIN MIXED UP IN THIS STORY.
I KNOW THAT IT WAS THE RIGHT THING TO DO. A LOGICAL, RELEVANT CHOICE. HOWEVER, THE RESULT IS NO LESS TERRIBLE.
I'VE LOST THE TWO PEOPLE I WAS CLOSEST TO.

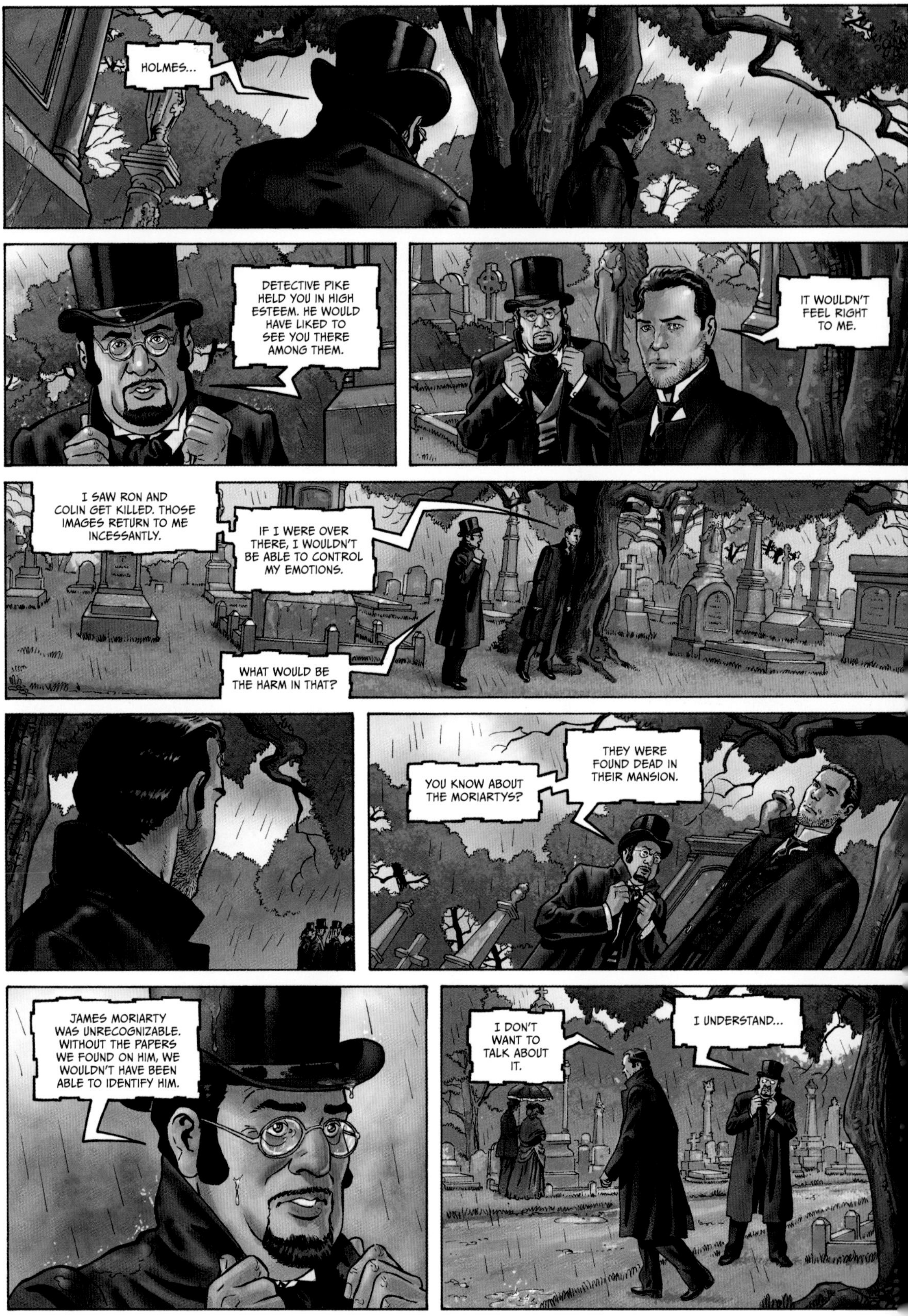
HOLMES...
DETECTIVE PIKE HELD YOU IN HIGH ESTEEM. HE WOULD HAVE LIKED TO SEE YOU THERE AMONG THEM.
IT WOULDN'T FEEL RIGHT TO ME.
I SAW RON AND COLIN GET KILLED. THOSE IMAGES RETURN TO ME INCESSANTLY.
IF I WERE OVER THERE, I WOULDN'T BE ABLE TO CONTROL MY EMOTIONS.
WHAT WOULD BE THE HARM IN THAT?
YOU KNOW ABOUT THE MORIARTYS?
THEY WERE FOUND DEAD IN THEIR MANSION.
JAMES MORIARTY WAS UNRECOGNIZABLE. WITHOUT THE PAPERS WE FOUND ON HIM, WE WOULDN'T HAVE BEEN ABLE TO IDENTIFY HIM.
I DON'T WANT TO TALK ABOUT IT.
I UNDERSTAND...

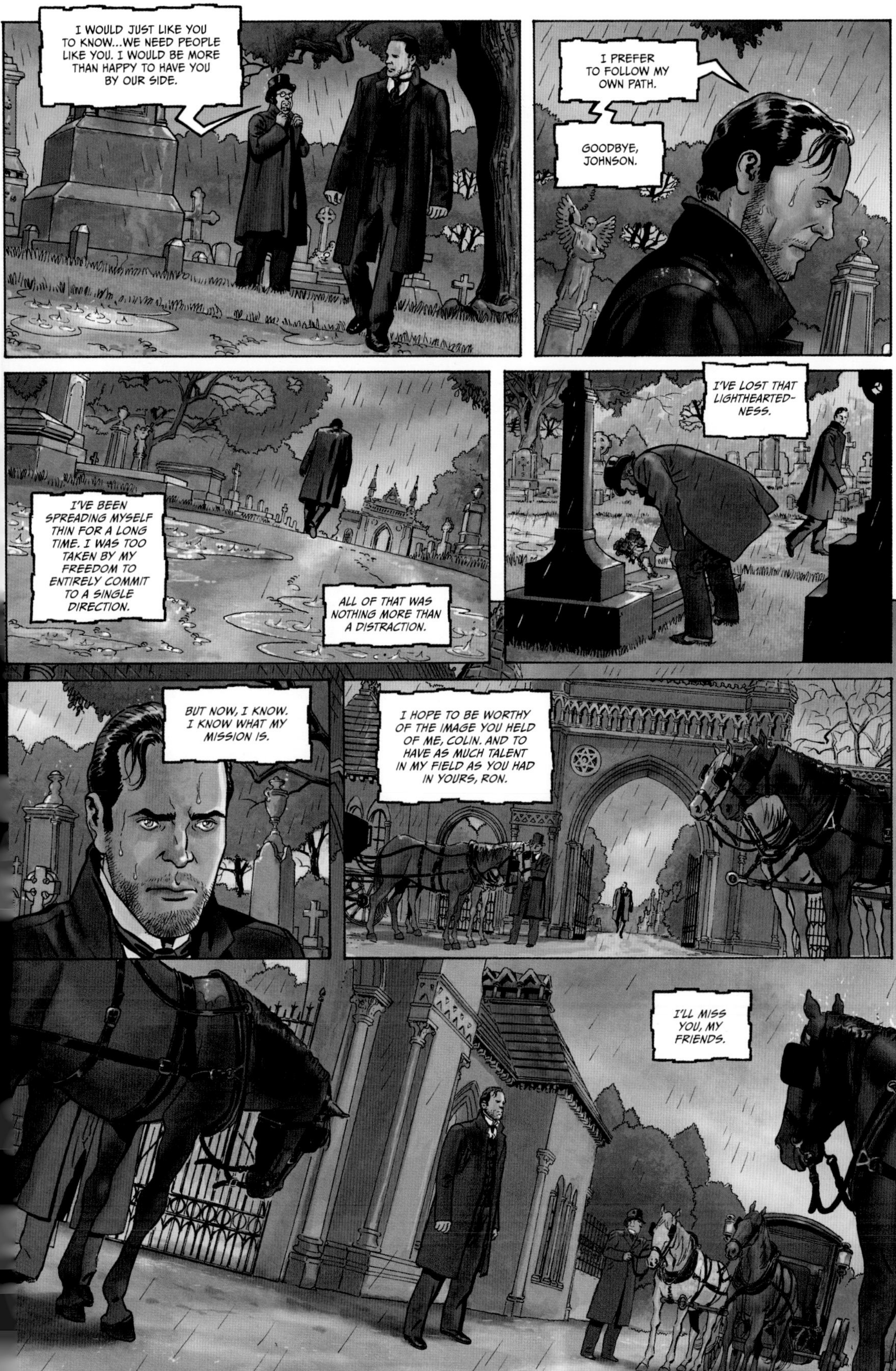
I WOULD JUST LIKE YOU TO KNOW...WE NEED PEOPLE LIKE YOU. I WOULD BE MORE THAN HAPPY TO HAVE YOU BY OUR SIDE.
I PREFER TO FOLLOW MY OWN PATH.
GOODBYE, JOHNSON.
I'VE BEEN SPREADING MYSELF THIN FOR A LONG TIME. I WAS TOO TAKEN BY MY FREEDOM TO ENTIRELY COMMIT TO A SINGLE DIRECTION.
ALL OF THAT WAS NOTHING MORE THAN A DISTRACTION.
I'VE LOST THAT LIGHTHEARTED-NESS.
BUT NOW, I KNOW. I KNOW WHAT MY MISSION IS.
I HOPE TO BE WORTHY OF THE IMAGE YOU HELD OF ME, COLIN. AND TO HAVE AS MUCH TALENT IN MY FIELD AS YOU HAD IN YOURS, RON.
I'LL MISS YOU, MY FRIENDS.

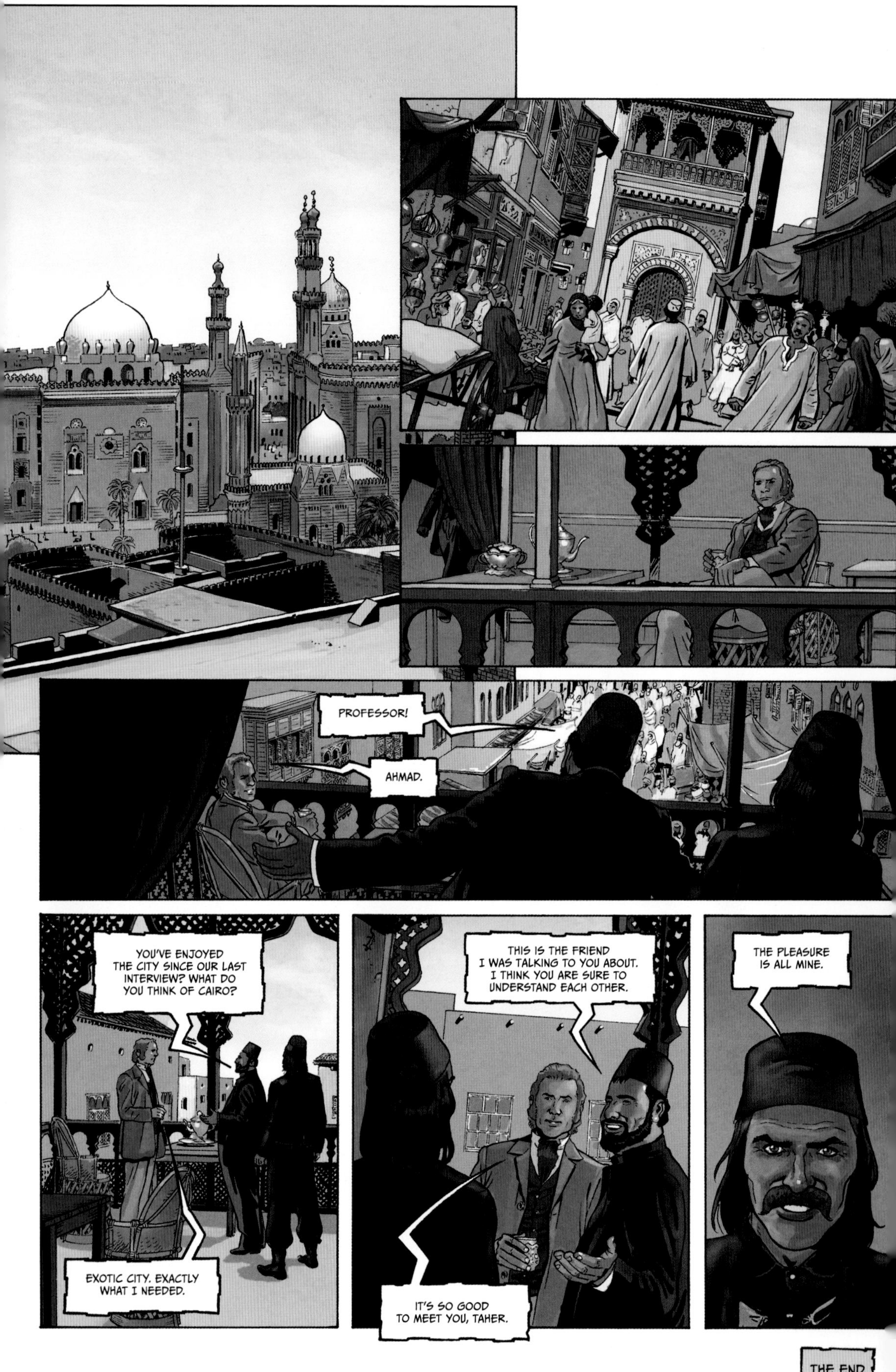
PROFESSOR!
AHMAD.
YOU'VE ENJOYED THE CITY SINCE OUR LAST INTERVIEW? WHAT DO YOU THINK OF CAIRO?
EXOTIC CITY. EXACTLY WHAT I NEEDED.
THIS IS THE FRIEND I WAS TALKING TO YOU ABOUT. I THINK YOU ARE SURE TO UNDERSTAND EACH OTHER.
IT'S SO GOOD TO MEET YOU, TAHER.
THE PLEASURE IS ALL MINE.
THE END.

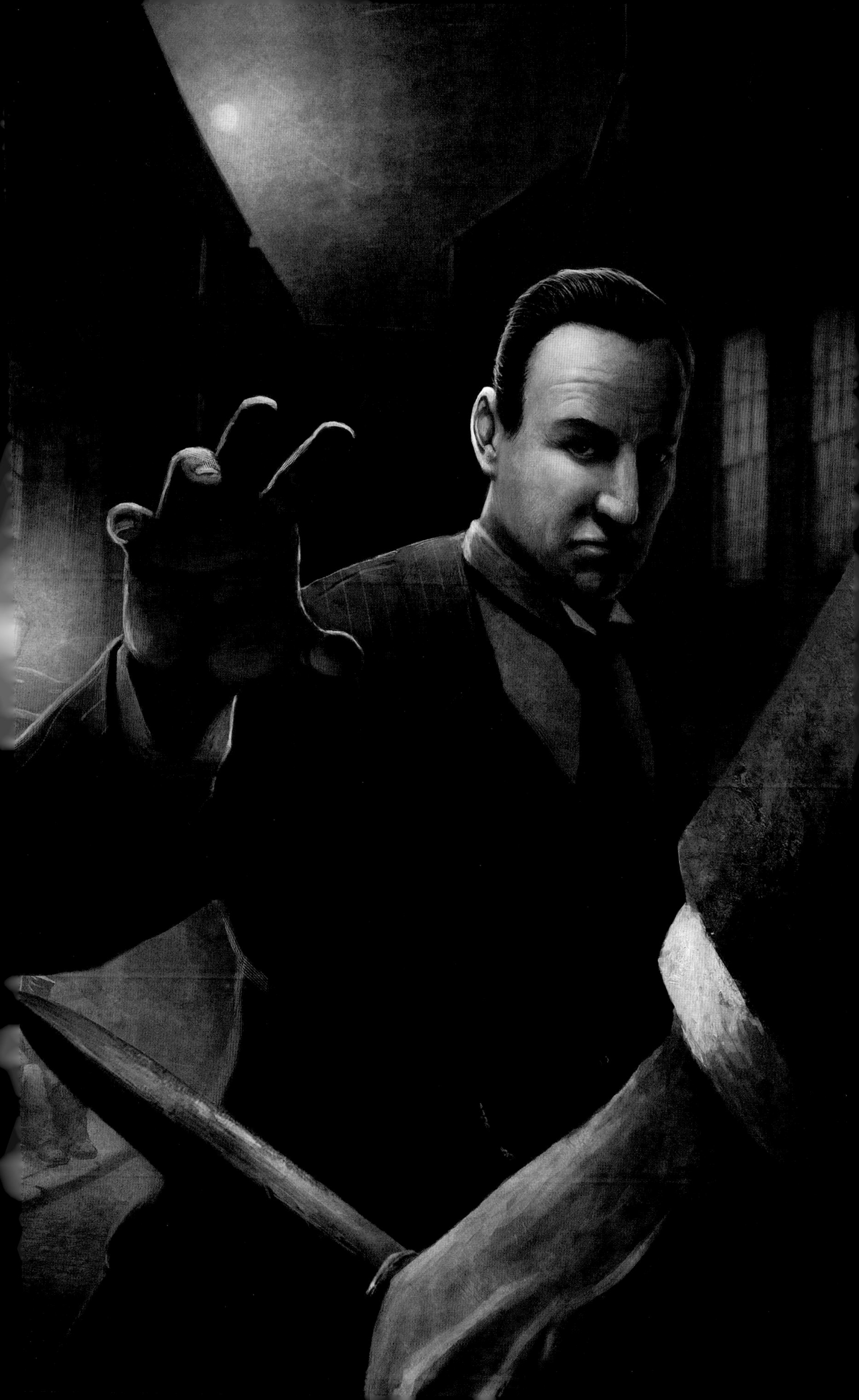

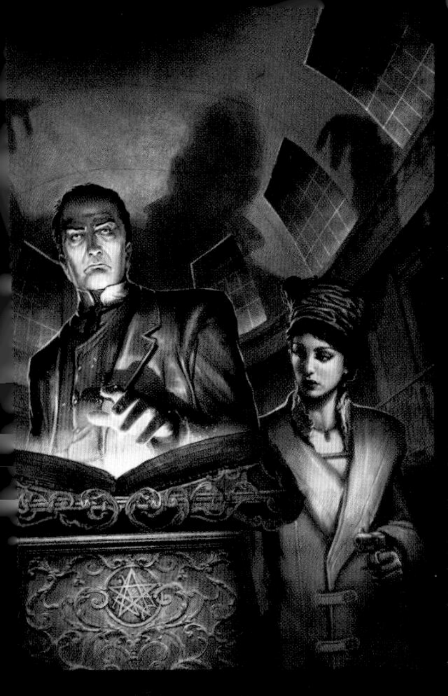

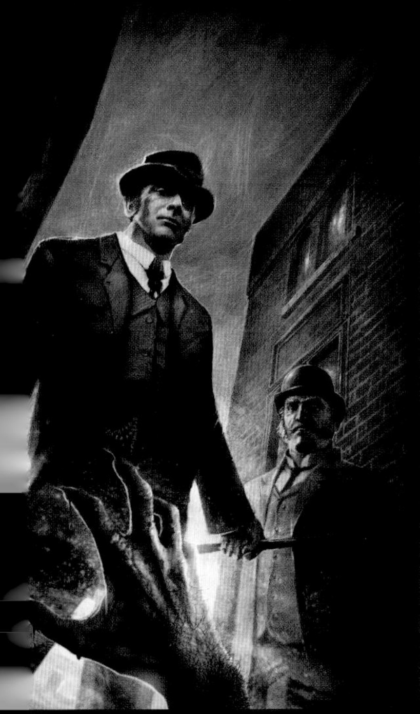

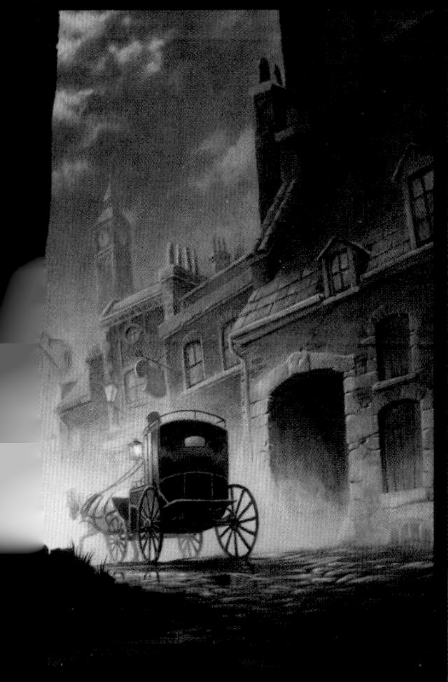

MORE EUROPEAN MYSTERY THRILLS FROM DARK HORSE BOOKS!

Sherlock Holmes and the Vampires of London HC
Sylvain Cordurié, Laci

Sherlock Holmes died fighting Professor Moriarty in the Reichenbach Falls. At least, that's what the press claims. However, Holmes is alive and well and taking advantage of his presumed death to travel the globe. Unfortunately, Holmes's plans are thwarted when a plague of vampirism haunts Britain.

$17.99
ISBN 978-1-61655-266-4

Sherlock Holmes and the Necronomicon HC
Sylvain Cordurié, Laci

Following his encounter with the vampire Selymes, Sherlock Holmes embarks on an Arctic expedition under an assumed name. During his excursion, the great detective uncovers strange and dark forces at work, and learns that some mysteries are best left unsolved!

$17.99
ISBN 978-1-61655-816-1

Jack the Ripper HC
François Debois, Jean-Charles Poupard

Spring 1889. Months have passed since Whitechapel was covered in blood, and while the mystery surrounding Jack the Ripper goes cold, Inspector Frederick Abberline is still a man obsessed. But when a series of killings identical to the Ripper's occur in Paris, Abberline must risk everything to close history's most famous murder case once and for all!

$17.99
ISBN 978-1-61655-819-2

ALSO FROM DARK HORSE BOOKS

HERMANN
JEREMIAH
OMNIBUS | 1

JEREMIAH OMNIBUS VOLUME 1

Hermann

One of Europe's most revered comics classics comes to America! At the end of the twentieth century, the United States is overcome by race hatred, and the ensuing civil war leaves only a few million survivors and a shattered society. Forced by circumstances into a series of violent moral compromises, innocent Jeremiah and his cynical friend Kurdy attempt to find their place in the postapocalyptic world without descending into savagery.

978-1-59582-945-0 | $24.99

MANARA
INDIAN SUMMER and OTHER STORIES
VOLUME ONE
MILO MANARA
with HUGO PRATT

THE MANARA LIBRARY VOLUME 1

Milo Manara with Hugo Pratt

The first of nine volumes, The Manara Library Volume 1 collects two of Manara's seminal works in a magnificently appointed, deluxe hardcover edition. The sweeping epic Indian Summer, a collaboration with celebrated creator Hugo Pratt, is collected here along with Manara's The Paper Man, both translated by Euro comics expert Kim Thompson.

978-1-59582-782-1 | $59.99

DOG MENDONÇA AND PIZZABOY
FILIPE MELO
JUAN CAVIA

THE INCREDIBLE ADVENTURES OF DOG MENDONÇA AND PIZZABOY

Filipe Melo and Juan Cavia

What do an overweight Portuguese werewolf, a seven-year-old girl who's actually a six thousand-year-old demon, and a downtrodden pizza boy have in common? In this smash-hit import, the unlikely team bands together to ward off occult evils, Nazis, and impending global doom! Featuring an introduction by An American Werewolf in London director John Landis!

978-1-59582-938-2 | $12.99

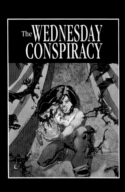

The WEDNESDAY CONSPIRACY

THE WEDNESDAY CONSPIRACY

Sergio Bleda

Think you've got problems? Meet the patients in Dr. Burton's Wednesday afternoon support group: Violet carries a jar of demons. Roger can read minds. Akiko talks with her dead parents through the bathroom mirror. Joe is an exorcist. Brian is pyrokinetic. And then, of course, there's Charles. They've been thrown together by the luck of the draw, stuck with supernatural powers they don't want and can't control. But when something begins to pick them off one by one, the surviving members of the Wednesday Conspiracy find themselves the last, reluctant line of defense between the reincarnation of an ancient evil and the fate of the world.

978-1-59582-563-6 | $19.99

MORE EUROPEAN INTRIGUE FROM
DARK HORSE BOOKS

THE AWARD-WINNING INTERNATIONAL BESTSELLER
BLACKSAD
"As good as it gets!"

BLACKSAD

Juan Díaz Canales and Juanjo Guarnido

The *Blacksad* books first took Europe by storm in 2000 and sold over 200,000 copies in France alone. Now Dark Horse Comics presents the beautifully painted stories of private investigator John Blacksad, up to his feline ears in mystery, digging into the backstories behind murders, child abductions, and nuclear secrets.

Volume 1
978-1-59582-393-9 | $29.99
Volume 2: A Silent Hell
978-1-59582-931-3 | $19.99

VAMPIRE BOY
CARLOS TRILLO
EDUARDO RISSO

VAMPIRE BOY

Carlos Trillo and Eduardo Risso

Left nameless by his father and sentenced to eternal life by a trick of fate and fortune, the protagonist of Carlos Trillo and Eduardo Risso's *Vampire Boy* has spent fifty centuries in a body that never ages, locked in an eternal struggle with a rival as immortal as he. Acclaimed writer Carlos Trillo teams with legendary artist Eduardo Risso (100 Bullets) to produce a poignantly engrossing twist on the classic vampire mythos, now presented in English for the first time!

978-1-59582-562-9 | $24.99

THE DYLAN DOG CASE FILES
MORE THAN 56 MILLION COPIES SOLD WORLDWIDE!

THE DYLAN DOG CASE FILES

Tiziano Sclavi and others

Unavailable in English for almost a decade, one of the most popular comics in the world—selling more than a million copies every month throughout Europe—returns! An ex-cop who now battles against evil as a "nightmare investigator," Dylan Dog is unlike any private eye you've ever met. If creatures from beyond the unknown are after you, and if you can hire him, he just might save your life.

978-1-59582-206-2 | $24.99

ENTER A WORLD OF MAGIC AND FANTASY!
DRAGONERO
Luca Enoch • Stefano Vietti • Giuseppe Matteoni

DRAGONERO

Luca Enoch, Stefano Vietti, and Giuseppe Matteoni

Beyond the civilized lands of Erondàr, the Stone Towers are crumbling. The great monoliths are falling one after another under the wild thrusts of an evil force. The Ancient Prohibition that binds the Abominables inside their dark world is soon to be broken. Alben the Wizard will send for Myrva, a young follower of the powerful Technocrats; he will choose Ecuba, the fighting nun, to protect him; and he will call back Ian Aranill, a former Empire officer—followed by Gmor the Orc, his loyal friend—to use his scouting experience. Together they will face the Painers, the evil beings who still live in the barren Dragonlands. Can Ian prevail against the last, horrible threat they will be facing?

978-1-59582-291-8 | $19.99

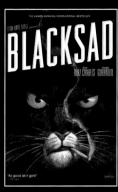